AF352269

CHIEFDOM POLITICS AND ALIEN LAW

MASOPHA

CHIEFDOM POLITICS AND ALIEN LAW:
Basutoland under Cape Rule, 1871–1884

Sandra Burman

AFRICANA PUBLISHING COMPANY
A division of Holmes & Meier Publishers, Inc.
New York

First published in the United States of America 1981 by
AFRICANA PUBLISHING COMPANY
A division of Holmes & Meier Publishers, Inc.
30 Irving Place
New York, N.Y. 10003

Library of Congress Cataloging in Publication Data

Burman, Sandra.
   Chiefdom politics and alien law.

   Based on the author's thesis.
   Bibliography: p.
   Includes index.
   1.   Lesotho–Politics and government–To 1966.
2.   Moshoeshoe, Basuto chief, d. 1870.   3.   Lesotho–
Relations (general) with the Cape of Good Hope.
4.   Cape of Good Hope–Relations (general) with Lesotho.
5.   Lesotho–Relations (general) with Natal.   6.   Natal–
Relations (general) with Lesotho.   7.   Law, Sotho.
I.   Title.
DT787.4.B86   968.1'602   79–25600
ISBN 0–8419–0591–6

Printed in Hong Kong

Contents

Masopha   *Frontispiece*

List of Maps   vi

List of Plates   vii

Acknowledgements   ix

List of Abbreviations   x

A Note on Names and Orthography   xi

Glossary of Sotho Terms   xii

Introduction   1

1   Creating a Nation   5
2   Conflicting Values   17
3   Interregnum   35
4   The Cape Administration   49
5   Neutralising the Chiefs   61
6   Winning over the People   75
7   Changing the Law   91
8   Prophesies   100
9   Moorosi Rebels   108
10 The Collapse of Magisterial Rule   132
11 Defeating Disarmament   148
12 The Triumph of the Chiefs   162

Epilogue   185

Notes   192

Bibliography   229

Index   245

List of Maps

Map 1   Southern Africa in 1966 (Lesotho Independence)   xiv
Map 2   Map of Basutoland, drawn in 1888, showing
        the topography   4
Map 3   Map of Basutoland in the nineteenth century   36
Map 4   Map of Basutoland, drawn in July 1871,
        showing magisterial districts   51
Map 5   The Moorosi Rebellion   109
Map 6   Basutoland after the War of the Guns, showing
        magisterial districts   152

List of Plates

1   Moshoeshoe and some of his advisers
2   Letsie in 1845
3   Molapo in 1845
4   Masopha in uniform with his standard bearer
5   Masopha at a pitso
6   Nehemiah Moshoeshoe (Sekhonyana)
7   Sofonia Moshoeshoe (Pii)
8   Tsekelo Moshoeshoe
9   Lerotholi
10   Lerotholi and some of his advisers
11   Joel Molapo
12   Jonathan Molapo
13   Jonathan Molapo leading a war dance
14   RaMatšeatsana
15   Moorosi, chief of the Phuthi
16   Nkoebi Letsie
17   Eugene Casalis
18   Dr Eugene Casalis
19   François Coillard
20   Adolphe Mabille
21   Adèle Mabille
22   John Widdicombe
23   Sir Philip Wodehouse
24   Sir Henry Barkly
25   Sir Bartle Frere
26   Sir Hercules Robinson
27   John Gordan Sprigg
28   William Ayliff
29   Jacobus Wilhelmus Sauer
30   John Xavier Merriman
31   Charles Duncan Griffith
32   Hamilton Hope
33   Fanny Barkly

34 Arthur Barkly
35 Charles Harland Bell
36 Charles George Harland Bell
37 Dr Henry Shinglewood Taylor
38 Joseph Orpen
39 Charles George Gordon ('Chinese Gordon')
40 Matthew Smith Blyth
41 Marshall Clarke
42 Thaba-Baosiu, Masopha's stronghold
43 Matsieng, Letsie's village
44 Molapo's house near Leribe
45 Headquarters camp under Moorosi's stronghold during the siege
46 The capture of Moorosi's mountain: the final assault
47 Maseru in the Gun War, December 1880
48 Fort Bell, Hlotse Heights, in the Gun War

Plates, 2, 3, 5, 6, 7, 8, 9, 10, 20, 21 and 38 are by courtesy of Rev. A. Brutsch and the Archives of the Lesotho Evangelical Church, Morija. The jacket picture of Frere and plates 4, 23 and 41 are from G Lagden, *The Basutos* (London, 1909). Plates 12 and 37 are from P. Hadley (ed.), *Doctor to Basuto, Boer and Briton 1877–1906* (Cape Town, 1972). Plate 15 is by courtesy of Dr P. B. Sanders. Plates 16, 24, 25, 26, 27, 28, 29, 30 and 45 are from Cape Archives, Cape Town. Plate 17 is from H. Dieterlen, *Eugène Casalis (1812–1891)* (Paris, 1930). Plate 19 is from E. Favre, *Les vingt-cinq ans de Coillard au Lessouto* (Paris, 1931). Plate 22 is from *Basutoland Notes and Records*. Plate 33 is by courtesy of Mr Karl Wayne. Plate 34 is by courtesy of Mrs K. Nixon-Eckersall. Plate 39 is from A. Nutting, *Gordon, Martyr and Misfit* (London, 1966). Plate 43 is from H. Dieterlen, *Adolphe Mabille (1836–1894)* (Paris, 1933). Plate 47 is from Lesotho Archives, Maseru.

Acknowledgements

In preparing this book, which is an expanded version of part of my doctoral thesis, I have been assisted and encouraged by so many people that it would be impossible to mention all of them. I am, however, particularly indebted to Colin Bundy, Jose Burman, Max Hartwell, Désirèe Park, Peter Sanders, Christopher Saunders and Gavin Williams for their advice and comments on the manuscript, and to John Benyon, Peter Sanders and Christopher Saunders for making their theses available to me; to Freddie Madden, my supervisor during my research for my thesis; to Anthony Atmore, David Ambrose, Jim Anderson, the Rev. Albert Brutsch, and Stanley Trapido for their advice, encouragement, and assistance with research material; to the helpful staff in the archives and public libraries I used; to Virginia Rosamond and the other secretaries at the Centre for Socio-Legal Studies for all their assistance in producing a final manuscript; and to Lady Margaret Hall, the British Federation of University Women, the South African Association of University Women, and the Administrators of the Beit Fund, the Bryce Research Fund, the Arnold Historical Essay Fund, the Oxford Society Fund and the Africa Educational Trust for their generous financial support that made the research for my thesis possible.

The author and publishers wish to thank the following who have kindly given permission for the use of copyright material: Department of National Education, Government Archives, South Africa, for quotations from documents in the Cape Archives Depot; Heinemann Educational Books Ltd, for an extract from Christophers Saunders (ed.), *Black Leaders in Southern African History*; Heinemann Educational Books Ltd and Holmes & Meier Publishers Inc., for a map and extracts from P. Sanders, *Moshoeshoe: Chief of the Sotho*; Mrs M. Howard-Jones, for an extract from her father's book, Rev. E. W. Smith, *The Mabilles of Basutoland*; Oxford University Press Inc., for a map from Robert I. Rotberg, Ali A. Mazrui *et al.* (eds), *Protest and Power in Black Africa*, © 1970 by Oxford University Press Inc.; David Philip, Publisher (Pty) Ltd, for extracts from P. Hadley (ed.), *Doctor to Basuto, Boer and Briton, 1877–1906 Memoirs of Dr Henry Taylor* (1972).

List of Abbreviations

1. *Archival Records*

Cape	South African Government Archives, Cape Town
Lesotho	Lesotho Archives, Maseru
P.R.O.	Public Record Office, London
S.A.P.L.	South African Public Library, Cape Town
U.C.T.	University of Cape Town Jagger Library, Cape Town

2. *Other*

Brit. Parl. Papers	*British Parliamentary Papers*
C.M.R.	Cape Mounted Rifles
Cape Parl. Papers	*Cape Parliamentary Papers (Annexures and Appendices to the Votes and Proceedings of the Cape Parliament)*
encl.	enclosed
J.M.E.	*Le Journal des Missions Evangéliques*
P.E.M.S. (and P.M.S.)	Paris Evangelical Missionary Society
tel.	telegram
U.B.R.	Unpublished Basutoland Records, ed. G. M. Theal (in Cape Archives)

A Note on Names and Orthography

Throughout this book the quotations show a variety of spellings and word formations in referring to names and other indigenous words, and often differ from those in the rest of the text. This variety is, first, the result of the still unsettled state of the orthography of the local language at that period, and the fact that many of the officials and others writing about the country could not speak it fluently. Second, the people living in and around Lesotho use prefixes in their language. They call themselves *Basotho* (sing. *Mosotho*); their country is *Lesotho* and both their language and the adjective they apply to anything characteristic of their culture is *Sesotho*. The use made of these prefixes by strangers to the language in the nineteenth century was often inconsistent or erroneous, giving rise to such forms as 'Basutoland'. Modern English usage now frequently dispenses with prefixes and, in conformity with this practice, I have used 'Sotho' for all forms where not actually quoting from earlier writing. Third, the Sotho language has two systems of orthography. One is used in the Republic of South Africa; the other is the official orthography of Lesotho and I have used the latter. It has certain variations from both English pronunciation and the South African system, however, that account for some of the common differences between quoted passages and the rest of the text. For example, in Lesotho's orthography, *l* before *i* or *u* is pronounced *d*; hence Lerothodi/Lerotholi.

Glossary of Sotho Terms

bohali	dowry of livestock (or money) transferred to wife's family upon marriage
joala	strong beer
khotla, lekhotla	chief's court; public meeting place
lebollo	initiation
letsema	communal labour performed for a chief
lifaqane	the wars in Lesotho in the 1820s
lingoetsi	junior wives
lithoko	praise poems or songs
maboella	protected winter grazing lands
mafisa	a contract for the loan of livestock, a condition of which is that their increase accrues to the owner
mafura	fat, oil; head of cattle slaughtered at the conclusion of a marriage
malome	senior maternal uncle
mokhoa (plural *mekhoa*)	custom, habit, way
molao	law, order, commandment
morena	chief
pitso (plural *lipitso* but anglicised in text)	assembly, public meeting
pula	rain
tlhabiso	ox slaughtered as part of the wedding festivities

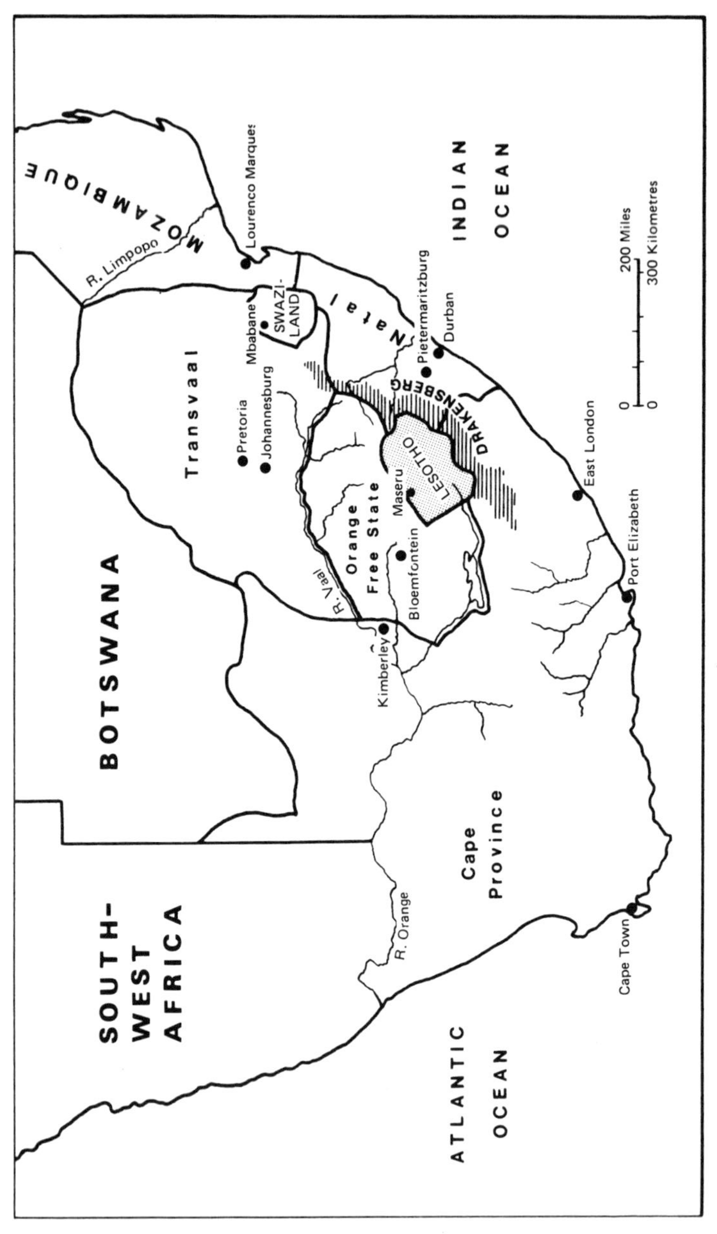

Map 1   Southern Africa in 1966 (Lesotho Independence)

Introduction

Lesotho today is a small enclave of African-ruled territory completely surrounded by the Republic of South Africa. Although its independence is recognised by the United Nations, it is as firmly enmeshed in the Republic's economy as any of the Bantustans, and in an equally subordinate position. It is desperately poor, too overpopulated to feed itself, and at any given time nearly half the able-bodied men are absent—factory, farm or mine workers in South Africa. Yet the Sotho differ from the Africans of the Republic in retaining significantly more of their cultural heritage and social cohesion. That they have done so is largely the result of the fact that they were able to escape from magisterial settler rule after little more than a decade and revert to the control of their chiefs under British protection. Whatever the deficiencies of that system (and they were numerous) it kept Sotho territory unfragmented and forced the Sotho to retain their customs and law to a far greater extent than the Africans in the Republic. This book is an examination of the first explosive years of Lesotho (Basutoland) under magisterial rule, in which an attempt was made to effect a rapid change in Sotho society by a combination of legislation and political manipulation.

Lesotho came under colonial control after a minor chief named Moshoeshoe united the Sotho small-scale chiefdoms of the southern African High Veld into a nation which became known as the Basuto. However, encroachment by white settlers on Moshoeshoe's land resulted in war with the neighbouring Boer republic and led him in 1868, shortly before his death, to place his country under British protection. In 1871 Britain transferred direct administration of the territory to the Cape Colony, then on the point of being given control of its own affairs under a form of Responsible Government, and the colony embarked on a policy of 'civilising' the Sotho.

The small Administration of magistrates that was set up by the Cape Government initially proved remarkably effective in manipulating Sotho politics and society in such a way as to be able to impose the Cape's regulations, which aimed at effecting desired changes in Sotho law and society as rapidly as was thought possible. Although this generated new tensions in the social institutions and politics of the country, under continued skilful guidance the Administration might well have been able to achieve its goal. Even when Moorosi, an important chief in the country, was driven into open revolt against the magisterial system, the rest of the nation assisted the Administration to quell the rebellion. However, the Cape Government then decided to disarm all the tribes under its control, and this measure broke down the still new and tenuous network of trust and interests which the magistrates had built up with such care over the preceding eight years. The leader of the opposition to colonial rule in the country, a younger son of Moshoeshoe, seized his opportunity and led the nation in revolt against the Cape Administration; and the Government proved unable either to defeat the Sotho, or, after making peace, to re-establish magisterial rule. After three years of increasing chaos, it was forced to hand back Basutoland to Britain, which instituted a form of indirect rule through the chiefs. As a result of Britain's subsequent policy of decolonisation, the country is today the independent Kingdom of Lesotho.

There have been various studies of the role of the Cape and British governments in relation to Basutoland during these years, notably John Benyon's unpublished thesis on the High Commission.[1] In this book I have therefore concentrated on the interaction of the Sotho and the Cape Administration within Basutoland, especially the attempts to change the society by administrative fiat and the reaction of that society to attacks on its basic structure. Limitations of length have prevented a detailed examination of the effects of the wider southern African economy on this process, but it should be borne in mind that the period under review covered years of great and fluctuating socio-economic changes in both Sotho and Cape societies. As is outlined below, among the Sotho the half century after the wars of the 1820s marked a change from small chiefdoms to a much larger unit dominated to a great extent by one lineage. Within that unit the society became increasingly stratified as changing political organisation gave the chiefs greater authority and control over property, both that property produced within the Sotho economy and that acquired from the colonial society. With the arrival of the colonial Administration, many of the processes increasing the chiefs' wealth and power came into abrupt collision with the aims of the Administration, bent on ultimately integrating the Sotho into the Cape economy. At one level the legal changes the magistrates sought to introduce can be seen as attempts to change the control and ownership of property, and hence inevitably they involved direct conflict with the chiefs. The climax came when the underlying economic pressures of Cape society gave rise to a policy that led to full-scale revolt. As Atmore and Marks have shown,[2] the confederation policy, of which disarmament was an offshoot, had economic roots in the greatly increased demand for African labour generated by the spectacular discoveries of diamonds between 1867 and 1871 in Griqualand West. Ultimately, the War of the Guns can be described as the outcome of the incompatible economic processes evolving in Sotho and Cape societies.

The period of Cape rule is very well documented, not only in official and semi-official papers, but also by missionaries, their wives and children, and later, by officials and their wives, who were often personal friends of many of the chiefs and the people. In addition, by the time the Cape Administration took over, missionary education had produced the first generation of literate Sotho, a number of whose letters survive. Together, these and other sources provide an unusually vivid first-hand account of the period, and as far as possible the words of the people who participated in or witnessed its colourful events have been used to evoke its atmosphere. The defects of oral evidence for the type of legal and political material covered by this book have been outlined by Peter Sanders,[3] and as contemporary written evidence is so abundant, oral evidence has not been collected. As a result, however, the events of the period are not often seen directly through Sotho eyes—and even less those of Sotho commoners. Perhaps some day someone will attempt the much more difficult task of filtering oral evidence on these years and filling in the picture more fully.

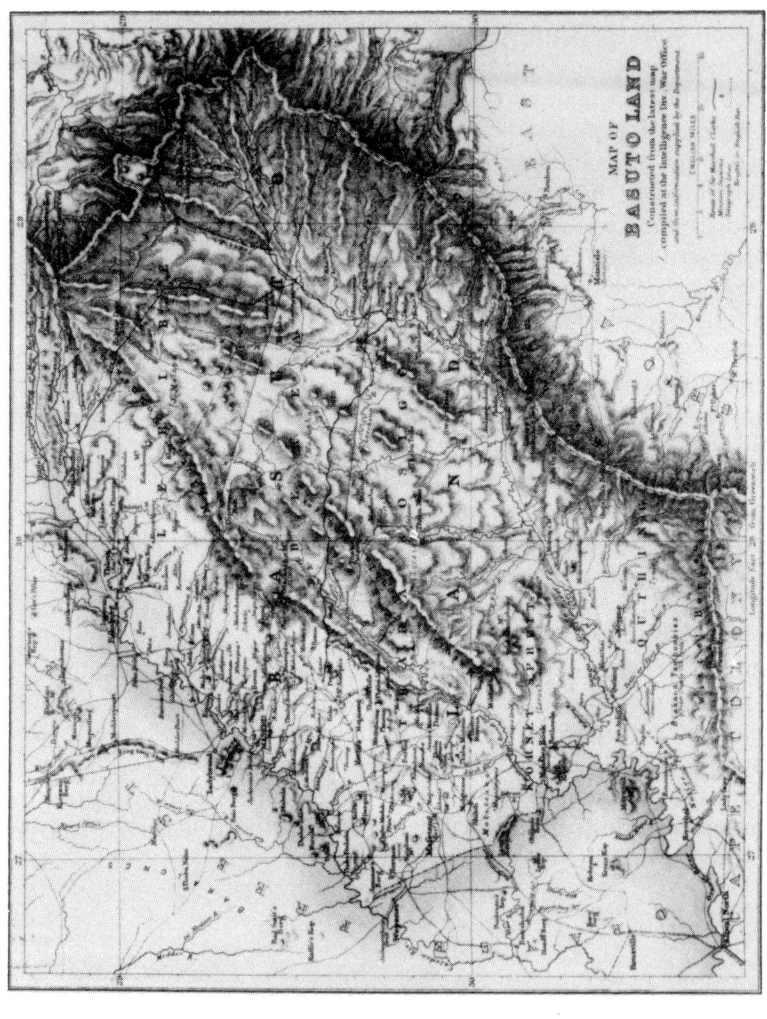

Map 2 Map of Basutoland, drawn in 1888, showing the topography

1 Creating a Nation

The Bantu-speaking societies arrived in South Africa as a result of migration and colonisation begun by their forefathers far to the north many centuries before. They probably reached the Limpopo during the twelfth century, and by the eighteenth century were as far south as the Fish River, where they first came into conflict with the Dutch colonists expanding eastward from the Cape Colony. The luckless original inhabitants of the area, small yellow-skinned men who belonged to two closely related peoples known to the colonists as 'Hottentots' and 'Bushmen', were slowly pushed north by the colonists and expelled or absorbed by the advancing migrants.

These migrants were divided into various language groups, of which the Cape was to come into contact with two during the eighteenth and nineteenth centuries—the Nguni and the Sotho. The Nguni lived along the eastern coastal corridor formed by the sea on the one side and the escarpment of the central plateau on the other, the highest portion of which was the Drakensberg Mountains. They spoke what were virtually dialects of the same language and to a large extent shared a common culture. The Sotho, who had settled on the interior plateau, were more diverse, dividing into the Tswana to the west, the Northern Sotho or Pedi, who moved east into what became the central and northern Transvaal, and the Southern Sotho, who moved off to the south-east into what became known as Transorangia and Lesotho.

Exact dates are uncertain, but oral and archaeological evidence indicates that by about 1670 at the latest, Sotho settlement was to be found on the plains that form the western part of modern Lesotho, an area studded with isolated flat-topped and castellated sandstone hills, like natural fortresses. By the time that the white man made contact with them, the Southern Sotho had been settled for a number of generations on the High Veld, over a much larger area than that of Lesotho today. Intermingled with them were several bands of earlier settlers of Nguni origin, known as the Phetla, the

Polani and the Phuthi. These three groups were settled in the south and east of the country. The San (the semi-nomadic hunters and gatherers whom the colonists called 'Bushmen'), were living in the country in scattered groups when the Bantu-speaking tribes arrived. They were overwhelmed by the more numerous and powerful immigrants and either killed, driven out, or absorbed into Sotho society as clients, servants, or wives.

Each Sotho village, which did not usually contain more than a hundred inhabitants, was ruled by its own chief. Many, but not all the inhabitants, would be related to the chief, who might be either independent or else subordinate to another chief, usually a senior relative. He, in turn, might be subordinate to an overlord. An overlord would have the right to hear appeals from his subordinate's court, and would expect his subordinate's people to fight for him and attend his work parties. New villages were constantly being established since land was plentiful but grazing often sparse. Younger brothers and sons would be sent out to establish new villages to provide a safe place where an already existing community's increasing flock might graze and where additional crops might be grown; the more ambitious often repudiated the authority of their overlord and established independent or semi-independent chiefdoms. An offended subordinate chief was very likely to do the same. Several chiefdoms of common descent might be known by a common name, derived from either an ancestor or an animal they revered, but they did not usually recognise· any common political authority. The result was that by the late eighteenth century small Sotho chiefdoms were scattered over the High Veld, some independent, some subordinate, but recognising no common paramout chief.

The unification of these chiefdoms into a supra-tribal nation was the result of events on the other side of the Drakensberg in what is now Zululand. After a bloody power struggle between the Nguni chiefdoms there, the Zulu chief, Shaka, emerged as the victor. He proceeded to reorganise his army, removing the warriors into large camps, away from the control of their chiefs, and thereby depriving his subordinate chiefs of their ability to defect. With this gone, they no longer had any effective check on his arbitrary power. New weapons, tactics, and savage discipline converted the army into the most effective fighting force in southern Africa. With absolute control of this formidable force, Shaka set out on a policy of tribal amalgamation by a series of devastating wars deliberately aimed at destroying the existing political organisation in conquered tribes. During his reign he is said to have destroyed 300 tribes and extended his power 500 miles north, south, and west.[1] The turmoil that resulted is known in Sotho as the *lifaqane*, the 'wars of calamity'.[2] Tribes fleeing from Shaka's armies often proved to be formidable marauders themselves. They first invaded the High Veld through the Drakensberg passes in 1822, and for several years political and social chaos ensued, very different from the minor cattle raids of earlier days: the invading hordes burnt villages to the ground, often killing anyone they found there, and seized both cattle and grain. Thousands starved to death, and famine drove some groups even to cannibalism.

It was this chaos that was to enable an ambitious and exceptionally able man to amalgamate the hitherto jealously independent chiefdoms into a nation. In about 1786[3] a son was born to an unimportant sub-chief of the Koena, 'The People of the Crocodile', one of the Sotho clusters of chiefdoms on the High Veld. From an early age, Moshoeshoe, as the young man became known,[4] showed unusual promise, and before 1820 had already begun to acquire subordinate chiefdoms; these followed him when in about 1820, shortly before the outbreak of the *lifaqane* disturbances, he set up a village of his own at Botha-Bothe in a strong defensive position in the mountains of the north-eastern Lesotho. When later attacks convinced him that Botha-Bothe was inadequate as a permanent home for his people, he moved some fifty miles to the south-west to Thaba-Bosiu, 'The Mountain of Night'[5], a great flat-topped mountain some four miles in circumference standing isolated in a fertile plain which could support a substantial population in times of peace. It proved to be defensible against all comers, and from there Moshoeshoe slowly built up a nation which became known as BaSotho (i.e. *the* Sotho), a name corrupted to Basuto by the white men who first came into contact with Moshoeshoe and his people.

That he should have been able to do so was largely due to the widespread need for security in such dangerous times, but the importance of Moshoeshoe's character and methods in securing unity should not be underestimated. Various writers on Lesotho have produced summaries of the descriptions left by his contemporaries of Moshoeshoe's appearance and manner; Tylden, a military historian of Lesotho, writes:

From Casalis and Arbousset and at later dates from other writers there are available accounts of Moshesh which give a good idea of what he was like. He is described as a tall, well-built man over six feet in height,[6] with a face of almost Roman appearance, a slightly flattened aquiline nose, and with no trace of the obesity common to most African chiefs. Like the rest of his clan the Bamokoteli, a branch of the Bakuena, who are an offshoot of the Bahlakoana, he was as a young man of a light colour, which became darker as he aged. He is said to have been long-winded, with a raucous voice, and would, on occasion, speak for hours at a stretch. All agree as to his simplicity, courtesy, imperturbability, charm, and command of language. He rode well and was well in advance of his age in his fondness for water—even in very cold weather he had buckets of cold water thrown over him daily. On state occasions he wore a dark blue uniform, otherwise he wore the loin cloth and fur cloak or kaross of his people . . .

He was very approachable and stood on no ceremony. The humblest of his subjects could obtain an audience at almost any hour of the day or night and be heard patiently.[7]

For example, Arbousset, one of his first missionaries, described a journey with him in 1852. As they rode along his subjects came flocking to greet him.

In everything this African prince has shown a tact which I admire extremely. His affability has not flagged for a single moment. Vivacity, gaiety, nothing is lacking, in him. He speaks to everyone without regard to age or rank. He even amuses himself with the children, as if he were one of them himself; and, even more astonishing, his memory is so good that he seems to know the name and history of each of his subjects. I leave it to the imagination whether, with such qualities, he is popular among them![8]

His ability impressed many more than his subjects. Typical of the opinions which appear in the letters and reports of white visitors and officials is that of J. M. Orpen, who frequently negotiated with Moshoeshoe on behalf of the Orange Free State Government and was later to be Acting Governor's Agent in Basutoland: Orpen believed Moshoeshoe to be an exceptionally original, able and enlightened chief.[9] Certainly Moshoeshoe often departed from traditional customs that failed to serve his needs, and when faced with apparently unfavourable events, showed great resourcefulness in turning them to his advantage. A shrewd judge of character, he was, as a missionary who worked in Lesotho from 1861 to 1905 testified:

> at once fearless and cautious; very wary of entering upon a quarrel; but having once embarked upon one, he carried it through with an intrepidity which nothing could daunt. He could see farther ahead than most men; and, no matter what checks he encountered, he never lost sight of the end in view.[10]

The end he had in view from an early age was to build as large and strong a chiefdom for himself as possible. There were two main motives for individuals and other chiefdoms to join him: for protection and for material benefits. To achieve the former for his followers in those troubled and unpredictable times, he used every means to forestall attacks from those stronger than himself, and resisted fiercely when all else failed. Thus he paid tribute to any chief stronger than himself, put on a great display of strength where this was likely to act as a sufficient deterrent to would-be attackers, and where necessary would even humble himself before defeated enemies in an attempt to prevent their return, or speed their departure. Casalis, one of the first missionaries to the Sotho, describes for example how, after an abortive attack on Thaba-Bosiu by the Ndebele, Moshoeshoe sent an offering of oxen after them as they retreated, with the message: 'Moshesh salutes you. Supposing that hunger has brought you into this country, he sends you these cattle, that you may eat them on your way home.' Casalis claimed that this dramatic gesture so impressed the Ndebele that they resolved never to attack him again—and indeed, they never did.[11]

Equally important was the provision of material benefits for his followers. A chief was expected to entertain visitors, provide food and drink for his followers at large meetings and celebrations, and look after the poor by providing livestock under the *mafisa* system, whereby cattle or other livestock were given on long loan on certain conditions. As a result, the size of a chief's following was largely dependent on the size of his herds. Moshoeshoe at an early age showed himself to be a daring and successful leader of cattle raids, the accepted method for a chief of acquiring stock. He also proved able to defend his herds from the inevitable counter-raids. However, his exceptional success in using this wealth to attract followers was the result of methods as original and psychologically far-sighted as his defensive strategies.[12]

His magnanimity became legendary. His herds were distributed throughout the country under the *mafisa* system and, according to his son Nehemiah, he never kept recaptured cattle of other clans of the Sotho for himself, as he could have done according to custom, but returned them to their owners.[13] The missionary Ellenberger bears this out in his report that even although the Sekake[14] refused Moshoeshoe assistance when he was attacked by another chief, Shekeshe, he went to their aid when they in turn were attacked by the same enemy, rescued their cattle which had been captured, and returned most of their herds to them. This act secured him the adherence of the Sekake.[15] There were other similar stories too, demonstrating his political far-sightedness and economic acumen, for the *mafisa* system worked to his own ultimate enrichment.

For the same reason, to increase the number of his followers when more peaceful times returned, Moshoeshoe encouraged the many Sotho who had taken refuge in the Cape Colony and Natal to return to their country. For those of his people whom the wars had left without cattle, he provided cattle under the *mafisa* system. For certain destitute young men he also provided *bohali* (or the cattle which a man had to give to his wife's family at marriage), on condition that the *bohali* of their daughters by those marriages should revert to him. 'Their wives and children were then regarded as his "by cattle", while they themselves were completely at his service'.[16] In this way he acquired both the services of those clients and an ever increasing source of wealth for himself.[17]

Nor was he exclusive in accepting followers. Although Sotho formed the bulk of his adherents, Nguni were also welcomed and even cannibals, despite the fact the Moshoeshoe's own grandfather had been eaten by cannibals and his followers were keen to avenge themselves for past murders. But with typical foresight, Moshoeshoe saw that this would incur all the horrors of a civil war, and tend to depopulate the land still further. Even when the very cannibals who had eaten his grandfather were brought before him, he set them free, remarking with dry humour that it was not becoming to disturb the graves of one's ancestors. They were provided with cattle (presumably under the *mafisa* system) on condition that they ceased to attack his people, and became loyal subjects.[18] Similarly, for those who sought to join him he enforced a general amnesty of past offences against his people, which encouraged their old rivals to come under his chieftainship.[19] This was particularly important where a successful cattle raid left a chief and his followers so impoverished that they wished to 'follow the cattle behind' and become the subjects of the successful raider in order to retain their cattle under the *mafisa* system.[20]

Not only his generosity, but no doubt also his reputation for justice attracted many disaffected men from other chiefdoms, as well as allies in search of protection under the least restrictive conditions. J. M. Orpen reported: 'His government has always been characterised by humanity, mildness, and justice; he has never been known to "eat up"[21] his subjects; he forbade the punishment of death for witchcraft,[22] and has uniformly endeavoured to suppress the bloody feuds so common among African tribes.'[23] Casalis testified that during the twenty-three years he spent among the Sotho, the chief put no one to death from personal motives.[24] And according to RaMatšeatsana, one of his counsellors, he abolished the traditional death sentence for murder, justifying this change with the argument that the execution made the executioner a murderer who must in turn be executed, and so on *ad infinitum*.[25] Not surprisingly, many in search of a strong, just and generous protector chose to place themselves under him. By 1848, after twelve years of uninterrupted peace, Moshoeshoe was acknowledged leader of some 80,000 people in what they called Lesotho—the country of the Sotho.[26]

While individuals who sought his protection were incorporated directly into villages administered by himself or members of his family, his method of retaining chiefdoms that had joined him was to keep a very light hand on the reins. Small groups of refugees without a chief were ruled by their own headmen, supervised by a member of Moshoeshoe's family 'placed' in the vicinity.[27] Similarly, where a group with a recognised chief came under his rule, he was usually content to leave it under its own chief provided the supremacy of the Paramount Chief (and possibly a 'placed' member of his family) was recognised; Orpen wrote that no act of great national importance was regarded as legal or binding on them, or on the nation as a whole, unless discussed and agreed upon in a council consisting of all the chiefs.[28] To enhance his personal status and extend or strengthen his influence, Moshoeshoe married women from many different chiefly families; in 1833 he already had thirty wives, by 1864 about 150, some of whom were the daughters of his subordinate chiefs.[29] By the time of his death, his system had produced not a united nation, but a loosely-knit federation in which not only different dialects, but different languages were spoken, and with a wide variety of customs. Holding this patchwork together required constant diplomacy and frequent compromise, not least with recalcitrant members of his own family threatening to secede.[30]

It was his desire to strengthen his nation further and protect it from raids by the armed and mounted Kora[31] that led Moshoeshoe to invite missionaries to his country, after an emancipated slave had told him how missionaries had helped the Griqua to organise themselves into effective states. The missionaries who responded to his invitation were of the Paris Evangelical Missionary Society—Thomas Arbousset, Eugene Casalis, and the artisan Constant Gosselin—and arrived at Thaba-Bosiu in June 1833. Moshoeshoe made them welcome and established them some thirty miles south of Thaba-Bosiu, where they named their station Morija.[32] Both Morija and the sites where other French missionaries subsequently established mission stations were on his more exposed borders, and the missionaries were in practice a means of spreading his influence. However, he also genuinely regarded them as agents of moral and material progress, and did not hide his motives for inviting them; when in 1862 the French Protestant missionaries objected to his admission of Roman Catholic priests to Lesotho, he replied that 'he could not oppose any body coming into his country to teach his people, and that Protestants and Catholics, as he had been told, were like two cows whose bellowing was a little different from each other, but both would give milk'.[33] Despite this, his willingness to listen to and act on the missionaries' advice (sometimes even in the face of hostility from his less open-minded followers), his deep interest in Christianity, and the converts they soon made,[34] led the missionaries to identify themselves closely with the Sotho cause and to provide invaluable advice and assistance in all Moshoeshoe's subsequent dealings with the British and Boers. However, although the missionaries and Moshoeshoe proved very useful to each other, the seeds of future conflict were present. The Paris Evangelical Mission Society had an uncompromising attitude towards in-digenous customs, especially polygamy and initiation schools; from the start it used its influence to try to change the Sotho law which governed these customs, thereby arousing deep resentment and fear amongst the more conservative elements in the country.

Even in Moshoeshoe's time, some changes of this kind were made at their instigation, for the Paramount Chief liked to stand well with his missionaries,[35] had an exceptionally open mind to new ideas, and was empowered by Sotho custom to make at least temporary changes. As Casalis explains:

> The chiefs have the right of making laws and publishing regulations required by the necessities of the times. These laws, which are generally temporary, have received the name of *Molaos* (our law, or commandment). Higher than these edicts rank the *Mekoas* (the *use and wont*), which constitute the real laws of the country.[36]

Thus, for example, Moshoeshoe even temporarily banned initiation rituals,[37] to which the Sotho attached the utmost importance,[38] and several of his sons did not attend initiation school, including the last son of his chief wife.[39] He also took steps to make plain to his people that women who converted should not be forced to remain married polygamously. To many of his own wives who converted he granted letters of divorce, since they could not be admitted to church membership unless they separated from him.[40] The missionary Casalis reported:

> His decision to separate from these women was not a private arrangement, simply between himself and the women, but it was proclaimed in a great assembly of the people in 1840. Some of the heathen present raised their voice in the meeting to oppose the introduction of the new custom, and even threatened one of the counsellors of Moshesh with instant death for advising the chief to divorce his wives. But Moshesh was firm.[41]

However, he was always very conscious that his rule ultimately rested on consent, and was careful not to exceed the limits of his subjects' tolerance to foreign ideas.[42]

But foreign ideas were drastically affecting the Sotho way of life in another sphere, despite all Moshoeshoe's efforts. Since the early nineteenth century Dutch farmers (or Boers) from the Cape Colony had seasonally crossed the Orange River to graze their herds, and from about 1820 a permanent population began to grow up north of the Orange River. A few of these farmers in the 1830s settled on land that Moshoeshoe claimed between the Orange and the Caledon, but they and the Sotho lived peacefully enough alongside each other until 1835, when the Great Trek—the large-scale migration of

Boers dissatisfied with Cape rule—greatly increased the white population north of the Orange. The newcomers were given Moshoeshoe's permission to graze their cattle until they were ready to move on, but were warned that they were not being granted any permanent rights in the land. As with other groups, in Sotho law their land was inalienable and the concept of selling land was unknown.[43] Having heard of this practice of the whites however, and fearing lest advantage be taken of him, Moshoeshoe refused to receive any payment from white farmers, not even the customary present of cattle as recognition of his suzerainty. But the farmers proceeded nonetheless to build permanent homes, despite Moshoeshoe's frequent protests.

In the early nineteenth century the British had taken the Cape Colony from the Dutch, and as early as 1842 the Sotho, through their missionaries, made a formal request to the British Government for an alliance with it in order to obtain protection from the Boers. There followed an inglorious confusion in which the British Government made futile attempts to prevent Boer encroachment, first by making treaties with the Sotho in 1843 and 1845, offering Moshoeshoe protection which was never in fact given, and then in 1848 by annexing his land to a newly created British territory between the Orange and Vaal Rivers and named the Orange River Sovereignty. But the British Resident failed to act in an impartial manner in land disputes, partly through a lack of understanding of Sotho land tenure, partly through the need to win the support of the Boers. When fighting eventually broke out between the disillusioned Sotho and the British who were trying to enforce the Resident's authority, the British were defeated. A change of policy led to the British abandonment of the Sovereignty in 1854 and a series of wars between the Sotho and Boers who had established the Orange Free State. Although the Sotho won the first encounters, Moshoeshoe foresaw that time was working against the federation he had spent his life creating, and that in British protection lay its one chance of safety. He repeatedly asked to be made a British subject but the British refused for fear of being involved in further expense.

By 1865, however, the Boers had the advantage of the Sotho in guns, ammunition, and leadership. Although the Sotho nation by then probably numbered about 150,000, Moshoeshoe was almost eighty and showing signs of senility, while his sons and their followers were quarrelling over the succession; the Orange Free

State, on the other hand, had a considerably increased white population and a capable and energetic leader, President J. H. Brand. Molapo, Moshoeshoe's second son, made a separate peace and reluctantly agreed to become a subject of the Orange Free State.[44] Deprived of his assistance, Moshoeshoe was obliged at the Treaty of Thaba Bosiu in 1866 to cede nearly all the lowlands where his people lived to the Orange Free State, but the Sotho violated the treaty almost immediately and war broke out again in 1867. The Orange Free State policy of destroying crops and reducing the Africans to starvation rapidly brought the Sotho state to the verge of disintegration, and the dispersion of its people seemed imminent.

In a last effort to prevent this, Moshoeshoe, his sons, missionaries and friends bombarded the High Commissioner with pleas for British intervention. Sir Philip Wodehouse, the High Commissioner, was sympathetic but helpless in the face of his instructions from England. Moshoeshoe and his sons in desperation began negotiations with the neighbouring British Colony of Natal, requesting to be annexed to Natal; and the Natal Government forwarded this request to the British Government with its blessing.[45] However, events elsewhere had been working in Moshoeshoe's favour, eroding Colonial Office confidence in its policy of neutrality. Doubts were growing about the wisdom of allowing the Boers to continue their activities unchecked: the severe terms inflicted on the Sotho by the Treaty of Thaba Bosiu might force a disrupting Sotho migration and had already led to the expulsion of the French Protestant missionaries;[46] Sotho raids in pursuit of the Boers were interfering with Natal's trade and development and threatened to affect the Cape Colony;[47] there were also reports of slavery in the Transvaal and of African chiefdoms being harassed by commandos; the Orange Free State's power had been enhanced by Molapo's agreement; worst of all, the British feared that the Boers might gain access to the sea through Pondoland, thus simultaneously isolating the Cape from Natal and allowing other European influences into South Africa.[48] In December 1867 the Cabinet instructed Wodehouse that he might annex Lesotho—but to Natal, not directly to Britain, and only with the consent of both Natal and the Orange Free State.

The Sotho were in such a desperate position that they would have accepted even this, but they feared annexation to Natal as they believed the colonists would oblige them to surrender their guns.[49]

Wodehouse had wider fears: apart from disliking the idea of a much strengthened Natal, he suspected the white community there would subject the Sotho to its own interests and annex their land. The Cape was not prepared to accept Lesotho as part of its territory, and the Free State objected to British interference in a war they had almost won. Finally, fearing that Thaba-Bosiu itself would fall if attacked, Wodehouse proceeded to ignore his instructions, cut off the supply of Free State ammunition at the Cape ports and, on 12 March 1868, proclaimed Lesotho annexed to the Crown. Its official name became 'Basutoland'.

Thus the nation which Moshoeshoe had created so laboriously came under the legal control of the white man. Moshoeshoe, failing in mind and body, no longer wielded the real power in the land, but the loosely-knit and heterogeneous Sotho nation was very much his creation; how far the white men would be able to impose their will on the Sotho depended, in the absence of large-scale force being available to them, on their ability to emulate Moshoeshoe in ensuring that the advantages of their rule outweighed the irritations and loss of independence it involved. The major irritation during the early years after magistrates were appointed, especially to the chiefs, was to be the changes imposed on Sotho law and the chiefs' powers.

2 Conflicting Values

The Sotho had accepted British rule out of military necessity, not because they desired it for itself. The British Government had been forced by fear of Boer activities and by Wodehouse's manipulations to receive the Sotho as British subjects; it did not wish to order their daily lives and was anxious not to incur any extra expense. The obvious solution was to leave the Sotho to rule themselves so far as the mid-Victorian Christian conscience could allow, and to ensure that they paid for any costs incurred. But this ran counter to the prevailing idea both in Britain and South Africa that it was a Christian duty to 'civilise' the African. The civilisation to which they were to be introduced was that of Victorian England, with its firm belief in the superior virtue of a way of life rooted in Christianity, a profit-seeking economy, and the consequently necessary high degree of protection of the individual from the demands of the group. Unfortunately for both British and Sotho, Sotho society had developed to meet different economic and strategic requirements, and as a result was based on rather different values.

As with the other African societies of southern Africa, the Sotho had an essentially subsistence economy, with the family providing the basic necessities for survival and most of a man's other requirements. The role of the family was therefore central to their daily life, and their laws and customs had developed to preserve it, if necessary at the expense of what Europeans viewed as individual freedom, especially of women, on whom the continuance of the family depended. For a man too, his connection with his family determined all his legal relationships—whether or not he was liable for his actions, whether he could sue or be sued, under what conditions he could make a valid contract binding either himself or another, whom he could marry and on what conditions, what he might do with his property during his lifetime or what his kinsmen might do with it after his death. Family law was thus the most highly developed aspect of Sotho law and the one that would most affect the Sotho if changed. It was also unfortunately the branch of the law containing most of the concepts that Victorians found offensive in Sotho society.

In this society the family was usually formed of all those who came under the legal authority of the head of the extended family. This was normally a man; women were regarded as perpetual minors and only in exceptional circumstances did a woman become head of a family. Under the authority of the family head would be not only his wives (for Sotho marriage was at least potentially polygamous)[1] and their children, but any of his own younger brothers and those of his father who had not set up their own establishments on marriage, with all their wives and descendants. There might also be some other people who were not necessarily blood relatives but who had lost or abandoned their own natural family heads and voluntarily placed themselves under his power, in effect becoming part of the family. He represented everyone in his establishment, making all binding contracts and holding all property in trust for it,[2] suing and being sued for all its members, and disposing of the young men and women in marriage. His authority was reinforced by the belief that he was the direct representative of the ancestors and the mediator between the living and departed members of the family. For a man to cut himself off from the family was to forfeit the protection of the ancestral spirits during his lifetime and a place in the family cult, necessary for the well-being of his spirit, after his death. It also ensured him of the spirits' anger (which was believed to result in illness or other disasters), for the acts most displeasing to them were neglect or disregard of the customs of the country.

In practice, however, the arbitrary exercise of power by the head of the family would be limited by customary consultation with the senior men of the family, his natural affection for its members, and fear of both public opinion and punishment by the spirits. This meant that in fact, if not theory, there was to a large degree joint ownership and control of property, and a collective responsibility which made the whole family liable for the misdeeds and debts of its members, including those incurred if the marriage of a family member broke up. Changes in marriage law, such as the Administration was to introduce, therefore had an economic effect on far more people than just the married couple.

In family matters the married men had a good deal of influence, especially in regard to matters affecting their own wives and children and the property attaching specifically to their establish-ments. A man could only marry and take part in the councils of his community after undergoing the rites of initiation into manhood, which included practices highly objectionable to the Victorians.[3] When a chief's son was sixteen or seventeen years old, he would be initiated with the other boys of his age in the chiefdom, who would then form a band of devoted—and therefore particularly valuable—followers for the rest of his life.

> At the outset they were required to overpower a black bull captured from another chiefdom and to tear a shoulder and a leg from its living body. The raw flesh was then given to the doctor, who treated it with medicines from the chief's horn before giving it back to the boys to eat. These medicines would have been culled from many sources, from material substances, plants, animals, and the human body, and they would have been prepared by being burnt and then ground into powder and mixed with fats. It was believed, for example, that tufts of hair from the base of a bull's horn would impart strength, that the liver of a wild cat would impart ferocity, and that various organs cut from the bodies of slain enemies would impart bravery.[4] When this ceremony was completed the boys retired to the initiation lodge, where they were circumcised and then remained in seclusion for about six months. During this period they were trained in the arts of fighting and cattle raiding; they were subjected to floggings, forced marches, and other gruelling tests of endurance; they were given instruction on their future conduct in the *khotla*[5] and on their duties to their chief; they were taught the mysterious songs of the initiation lodge; and they were assisted in the composition of their own praise-poems. At the conclusion of this education the lodge was burnt to the ground, while the initiates ran back to the village without so much as glancing behind them at the flames. This symbolised the end of all that had to do with their childhood and adolescence . . . . Girls under-went a similar rite of initiation, and for them too it was the gateway to adult life. Their training, of course, was very different, for they were taught their responsibilities in the home and their duties towards their husbands. Normally they were married soon after it was completed.[6]

A match would be arranged by the elders of the two families

involved and in general was a contract of convenience between two families; romance seldom entered into it, although frequently a very real affection would later develop between the couple. Casalis, for example, on first visiting Moshoeshoe, drew a picture of his contented domesticity with his principal wife, 'MaMohato:

> Mamohato was a tall and strong woman already of somewhat ripe age, but not wanting in attractions. . . . Moshesh seated himself by her side, and took their youngest son Ntalimi, a little boy between four and five, between his knees. The apparently perfect union between these two, and the perfect cordiality mingled with respect with which they addressed and offered little services to each other, greatly struck me.[7]

But the interests of the family did not necessarily coincide with the wishes of its marriageable members, and girls were sometimes forced into marriages they did not want; a practice which met with magisterial and missionary disapproval. Marriage by elopement was used to some extent to overcome the opposition of the elders to a particular match, and in such cases the elders generally acquiesced in the situation but exacted a fine for the elopement as well as the customary marriage payment for the bride. Where, however, the marriage was not allowed, the man would be liable to pay damages for seduction to the girl's family. But in contrast to European law, this was because an unmarried woman represented the potential value of her marriage-cattle, which would be lessened by her seduction, and Sotho law afforded to the head of the family redress for the violation of any right representing material value. It differed from the European (and therefore missionary) way of viewing seduction as an offence against the girl herself for affront to her dignity.

There were very few essential requirements for a marriage to be valid: simply the consent of the contracting parties, though not necessarily of the couple involved, and usually payment or arrangements for payment of an agreed number of marriage-cattle for the bride (called *bohali* by the Sotho).[8] There is also evidence that formal acceptance of the marriage by her husband was required at the *tlhabiso* ceremony, which was described by Moshoeshoe's son, Sofonia, to the 1872 Commission on Sotho law:

> A marriage is said to be completed when the father of the bride

has slaughtered an animal or animals as 'mafura', with the fat of which the bride and bridegroom are anointed, and the bridegroom has the gall bladders put round his wrist. If the bridegroom refuses to have the gall bladders put on his wrist it is a sign that he does not like the bride, and the marriage is dissolved, the cattle are returned, and the animals slaughtered by the bride's father are paid for by the bridegroom or his friends.[9]

All other customs associated with the marriage could be omitted without affecting the validity of the marriage, but these three elements were usually considered essential. Attacks by the missionaries and Government officials in later times on the giving of marriage-cattle were therefore attacks on the basis of African law marriage.

It is important to note that the payment of the marriage-cattle was not regarded as similar to paying for a purchase, and the Sotho used a separate word to denote the handing over of the marriage-cattle and payment for goods. Neither were women regarded as objects: they could not be bought, sold, exchanged or destroyed at will, nor given away. The marriage payment was regarded as security given by the husband for his own good conduct towards his wife, for if she left him because of ill-treatment, he lost his claim for the return of the cattle. It was also partially a payment to her father for his consent to the marriage, whereby he lost the services of his daughter and her future children: unless the marriage-cattle were paid, the children generally remained under the power of the woman's family.[10] Finally, it also guaranteed the good behaviour of the wife to some extent, for if she left her husband without just cause, he could claim back the marriage payment. Rather than surrender it, her family would do everything possible to effect a reconciliation. Misunderstanding by missionaries and colonists of the purpose of the marriage payment was to cause much trouble in the future.

In Sotho society many court cases arose from the web of debts created by marriage payment obligations. Payment of the cattle did not always take place before the marriage. A man's family would usually provide the cattle for at least his first wife, but these cattle might become available only when his sister married and marriage-cattle were received for her. Or if the cattle were not forthcoming from his family, a man might marry on credit, promising to pay all or the balance of the cattle when the first daughter of the marriage was herself married, the marriage-cattle received for her thus in effect paying for her mother. As debts were not wiped out by death, that many years' delay in payment might result from such arrangements was not considered an insuperable obstacle, even if, for example, a daughter was not born of the marriage.

The marriage had the result of transferring the guardianship of the woman (and her subsequent children) from her father to her husband, although her own family retained an ultimate guardianship over her all her life. To many white men this seemed to place her in the position of a slave, but in practice her position was very different. With a few exceptions, each married woman, whether or not a man's only wife, lived in a separate hut once she had borne children, and to each hut of a wife (or 'house')[11] was allotted livestock and land for cultivation to maintain herself and her children.[12] To protect these, she could probably appeal to the head of the village against her husband's (or his heir's) misuse of this property and, if not satisfied, to the chief himself, despite the normal rule that she could not act for herself in court. No house could be enriched at the expense of another, and by custom any dealing with the property that attached to a house was usually done by the husband in consultation with the wife in question and her eldest son when he became old enough. The head of the family was also expected to provide marriage-cattle for his sons, wedding outfits for his daughters, and maintenance for his wives and dependants, who in turn provided for his daily needs from their allocation of land and livestock.

The situation with Moshoeshoe's many wives (and that of his heir) was basically the same, though complicated by the large numbers involved.

Whereas the traditional Sotho village was set out in a circle, with the huts of the chief's wives being formally ranged beside his own, Moshoeshoe's was in no particular order at all. His residence was surrounded by his wives' huts, and between the reed walls enclosing these was a tangle of winding alleyways. The evidence about his marital arrangements is similarly confused. There can be little doubt, however, that his wives, like those of other Sotho chiefs later, could be divided into the three broad categories given by Ellenberger, namely 'the great wife', in his case 'MaMohato; 'important wives', who were 'women of position', and became 'the mothers of important men'; and *lingoetsi*, who were junior wives who were attached as servants 'to the houses of the more important wives, two or three or even more to each house, according to its importance'.[13] The distinction between the second and third categories was blurred in some cases, but generally, while he jealously guarded his rights over 'MaMohato and his 'important wives', he allowed visitors and retainers to form illicit relationships with the *lingoetsi*, although their children were regarded as his. . . . No doubt Moshoeshoe treated his wives with the tact and discretion that were habitual to him, but even so it was impossible for him to smooth out all their rivalries and jealousies. Indeed he once confessed to Casalis that there were times when, in spite of his immense wealth, he was almost starved because no one would feed him: he would wander pathetically from hut to hut, being told by each offended and sulking wife to go to his favourite, whoever she might be, since no doubt she would have some tasty morsel for him.[14]

An exasperated husband could beat his wife, but, as with her property, her person was in practice, although not in law, quite well protected. Although in theory the power of the husband over his wife was considered absolute in everything except the actual taking of her life, in reality his family would probably have interfered to prevent consistently brutal treatment. This would be prompted by the legal right of her family, should she run home to them because of ill-treatment, to demand additional cattle to those already given for her, and to detain her until their demands were met. If she utterly refused to return to her husband, she could not be compelled to do so. Her husband could only demand that the marriage-cattle be refunded to him, but a refund would often be only partial (even if he were not at fault) if there had been children born of the marriage who were, as usually happened, retained as members of his family.

By Sotho law the rules governing when a marriage might be dissolved differed from European legal systems and were to cause problems with magistrates and missionaries. A husband, for example, might obtain a divorce unilaterally by expelling his wife from his household with the intention of permanently discarding her (in which case he forfeited the marriage-cattle); and in contrast to both contemporary English and Roman-Dutch law,[15] adultery on the part of the wife, unless it was incestuous or otherwise grossly offended Sotho morality, was not necessarily a sufficient cause for divorce (although the husband could claim damages from the man involved and any child born as a result of the adultery was regarded as the child of the husband). In all cases of dissolution, whether any, part, or all of the marriage-cattle were forfeited depended on the circumstances of the case, including whether there were any children of the marriage. In addition, the death of the husband did not dissolve the marriage—his widow continued to be a 'wife' of his family—and although the death of the wife dissolved the union, it did not necessarily end the existence of the house created by the marriage. When a wife died (or even while she was alive in certain circumstances) a husband could marry another wife and place her in the house of the missing wife to 'raise up seed' to that house. Where a wife died after a short time without having borne children, the husband might be offered another girl from his deceased wife's family (usually for half the original number of marriage-cattle) and her younger sister generally went to take her place. The children of such wives were counted as the children of the original wife of the house.

Even odder to strangers to Sotho society was the fact that anything that could be done by a man by way of 'raising seed' for himself during his lifetime could be done for him after his death. Marriage-cattle could be paid out of his estate for a 'seed-raiser', and a man, usually a male relative, selected to take his place in the marriage. Even if a son died unmarried, a 'marriage' could be created for the dead man in this way. An even stranger arrangement could be made where the father had never had a son at all but, pretending that he had, paid *bohali* for a wife for the imagined son. Yet another type of fictitious marriage was occasionally arranged when a widow who had no children would act as a man by paying *bohali* for another woman. The widow would then appoint a male relative to cohabit with her 'wife' and the children would belong to her since she had paid the *bohali*. The motive for all these arrangements, which the missionaries regarded as immoral, was at all costs to obtain a male heir. Z. K. Matthews described the beliefs that gave rise to this practice:

> the man who has no male heir cannot have his name perpetuated in the group to which he belongs; he leaves no one to sacrifice to the ancestral spirits; no one to settle the disputes that will arise out of the distribution of his estate and to act as guardian over his children.[16]

Since the death of the husband did not dissolve the marriage, a widow was expected to remain with her husband's family to bring up her children, assist with the work and, although she could not be forced to do so, to have further children by a relative of her husband chosen by his family, which would be regarded as the children of her dead husband. If instead she chose to return to her own family (or to live on a mission station, if she were a Christian), her guardian was liable to pay back at least part of her dowry. Alternatively, it was possible that she might be allowed to return to her family without a demand being made for repayment of the marriage-cattle, but in that case she was still regarded as part of her husband's family. If she married again, whether the marriage-cattle paid by her new husband went to her parents or her deceased husband's heir probably depended on whether she had borne children to her first husband. Intervention by the new Administration on behalf of widows was to cause much bitterness.

When the marriage was dissolved, the husband usually remained the guardian of the children if he had paid marriage-cattle, although if they were too young to be taken from the mother's care she might be allowed to keep them until they were older. They then had to be returned to the father, an arrangement which the missionaries opposed. The woman was entitled to take from the joint property only her personal belongings. In contrast to English and Roman-Dutch law marriages, Sotho law marriages were usually dissolved extra-judicially by agreement between the families of the spouses and outside intervention was required only if the families failed to agree, in which case the chief or headman was called in to act as arbitrator. Thereafter a woman's guardian in her own family had a duty to support her, unless she remarried. The legal necessity of judicial intervention to dissolve a Christian or civil law marriage was to cause many problems in the future, when people failed to understand that family agreement had not dissolved their marriages.

Many such problems came to light when inheritance disputes were brought to court. As the southern African peoples did not have a knowledge of writing until after the arrival of the missionaries, the making of wills was unknown. However, among the Sotho, from the time of Moshoeshoe a man might in the presence of witnesses tell his heir what he wished to be done with his property after his death, and these wishes would be strictly obeyed—but only as long as they did not contradict the Sotho law governing succession. Unlike the Roman-Dutch Law of intestate succession, by which the deceased's property was divided between all his children, only men could inherit (with certain exceptions),[17] and the eldest son of a house (or his son, if he were dead) inherited all the property and debts of that house: younger sons who had not yet married would, for example, be provided with marriage-cattle from the property of the house. The heir of the great (or first-ranking) house succeeded to his father's position as head of the extended family, with all the rights and duties which that entailed in family and chiefdom matters.

Land, however, could not form part of the inheritance, since it was always held by the chief in trust for his people and merely allocated for use by them. It would revert to the chief if abandoned or if the holder died, and could then be reallocated, although it was usually allowed to pass automatically to the heirs of the deceased. The chief was unable to sell chiefdom land, but this fact was not always appreciated by white settlers who received what they thought was ownership of the land and what the chief thought was the right of occupation at his pleasure. The Sotho assumed 'that every man had the right to the use of land just as he had a right to breathe the air, and the notion of the exclusive rights of individuals, which could be sold, over land that was neither a building site, nor under cultivation, was foreign.'[18]

The contract by which a man held land from his chief was typical of Sotho contracts. In contrast with the type of society represented by the Cape Colony, where most contracts were single exchanges of goods and services between relative strangers, in Sotho society most contracts existed because the people involved were linked to one another by family ties or by their position in the society. The most common forms of contract in Sotho society were those between the families of spouses about the payment of marriage-cattle, and between a man and his chief governing the holding of chiefdom land. Under Moshoeshoe another very common contract was that of *mafisa*, mentioned above,[19] whereby cattle or other livestock were given on long loan on condition that the ownership of both them and their increase remained with the lender: the person to whom they were lent had, for example, the use of the cattle for ploughing and the milk of the cows, but could not sell or exchange them. This was frequently used by the chiefs as a form of patronage, and was one of Moshoeshoe's most effective means of building up his chiefdom. Interference with any of these contracts, as was brought about by contact with Cape colonial society, interfered too with a man's most important relationships within his society.

The way in which Sotho law operated was through the chiefs'
courts, which would be held much more informally than was the
case with European courts: cases would be heard interspersed with
all the other public business with which the chief dealt.

There was no distinction between what are now called 'administrative' and 'judicial' affairs. The chief discharged a plurality of
tasks, which were not segregated into distinct 'roles' or 'capa-
cities'. He acted as judge in disputes between his subjects, he
adjudicated rival claims to land, he allocated land to applicants
and withdrew it from those who had forfeited their right to enjoy
it; he maintained order in his ward[20] and punished those who
broke it; he issued instructions to his subjects, presided over the
popular assembly or *pitso*,[21] called on his people to labour in his
fields, appropriated the fines paid to him in court and witnessed
all the major and many of the minor events and transactions in his
ward; he was spokesman for his people in a question with another
area or with a higher chief, and he transmitted the policies and
directives of his superiors back to his people. In all these various
activities, the chief was performing, not a variety of roles, but the
one, unitary role of 'being a chief'.[22]

Moshoeshoe, as Paramount Chief, would in theory have had the
power to make the ultimate decision in matters of law, and his court
would have acted as the ultimate court of appeal from all other
courts. But in practice, unless he was in a particularly strong
position to manipulate personal loyalty, patronage, and factional
rivalries over some issue, he was unable to override the customs of
the nation against the will of the people. Had he attempted to
change a law or custom[23] without consulting his counsellors and
without allowing the change to be canvassed both publicly and
thoroughly before it was adopted, he ran the risk that any disaffected
portion of his people might withdraw its allegiance and transfer it to
another chief. Among the Sotho it was normal before important
changes were made to hold a *pitso*, where any proposed change
would be freely discussed by commoners as well as chiefs. In
addition, the men consulted personally on such decisions would
probably include all his important subordinate chiefs—usually his
close relatives or men related to him by marriage—and in daily
affairs he would also have a council of confidential advisers to whom
he was expected to listen. These advisers, many of whom would be
relatives, would be influential men in close touch with their own

local section of the chiefdom, and would also include men who had been initiated with him. If he went against their advice, he was likely to have trouble, while if he had their agreement and support he could normally be sure his wishes would be respected. The same procedure and considerations would operate in sub-chiefdoms as well.

Apart from their other duties, these advisers would assist the chief to judge cases, including appeals, arising from the laws; most cases were heard in the first instance by the lesser chiefs and headmen in their districts, usually with the assistance of the local heads of villages or men of importance. An appeal would go to the chief above him in the hierarchy, which was constantly being extended by the system of 'placing'. (As the 'placing' of a chief automatically demoted all those under him by putting him at the top of the hierarchy, Moshoeshoe and his successors made much use of this method to promote the interests of their sons at the expense of their brothers' children and other chiefs who were not their relatives—which caused intense bitterness amongst the senior chiefs.) At the bottom of the pyramid of those in authority were the heads of families, who were responsible for all those resident in their households, just as each chief was responsible for everyone under him.

Blood feuds between or within families were not allowed as a means of obtaining retribution between members of the same chiefdom; although self-help was permitted if an offender was caught in the act, criminal cases were always heard in the courts, and in civil cases, if agreement could not be reached by direct discussion between the people concerned,[24] the complainant had to resort to the courts.[25] In his fundamental approach to law and justice as something to be administered by public courts, the Sotho attitude did not therefore differ a great deal from that of the colonist. Nor in most cases were the elements of how a case was conducted very different in Sotho as opposed to colonial courts: both heard evidence for the two sides in the case and passed judgement accordingly. But in the details of how each society attempted to reach a just decision, there were great differences. Cases would be heard in an outdoor area in the centre of the village, known as the *khotla*, where the men of the village would gather for all the public business of the village and also for informal discussion and relaxation. As in other parts of southern Africa, there were no strict rules of procedure or evidence in Sotho courts.

Time was not considered an important element in the trial, which was allowed to drag on until every source of information likely to throw light on the point at issue had been investigated, and until every member of the tribe who felt like it had cross-examined the parties and had made any statement calculated to assist in the elucidation of the matter in dispute.[26]

Even strangers were free to give their opinions and participate in the trial. There were no professional lawyers in Sotho society and each party in the trial (and his relatives and friends) would put his case. In a criminal case the accused would be repeatedly cross-examined. Women, children, close relatives and spouses were all competent witnesses, hearsay evidence was valid (though it carried less weight), and witnesses were present throughout the proceedings. Although evidence was not given on oath, a witness might be challenged to swear an oath at any stage in the proceedings to impress the truth of his evidence upon the court, and would then swear by whatever the chiefdom held most sacred. However, perjury was not always punished when detected, and it was accepted as a part of litigation tactics that the litigants might use unscrupulous methods. Failure by the magistrates to appreciate this, and Sotho ignorance of the white man's complicated rules of evidence and procedure were to make for much misunderstanding in future legal contact between the races.

As Sotho law was rooted in established custom, precedents were of the utmost importance. In a society without writing, as Sotho society was before the arrival of the white man, most men could perform feats of memory which were most impressive by the standards of a literate society. Precedents had to be carried in men's memories, and old men could quote in great detail cases of a similar nature which had been tried many years before. Although established principles were strictly followed, because of this unwritten state of the law it could be adapted to changing conditions almost imperceptibly. Bold innovations, however, were rare, and as a result of this communal nature of legal settlements and trials, and communal participation in the legislative process, most Sotho men had more than a nodding acquaintance with the law and did not regard it as a set of inexplicable rules.

Once a case had been thoroughly discussed,[27] the chief or headman would deliver his judgement. In practice it was not unknown for chiefs to use their patronage to influence their subjects' attitude towards cases, but ideally, after a matter had been argued at length, the decision would give general satisfaction in the community, which would feel that justice or something approaching it had been done. Refusal to carry out a decision of the chief's court (or an order to appear before it) was regarded as treason—a major crime for which the penalty was confiscation of property and possibly even death. Contempt of court was therefore not a totally new concept to the Sotho. The chief was entitled to keep part of the fine in civil cases in payment for his services, and such payments (together with fines in criminal cases) formed an important part of his regular income—which magisterial justice was to affect seriously. In addition, as the defendant or accused had to be given notice of the case against him and the date of the hearing, a court messenger would often have been employed, and would also have to be paid from the judgement debt. The same would apply if his services were required to enforce the judgement. The concept of 'costs' was therefore familiar to the Sotho. But since in civil law cases the gainer paid the costs, often a high percentage of what he recovered, the system of law subsequently introduced by colonial magistrates was to prove preferable to injured parties in this respect.

In practice, though not in formula, a distinction was drawn between civil and criminal offences. Civil offences violated private rights in property arising from personal status, ownership of property or contracts entered into. Remedies available were to obtain either the restoration of the property or compensation for the violation of rights in it. Crimes, on the other hand, were offences against the chief as a guardian of his people, each member of which 'belonged' to him and could not with impunity be injured in person or, sometimes, in reputation. Examples were breaches of laws made by the chief, witchcraft,[28] incest and often also homicide and other cases of bloodshed, although these last-mentioned were treated primarily as civil wrongs among the Sotho.[29] Crimes could never be compounded and had to be reported to the nearest local ruler, who saw to the trial of the offender.

As a result of the criterion used in distinguishing between crimes and civil offences, some common offences defined as crimes (offences against society) in European legal systems were regarded in Sotho law as offences against the individual only—for example, theft. The European attitude towards such offences was foreign to the Sotho, especially when offenders were jailed. Punishment among the Sotho, even for crimes, was generally limited to fines paid in livestock.[30] These ranged from a single head of cattle to confiscation of all property and banishment ('being eaten up'), according to the nature of the offence, the offender's previous record, and his social status, but food was never included in the sentence of confiscation. As the chief was regarded as the injured party in criminal cases, he alone could claim the fine, although he might make a gift of part of it to the injured man or relatives of a murdered man 'to wipe their tears'. Flogging was sometimes resorted to in the punishment of young offenders, but there were no prisons and the death penalty was usually reserved for acts regarded as so antisocial as to endanger the community, such as rebellion and witchcraft.[31] In these latter cases, however, ordinary forms of trial procedure were often suspended and the accused was tortured to death.[32] Sometimes only a heavy fine was imposed on a man convicted of witchcraft, but more usually all his cattle were forfeit to the chief. Because of this forfeiture, some chiefs used witchcraft accusations against rich men, and sometimes also as a way of removing troublesome counsellors. As an increasing number of Sotho became prosperous after the *lifaqane* and as contact with the white man set up new tensions in Sotho society, fear of such victimisation by the chiefs became increasingly real to many Sotho. But as the causes of illness in either people or animals were not understood, witchcraft was also genuinely believed to be responsible for such misfortunes; the sickness or death of a chief, for example, almost always resulted in a 'smelling out' of witches and a witchcraft trial. Thus the intervention of the missionaries and, later, officials, forbidding the seeking out and punishment of witches was felt by most Sotho to be extremely dangerous, although under white rule it also provided much wanted protection for those benefiting from the white man's economy or adopting his ideas.

But even before the British annexed Lesotho, Sotho society was being affected by the values brought to southern Africa by the missionaries and the white settlers to the south. As already indicated, the influential missionaries objected to the whole Sotho concept of marriage, the central institution around which the civil law revolved. They brought with them the European view of a marriage as a contract between individuals rather than families which would thus automatically terminate on the death of the individuals and was essentially monogamous. Polygamy, the sororate and levirate, a woman's inability to refuse to marry a man she disliked, Sotho attitudes to adultery and seduction, and in most cases the giving of marriage-cattle all met with their extreme disfavour. They were shocked by initiation practices and by the ancestor worship[33] which bolstered the position of the chief and family head, and appalled by witchcraft beliefs and punishments. Their attempts to prevent their converts from participating in any of these institutions or attitudes challenged the authority of the chief and his courts, and affected not only the converted, but also the unconverted, since often only one member of a family became a Christian. This brought the missionaries into conflict with the laws of succession and the perpetual minority of women, as well as the law governing marriage: they tried to prevent converts and the children of converts from coming under the authority of pagan fathers or heirs who might send them to initiation schools or marry them to pagans willing to pay marriage-cattle. In all such cases, or where converted spouses were obliged by the missionaries to renounce already existing polygamous marriages, the legal and economic rights of the uncoverted Sotho were challenged. Moreover, as the chiefs not unnaturally usually opposed most missionary efforts to undermine Sotho law, the missionaries quite deliberately worked to undermine the power of the chiefs and their courts.

Less obvious but even more insidious in challenging Sotho social and legal values were the economic changes brought about by the settler society to the south. The Sotho economy was essentially a subsistence economy in which trade and barter played a relatively insignificant part. As a result, where family cattle were not available and a potential father-in-law could not be persuaded to part with his daughter on credit, only cattle raiding and the chief's patronage remained to a young man in search of marriage-cattle. But contact with the money economy produced an alternative solution—that of selling the occasional surplus of produce or other goods in demand to traders in return for stock or money. And where poverty did not drive the Sotho into the arms of the trader, the demand created by war and the traders, for guns and manufactured goods, soon had the same effect. So did the missionaries, insisting that their converts should adopt 'decent' European clothing and other features of European civilisation as a concomitant to accepting Christian teaching. Although war and white encroachment continued to make for ever shrinking Sotho lands and diminishing wealth in the 1850s and 1860s, demand for manufactured goods increased as indigenous industries died in the face of competition from European goods. So, even before a white administration took charge in Basutoland and imposed taxation, a second way of obtaining money or stock had been tentatively tried by many Sotho—that of selling their labour to white farmers, which brought them into close contact with the values of the white man.

But though these means of obtaining goods, cattle, and food helped to solve the Sotho's immediate problems, in the long run they carried the seeds of a slow disintegration of much of their way of life. Even before the arrival of a white administration, a chief's authority over his subjects weakened as men found an alternative source of marriage-cattle. As early as 1834, with the influx of cattle earned on Cape farms or acquired through trade, Moshoeshoe realised the potential threat. To curb it, he began to claim the entire earned income of his subjects, until it became apparent that this was driving men away, after which he exacted only a portion.[34] In the same period, as alien concepts of sale became more common, the attitude to the giving of marriage-cattle altered by treating it increasingly as a sale price for women, rather than a binding force between two families for the preservation of a marriage. Increasingly too marriage-cattle were given by an individual, not a family. Traditional responsibilities to one's kinship group began to break down. Although theoretically the earnings of family members came under the control of the head of the family for common use, the growing economic independence of its members and new attitudes of profit-seeking and exploitation acquired through contact with the money economy began to undermine this principle. Nor was it subsequently helped by the Cape Administration's alteration of Sotho law to allow all adults to obtain their majority and freedom from the control of the head of the family. Variations on the metaphorical lament voiced at a public meeting by a Sotho counsellor in 1875 could be heard throughout the latter part of the nineteenth century:

My misgivings are these: why am I disowned by my own children? They kick me, and no longer recognise me as their father. I am still complaining of this.[35]

It is against this background of slow but radical change in Sotho society that the imposition of white rule must be viewed.[36] That an attempt would be made to introduce basic changes into the Sotho way of life was inevitable. That it should prove successful so speedily

is less surprising than it appears at first sight when it is remembered
that the foundations for many of these changes had already been
laid by the time the High Commissioner arrived in Basutoland in
1868 to make arrangements for how the Sotho were to be governed.

3 Interregnum

The first visible effects of the British annexation of Basutoland was
the appearance of a detachment of Cape Frontier Armed and
Mounted Police under Sir Walter Currie as High Commissioner's
Agent, sent to give effect to the annexation. These were followed in
April by the High Commissioner in person, accompanied by the
Reverend John Daniel, the Wesleyan Methodist missionary from
Aliwal North, who was to act as interpreter.

> When Moshoeshoe heard of his approach he rode out to greet him
> at a few miles' distance from the mountain. The High
> Commissioner was already escorted by several of the chief's sons,
> and thousands of Sotho were riding in his train or lining the
> hills, cheering, singing, and firing off salvoes. Moshoeshoe shook
> his hand and fell in behind him, and so they arrived at Thaba
> Bosiu.[1]

Wodehouse's concerns were how Natal was to be prevented from
obtaining control of Basutoland, and how Currie was to rule the
country in the name of Britain. The former appears to have been
achieved by dint of a little diplomatic intrigue, by which the Sotho
were privately advised of Wodehouse's own preference for placing
Basutoland under the Cape. Moshoeshoe was encouraged to express
his own preference for the Cape publicly, which he duly did at the
pitso that immediately followed Wodehouse's arrival at Thaba-
Bosiu. When the Natal representatives arrived in Basutoland some
days later to receive Basutoland under Natal, they were confronted
with the Sotho repudiation.[2]

Wodehouse had also given advance consideration to the question
of the British regulation of Basutoland, but on this had not consulted
Moshoeshoe. The old chief had for many years believed—and was
to do so until the end of this life—that the country should be ruled
directly by the Paramount Chief, with any British agents acting
merely as political advisers.[3] But the missionaries, with whom

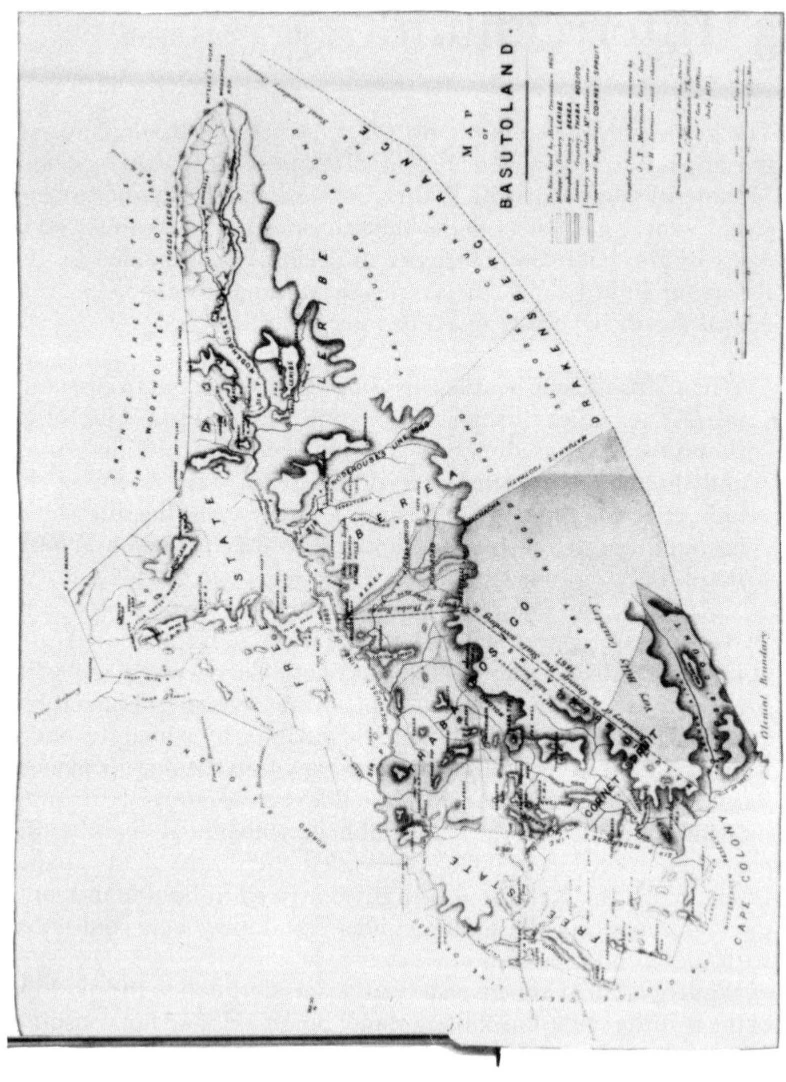

Map 3   Map of Basutoland in the nineteenth century

Wodehouse discussed the question,[4] had their own ideas on the subject. A memorandum, drafted on 30 March 1868 by Emile Rolland, one of the French Protestant missionaries who had worked in Basutoland before the war, was to be crucial in shaping Government policy in the territory.[5] In it he began with the assumption that some form of magisterial control would be instituted, for he argued that the main obstacle the British Government would encounter in ruling the Sotho and 'rendering them obedient to British law' would be the power of the chiefs, great and small; therefore the aim of the Government should be to diminish this power, preferably in such a way as not 'to excite the jealousy or embitter the prejudices of the natives'.

As a chief's power was based largely on his ability to reward those loyal to him with cattle, women and land, Rolland advocated a number of measures which would increase the wealth of commoners and lessen that of the chiefs: as well as preventing the chiefs from 'eating up' anyone who became wealthy, he thought the institution of polygamy should be abolished as far as could be done by legal enactments attacking various rights flowing from polygamous marriages; and he also favoured a radical reform of the land laws to allow for individual tenure. To reinforce these measures, Rolland suggested that the headmen should hold their appointments subject to the pleasure of the Crown, and that especial favours be shown to those who adopted 'the habits of Christianity and civilisation'. He pointed out that paganism supported the chiefs and that whatever struck at it, such as Christianity and education, would weaken them. He then went on to analyse the basic supports of paganism, which he enumerated as the practices of *bohali* and polygamy, witchcraft and circumcision. As he pointed out, Moshoeshoe had already moved against the 'smelling out' of witches, although not against rainmaking or divination, which Rolland believed should also be put down.[6] But on the evils of circumcision especially he waxed eloquent, both as to its degrading effect on morals and its potential use to anti-Government conspirators. He ended his memorandum by defending his advocacy of 'class legislation', arguing that the immediate introduction of Cape law would be impossible. Nor would a Natal-type system of indirect rule through the chiefs result in anything less than a reaction in favour of paganism. It was therefore best to introduce temporary regulations 'conceived in the spirit of our laws' to pave the way gradually for the introduction of Cape law. Such changes would not be opposed: not only were the Sotho more pliable than the tribes to the south, but the effect of over thirty-five years of missionary work amongst them had resulted in one tenth of the tribe becoming Christian and had affected public opinion throughout the tribe. Now more than at any other time, he argued, the Sotho were prepared for, and many desirous of, great and sweeping changes, and their gratitude to the British for saving them from the Boers would lead them to accept far greater alterations in their laws than other tribes annexed in the past.

Rolland's authoritative memorandum obviously persuaded Wodehouse, for many of its suggestions were embodied in the system which the High Commissioner proceeded to institute; though he refused to attack certain features of Sotho life that Rolland had wanted altered, and declined to use some of the methods Rolland had suggested. On 15 April 1868, at the *pitso* held on Wodehouse's arrival at Thaba-Bosiu, the High Commissioner received the formal submission of the chiefs, and under his legally questionable authority issued a temporary set of regulations.[7] These were designed 'to strike at the root of some of the most objectionable Native Customs'[8] and to pay for the administration to be set up in the territory by means of a ten shilling hut tax.[9]

The Sotho did not voice any strong objections to the regulations at the *pitso*, and until sufficient magistrates were appointed to administer the law, they were impossible to implement, except where Moshoeshoe intervened to assist.[10] Wodehouse reported that the principal men had urged the necessity for the appointment of four or at least three British officers,[11] and it may be that they thought this would afford them added protection against Free State raiders. Whether they would have urged the same course had they fully understood the effects of having the regulations enforced is much more doubtful. Their anxiety to obtain added protection was however understandable in view of their vulnerable position. The Cape Assembly, which was battling with a long-standing economic depression, was unwilling to finance the protection and colonisation of Basutoland, and Wodehouse was obliged to recall the Frontier Police as soon as possible. By May it became clear that despite frequent raids by the Boers, no further major attack from the Orange Free State was likely, and Currie received orders to return to the Cape with most of his men. He left James Henry Bowker, the officer next in rank in the Frontier Police, as High Commissioner's Agent, and Bowker found himself fully occupied just in keeping the peace between the raiding Boers and Sotho.[12]

For, not unexpectedly, the Free State disputed the right of the

High Commissioner to interfere. They had been fighting the Sotho for nearly three years and all the main Sotho mountain fortresses except Thaba-Bosiu itself had fallen to them. Wodehouse's annexation robbed them of the fruits of their efforts just when total victory and the coveted Sotho lands were within their grasp. On 24 March the Free State *Volksraad* resolved to send a deputation to London to protest about the annexation, and meanwhile they continued to raid the Sotho, who naturally retaliated.

The Free State deputation, however, met with no success in England, and after its return the Free State reluctantly agreed to come to terms with Wodehouse. In February 1869 they signed the Aliwal North Convention. Fearing the annulment of the Bloemfontein Convention,[13] they agreed to Molapo rejoining the Sotho nation and surrendered a large part of the recently conquered territory, but retained all the land west of the Caledon. This was some of the richest agricultural and pastoral land that the Sotho had ever possessed and was occupied by the Taung of Moletsane, Moshoeshoe's subjects. The Sotho were furious: not only were they deprived of nearly half their land, which the High Commissioner had promised the previous year to restore to them, but were even excluded from the meeting itself. As a result of Boer objections, not even a French missionary had been admitted to watch over their interests.[14] Of the land left to them, most was rugged and inhospitable mountains, except for a strip of country between the Caledon and the first range of mountains; and even parts of that were regularly made inaccessible by the flooding of the many rivers running from the mountains into the Caledon.

When Wodehouse arrived in Basutoland to tell the Sotho at a *pitso* what he had arranged for their future, he was met with angry objections, especially to the loss of land and the enforced removal of the Taung. Letsie,[15] Moshoeshoe's heir, in the type of delaying tactic which was to become well-known to white administrators in the future, declared himself unable to speak for Moshoeshoe, who was too weak to attend the meeting.[16] Nor did Wodehouse's arrangements get a better reception from Moshoeshoe himself when the High Commissioner climbed Thaba-Bosiu the next day to see the old chief.[17] Tsekelo, a son of Moshoeshoe, and two white supporters of the Sotho cause, David Dale Buchanan and the Reverend Mr Daumas, went to London to dispute the Convention.[18] They were unsuccessful but their intervention delayed its ratification until early in 1870.[19]

Meanwhile, Bowker and his deputy in the south, Inspector Surmon, together with 100 policemen, represented the only British presence in the country, and were hampered in the exercise of even moral persuasion by the British Government's long delay in ratifying the Convention. Moreover, until it was ratified, no magistrates could be appointed. Moshoeshoe was by then failing both mentally and physically,[20] increasingly ignored by his sons, and on 18 January 1870 he finally summoned a *pitso* and formally transferred his powers as Paramount Chief to Letsie. It is indicative of Sotho attitudes at this period that Bowker was neither invited to the *pitso* nor informed of its deliberations.[21] Once the first relief at being rescued from imminent danger was past, the Sotho had become increasingly disaffected, led by their chiefs, who objected to the Aliwal North Convention and the control that the High Commissioner's Agent sought to impose by his regulations on their traditional right to allocate land. Had the Convention been ratified immediately and money been made available, Wodehouse could have appointed magistrates and police officers before the people's gratitude had ebbed. Towards the end of the war traditional organisation had begun to break down as defeat forced groups to disperse, and the people had so completely lost confidence in their chiefs that in many cases they had refused to obey or even acknowledge them. But when the British stepped in and fear of a major Boer attack receded, most Sotho found that the only available authorities able to settle cases were the chiefs, who took the opportunity to recover their control.[22] This was to be crucial in the future history of the country. When the white Administration at last began to impose its control, it found itself dealing with a nation firmly under the control of its leaders, to whom the memory of past obligations was fading but to whom present grievances were very real.

Early in 1870 Moshoeshoe's sons were faced with a challenge of a different kind: now that he had formally surrendered his powers to Letsie, Moshoeshoe was finally converted to Christianity by the Protestant missionaries.[23] During February his sons were summoned in turn to Thaba-Bosiu to be informed of his decision, and were appalled. They all knew that conversion by the Protestant missionaries meant that their father would publicly 'put away' his polygamous wives, and would make provision for them out of the cattle of their houses—the houses which his sons stood to inherit with all the house property attached. For his sons more than loss of property was involved: given the intimate connection for a chief between wealth and power, their whole future position in Sotho society was in jeopardy. As a result, their opposition to arrangements for the future of those wives to be 'put away' delayed Moshoeshoe's baptism,[24] but it was eventually fixed for 20 March and later, as the chief weakened, was brought forward to 13 March. The missionaries wished to make it as public as possible, both to protect themselves from accusations of taking advantage of the old chief's weakness, and no doubt for the propaganda value of such a ceremony. Protestants were gathering for it from all over the country when, at nine o'clock on 11 March, two days before it was due to take place, Moshoeshoe died. Those who had come for his baptism instead accompanied his body to his grave on top of Thaba-Bosiu. Significantly, among the 4,000 people present were eight missionaries but not Bowker and his men: the British Administration was still merely a paper formality, not a power in the land.

Eight days after Moshoeshoe's death, on 19 March, the Convention of Aliwal North was finally ratified in Cape Town and the borders of Basutoland became virtually those that were still in force when modern Lesotho was established in 1966. Thus as Moshoeshoe was removed from the scene, the British were accepted, albeit unwillingly, by both the Sotho and their neighbours as guardians of Moshoeshoe's nation. They could at last begin to make arrangements for their effective control of his country.

As is the way with governments, the British required money. The Sotho had agreed at their first meeting with Wodehouse to pay hut tax,[25] and orders were now sent to the High Commissioner's Agent to collect it to provide for the expenses and salaries of the future administration of the country. The Sotho were fully aware of the purpose of the collection, so it was something of a test of whether the chiefs and people were willing to work with the British. There was of course the carrot held out to the great chiefs of receiving 10 per cent of the hut tax collected, and the great chiefs in turn customarily commanded a high degree of obedience,[26] but Letsie had very little control over his two most powerful brothers, Molapo and Masopha[27] (who, together with Letsie, were the surviving sons of Moshoeshoe's first wife). As it turned out, the great chiefs, with the exception of Masopha, willingly assisted in the collection; by June 1870 £3,721 had been received, much of it in kind, which was more than sufficient for the administrative expenses of that year.[28]

The men who organised the collection were Surmon, who was

deputising for Bowker as High Commissioner's Agent after the latter's appointment as Commandant of the Mounted Police, and John Austen, ex-Superintendent of the Wittebergen Reserve, who had been commissioned in May as Magistrate of the Southern District of Basutoland. Encouraged by their first major proof of cooperation by the Sotho, they decided that the time was ripe to promulgate a detailed set of regulations which Wodehouse had drawn up before his departure from South Africa in May;[29] there was to be a meeting of chiefs and headmen at Thaba-Bosiu on 22 December 1870 to announce Moshoeshoe's death to the nation formally, which provided a suitable opportunity. It was a bold move, for the regulations were a much more extensive embodiment of Rolland's ideas than the earlier ones promulgated; in them the attack on the chiefs' powers was fully spelt out and various time-honoured customs were challenged.

The country was to be divided into three districts, each to have a magistrate who was to have jurisdiction in civil and criminal cases except where the offence was murder, rape, or arson with intent to kill, which were punishable by death under Cape Law.[30] In such cases trial was to be by a court of two magistrates, with the High Commissioner having the final say in certain circumstances.[31] The chiefs, of whom the three principal ones were each to reside in a district, could still try any civil or petty criminal case, but the enforcement machinery of the state was not at their disposal and a suitor could bring the same case to the magistrate on appeal. When the Legal Adviser to the Colonial Office objected to this provision, Wodehouse explained that it was to stop the chiefs using their jurisdiction to prevent cases going before the magistrates.[32] However, the leading chiefs would object much more strongly than the Legal Advisor to this right to appeal over their heads for a reversal of their judgements, for according to an old Sotho proverb, 'a chief can't vomit'.[33] It also encouraged a litigant to refuse to pay a fine levied by a chief, yet the regulations declared that seizing property against the owner's will, except in execution of a magistrate's order, was theft. This deprived a chief of his right of 'eating up', which not only lowered his normal income from court fines, but gravely affected his ability to enforce his orders[34] and hence the attractiveness of his court for plaintiffs compared with that of the magistrate. In addition, much more surely than any single prohibition, the right of appeal to a magistrate spelt the decline of those practices to which there were different Sotho and

1. Moshoeshoe and some of his advisers in 1860. Moshoeshoe was then aged about 74.

2. Letsie in 1845

3. Molapo in 1845

47. Maseru in the Gun War, December 1880. The Governor's Agent's quarters are on the hill in the middle background. Traders' buildings are to the right foreground, left centre and extreme left centre

48. Fort Bell, Hlotse Heights, in the Gun War

magisterial attitudes and which were discouraged by the Administration, such as the retention of a widow's children by her husband's family. Since it would usually be to the advantage of one party in a dispute involving such practices to take his or her case to a magistrate, whether in the first instance or on appeal, rights inherent in those practices would become virtually unenforceable and access to the chief's courts meaningless for traditionalist adherents to such customs. Equally objectionable to chiefs was the section in the regulations that declared all men to be equal before the law, thereby making it possible to charge even the Paramount Chief himself in court.[35]

Nor was this all: as Rolland had shown in his memorandum, chiefs had reason to be even more antagonised than the rest of the tribe by the alterations made in family law. Even the commoners much disliked them. The forcible marriage of unconsenting women was forbidden, as was the circumcision of anyone against his will or that of his parents; both these prohibitions could work against the traditional power of a father over his children and his right to claim his daughter's *bohali*. According to Tsekelo Moshoeshoe, chiefs had an additional reason for resenting the prevention of forcible marriages: when a chief took a fancy to a woman, a prudent father promptly married her to the chief irrespective of her wishes.[36] The provision declaring Christian marriages (valid without *bohali*) to be as binding as customary ones was equally unpopular with all sections of the community except Christians, since it too affected the traditional power of a father over his children. In addition, since the institution of *bohali* was embedded in a network of kinship relations, with *bohali* for one woman paying for her male relatives' marriages, the ramifications of this provision affected far more family members than only the head of the household.[37] To ensure that the woman consented to her marriage, and to assist the magistrate in judging future cases arising out of *bohali* claims, it was provided that in future all marriages were to be registered before a magistrate, to whom the parties had to declare their consent and pay a registration fee of two shillings and sixpence; and in addition, all *bohali* paid had to be registered—otherwise no action regarding the marriage or the *bohali* could be brought before a magistrate. (The 1868 regulations had provided for a similar marriage registration charge, but without the lack of legal recognition if no registration took place.[38]) This unprecedented charge for legally recognising a marriage was naturally resented, especially as it acted as a tax on polygamy.

There is some evidence that the legalising function of registration was introduced at missionary prompting in an attempt to give Christian marriages priority over Sotho law marriages:[39] in practice the missionaries ensured that Christian marriages were registered, while pagans were deterred by the expense and difficulty involved.[40] How the regulations gave preference to Christian marriages at the expense of the rights of a Sotho law spouse is demonstrated by later instructions from Griffith (the official by then in charge of the country) to Surmon that a Christian marriage must be registered despite the wife already having a Sotho law husband.[41] This second marriage would then have been the only one recognised and protected by the courts. The resentment such a situation would have engendered among the pagan majority of the nation is understandable, and protests against it were not lacking.[42]

Quite as bad to the Sotho as the 'consent provision' was the right given to women whose marriages were not registered, or who were widowed, to the custody of their children until the boys were eighteen and the girls fifteen years of age; after that age the children would be considered as no longer minors. And of the same order was the provision giving a widow the right to remarry, although custody of her children would then pass to her deceased husband's family or other relatives of the children. As has been pointed out, in Sotho law a woman never obtained her majority, always remaining in the guardianship of some man of the family; she had no right to marry without her guardian's consent. But this was now changed by the regulations, making such marriages possible for girls over fifteen years of age, and for widows. Bowker subsequently suggested to a Cape parliamentary Select Committee that the obligatory removal of the children from widows' custody on their remarriage, as provided in the regulations, might have been inserted at the request of the missionaries,[43] but this seems unlikely, since it could well have resulted in the children of a Christian woman being reared in their heathen father's family. It seems more likely that the Administration was bowing to strong Sotho opposition.

This is supported to some extent by a more significant difference between the provisions of 1870 and those of 1868 that subsequent writers on the regulations have overlooked.[44] The wording of the 1868 regulations were so wide as to provide for a widow having both custody and guardianship of her children, whether she remarried or not. This was completely contrary to Sotho law, which would never regard a woman as capable of becoming a guardian—that is, having control over the education and over major decisions on the upbringing of the child, as opposed to the custody or care of the child—as she was herself perpetually under the power of a guardian. In the second set of regulations the word 'custody' is used throughout, which partly restores the guardianship of a widow's children to that in Sotho law. The reason for the situation created by the first set of regulations can be traced to Rolland and the other missionaries. Their objections to the practice of the levirate would account for the provisions that widows should not be regarded as minors, could remarry without consent, and could still retain guardianship of their children. Retention of guardianship in such cases would also ensure that a Christian mother could prevent her children being brought up by heathen relatives. Similarly, to prevent heathen guardians from persuading the daughters of Christian widows to marry polygamists who would give *bohali* for them, it was necessary that the guardianship as well as custody should remain with the mother, since the guardian obtained the *bohali* cattle. Changing the legal status of women to such an extent, and depriving the family that had paid *bohali* of that woman's children would have caused great and almost universal discontent; it may be that when it came to drafting the second code of regulations, it was decided that it was inadvisable to try to introduce so radical a change at once. Or it may simply be that Wodehouse himself or his secretary drew up the new regulations in the belief that he was merely putting into clearer language the provisions of the 1868 code, unaware of the important legal and practical distinction between custody and guardianship.

The alterations in the criminal law were hardly to the liking of the Sotho either, though perhaps not entirely unexpected in all cases. The regulations provided that 'persons practising or pretending to practise witchcraft or other such acts' or falsely accusing another of doing so should be held to be rogues and be punishable accordingly,[45] while the killing of supposed witches was to be treated as murder. Despite Moshoeshoe's earlier prohibition on killing supposed witches, most Sotho believed in the power to bewitch[46] and would regard this regulation as dangerous, while those chiefs who cynically manipulated witchcraft accusations to enlarge their wealth or to eliminate opposition would bitterly resent it. Similarly, the death penalty for arson when committed with intent to kill and the severe punishment for rape—a flogging not exceeding fifty lashes, or confiscation of property, or both—were alien to the traditional way of thinking. In Sotho law both crimes were punished with fines, and rape was considered a relatively minor offence.[47] The death penalty for murder was not entirely new; in 1855 Moshoeshoe had legislated that it should not be inflicted on supposed witches, and, as mentioned above,[48] at the 1873 annual meeting an old counsellor of Moshoeshoe claimed that it had been Sotho law, until altered by Moshoeshoe, to execute all murderers, a statement which Letsie corroborated. But it was almost twenty years since Moshoeshoe's changes had been introduced and a new generation had never known such a provision. The introduction of the death penalty for arson with intent to kill can be accounted for by the Administration's desire to stamp out the killing of supposed witches, who were often burnt alive in their huts—a traditionally acceptable way of eliminating them. Altogether the regulations introduced enough new ideas to upset the conservative Sotho, even without the blanket clause that all acts which were offences in Cape law were now to be punishable, subject to the special circumstances of the country.

Not unexpectedly, the regulations, when read to the national meeting, aroused heated protests. Molapo, Masopha, and the minor chiefs openly objected on the grounds that they ignored the chiefs, required payment for registration of marriages, and gave women rights that should belong exclusively to men. Vocal opposition was only halted by Letsie's order to the meeting that, as he was satisfied, the regulations were to be accepted.[49] Later in the day, however, a written address to Bowker was signed by the chiefs, in which they politely said that they thought the regulations reasonable but objected to mention of their rights and authority being omitted.[50]

It was this mild protest which Sir Henry Barkly found awaiting him when he assumed office as High Commissioner on 31 December 1870 and turned his attention to what the British Government insisted on regarding as an infant crown colony which was to be annexed to one of its neighbours.[51] He saw that the country would remain under the rule of these disgruntled chiefs until an adequate number of magistrates, properly organised and with well-defined duties, could establish a strong enough administration to make an impact on the daily lives of the people. As the plan to divide the country into three districts had not yet been implemented, Barkly decided, on Bowker's advice,[52] that the new regulations could be more effectively administered in four rather smaller districts. Charles Duncan Griffith, Civil Commissioner of King William's

Town was chosen to organise them.

What Barkly failed to understand, even after a visit to Basutoland, was the strength of feeling against the regulations and the opposition the magistrates would encounter. He realised that Molapo and Masopha were disaffected, but reported reassuringly on the mood of the people after his meeting with Molapo:

> I learnt, however, that as soon as I was gone he harangued his people in rather strong language, telling them 'that this Governor was no more good than the last, and that they had better go home and starve', an ebullition of wrath which is said only to have excited the laughter of the crowd, one of the minor Chiefs being bold enough to tell him that it was the sons of Moshesh who were no good, and that he himself would be the first to insist on payment of every penny of Hut Tax at the next collection.[53]

Letsie, he believed, supported the Government,[54] and he concluded:

> The fact is that however Molapo, Masupha, and one or two other of Moshesh's sons may indulge in dreams of reconquest, or chafe at the unaccustomed restraints which a Constitutional form of Government may impose on the exercise of their quasi-feudal prerogatives, the minor Chiefs and the people generally thoroughly appreciated the advantages of British Rule, and are only too glad to be left in the quiet enjoyment of the fruits of their industry, without being forced into fresh Military Service against the Free State.[55]

In the light of this apparently satisfactory situation, Barkly turned his attention to annexing Basutoland to the Cape, in keeping with Britain's intentions from the first not to be saddled with it. The Cape Legislative Council, however, was not enthusiastic at the prospect of receiving yet more Africans within its boundaries. It became more reconciled to the idea after the Select Committee to which the Legislative Council referred the matter reported in August that Basutoland should be secured for the wide field of profitable commercial enterprise it offered, especially as it was geographically connected with the Cape Colony and would be able to pay for its own administration.[56] By 10 August the Annexation Bill had been passed by both the Legislative Council and House of Assembly. It can therefore be seen that the Cape's motives in annexing Basutoland implied an official policy of breaking down the self-sufficient Sotho economy to create a market for Cape goods and a source of labour for Cape needs. How little interest there was in developing Basutoland in any other way is perhaps best indicated by the fact that, on the figures given, Basutoland's revenue could only be regarded as adequate for its needs if (as was the case) no provision was made in the estimates for public works, buildings, education or postal communication.

Another indication of Cape lack of interest in Basutoland is the legal arrangements made for the territory. Cape policy at that date was to impose colonial law on all colonial African territories, but it was realised that the Sotho, fast recovering from the war with the Orange Free State, were a very different proposition from the collaborating Mfengu and defeated Xhosa of the Ciskei. Troops to repress opposition would be expensive, and some realisation of the farcical results of the non-recognition policy in the Ciskei[57] may also have played a part in the Legislative Council's reluctance to annex Basutoland unless the annexation was purely formal. It wished to maintain intact the existing system of rule by an imperial officer, with regulations that, though making many innovations, would still require much less enforcement than the alien laws of the Cape.[58] Thus the Annexation Act vested the duty of legislating for the territory in the Governor, who was to lay all legislative enactments before the Cape Parliament within fourteen days of the opening of the session; unless altered they would remain in force. No parliamentary act would apply to the territory unless expressly stated to do so in the act itself or in a proclamation by the Governor. And so the High Commissioner was able to instruct his Agent in August to tell Letsie that the annexation made no difference to the position of the Sotho, except that it entitled them to the privileges of British subjects when they went into the Cape Colony. Griffith, who had duly arrived at the beginning of the month to take up his post as High Commissioner's Agent,[59] added that his relations with the Sotho would continue on exactly the same footing as Currie's and Bowker's had been.[60] Even after the Cape was given Responsible Government, at least this latter statement would for several years remain an accurate description of the facts if not the theory: Griffith would continue to exercise very wide discretion in deciding matters of policy. The Cape Government, faced in Basutoland with an established Administration and code of regulations, was at first content to keep a watchful eye on him.

4 The Cape Administration

By the time that the Annexation Act was confirmed by an order-in-council on 3 November 1871, it was already obvious that the Cape Colony would soon be given Responsible Government. The arrangements for this constitutional change were completed in 1872, and for the first time the Cape undertook for itself responsibility for administering the affairs of the Africans living both within and beyond its borders. To do this a Department of Native Affairs was set up and a Secretary for Native Affairs appointed from 1 December 1872 as the minister responsible to the Cape Parliament for the Department. However, Responsible Government did not give the Cape complete self-government. Through the Governor, the Imperial Government retained the power to prevent the Cape Colony from operating in opposition to imperial interests; although in theory the Governor was to act on the advice of his responsible advisers, in practice he was in the anomalous position of remaining ultimately responsible to the British Secretary of State for the Colonies.

The Governor, however, was also the British Government's agent responsible for extra-colonial affairs in South Africa—termed the High Commissioner. As High Commissioner his position was theoretically clearer: Responsible Government in the Cape did not affect his extra-colonial powers. But in practice it proved virtually impossible to separate the problems of the frontier within and beyond the Cape Colony and, acting on the instructions of Lord Kimberley, the British Secretary of State for the Colonies, the High Commissioner announced that he would act only on the advice of the Cape Ministers.[1] Although this policy was later countermanded by Lord Carnarvon, Kimberley's successor, a precedent had been established which led to trouble when a Governor later attempted to assert his right to independent action as the High Commissioner.[2]

Initially, therefore, the most influential figure in determining the Government's policies on African affairs was the Secretary for Native Affairs. That this policy-making role was not shared more by the Prime Minister, John Charles Molteno, and the other members of the five-man Cabinet was largely a result of the expertise of the first man appointed to hold the office. Charles Pacalt Brownlee, who took office on 2 December, was appointed for his outstanding knowledge of African affairs rather than his political influence. Born in 1821,[3] the eldest son of a missionary of the London Missionary Society to the Ngqika, he grew up amongst the Africans on his father's mission stations until 1835, when the family had to flee to escape an attack by tribesmen during the frontier war. He then spent three years in Natal as interpreter for a party of American missionaries and returned to farm on the eastern frontier of the Cape until the 1846 frontier war, in which he participated. At the end of 1846 he was appointed Clerk to the Ngqika Commissioner and a year later was replaced by his younger brother, James, while he himself became Ngqika Commissioner, stationed at Fort Cox as British Agent to Sandile, until the chief was deposed. War ensued after the tribe refused to accept Brownlee as a substitute for Sandile, James was killed, and Charles Brownlee spent six months in command of a levy of Mfengu at Fort Peddie; but in 1853 he assisted Cathcart in ending the war by negotiating with the chiefs, and was restored as Ngqika Commissioner, with his brother-in-law this time as his Clerk. In 1867 his post was abolished as part of Wodehouse's retrenchment policy, and in May he was appointed Civil Commissioner and Resident Magistrate in Somerset West. In 1871 he was promoted to King William's Town, taking up his post early the following year. By 1872 he was therefore almost uniquely experienced in African customs and administration, and had great influence with many of the more important chiefs. James Rose Innes, son of a later Under-Secretary for Native Affairs and subsequently Chief Justice of South Africa, who served as a clerk in the Native Affairs Department under Brownlee, wrote that the secret of his influence with Africans was their belief in his character 'as a just man who told them the truth however unpalatable, but who genuinely sympathised with their race'.[4]

His knowledge of the Xhosa language and Xhosa law was excellent[5]—he contributed a detailed and accurate section to Maclean's *Compendium of Kafir Laws and Customs*, which served as a handbook for magistrates in the Ciskei and Transkei throughout the period under discussion—but he had no experience of the Sotho and occasionally fell into the trap of attributing Xhosa customs to all Africans.[6] Fortunately, this deficiency was remedied by the structure

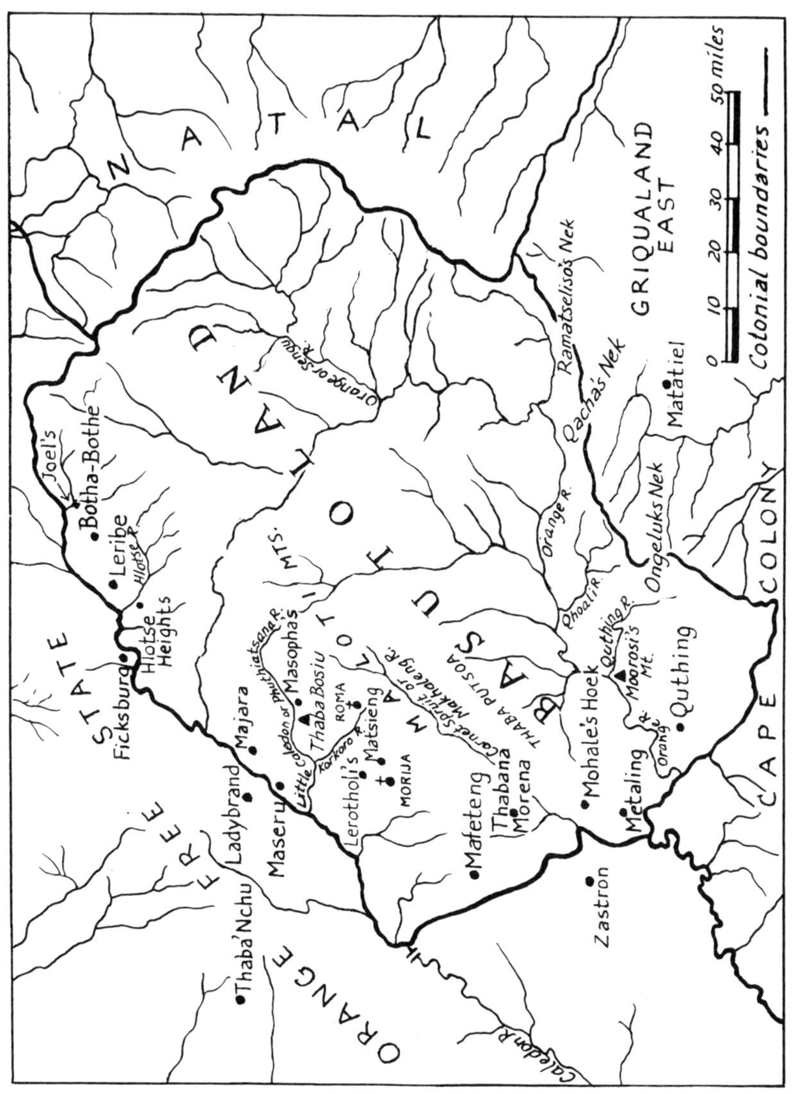

Map 4   Map of Basutoland, drawn in July 1871, showing magisterial districts

and personnel of his new Department of Native Affairs, which took over its functions from an existing branch of the Cape Government. Until 1872 all questions concerning Africans had been dealt with by the Cape Colonial Office, a sub-department of the Border Department, which had supervised officials appointed to control the African population both within and outside the colony.[7] Brownlee did not inherit the personnel of the Cape Colonial Office; in common with some other government departments, his newly created Native Affairs Department was very slenderly staffed, but this proved to be beneficial for the Sotho in an unexpected way. Apart from Brownlee himself as its ministerial head, for its first five years the staff consisted of only a Chief Clerk and a Messenger. Although one or two temporary clerks were employed to assist the Chief Clerk, it was January 1877 before a permanent clerical assistant was at last appointed, and only in 1878 was the post of Under-Secretary for Native Affairs created. Until 1878 the Chief Clerk therefore exercised far more power than the title of his office suggested, supervising the general running of the Department and acting as deputy in Brownlee's frequent absences on the frontier.[8]

This would have been particularly true of H. E. R. Bright, who was appointed as Clerk in succession to W. H. English in December 1874 (entitled Chief Clerk after May 1876) and Under-Secretary in July 1878. Prior to that he had spent three years as Clerk to the Governor's Agent in Basutoland. Brownlee, lacking any experience of this area, probably paid particular attention to Bright's advice on it. Bright's general influence is indicated by the Department files, which contain various despatches sent to the Secretary for Native Affairs by officers in African areas and on which the Chief Clerk's opinion, as indicated by memoranda or minutes, is endorsed as future policy by Brownlee. But Bright's sympathy with the Sotho and friendship with the magistrates stationed there may have proved to be his undoing. In 1881 the Sprigg Government, having antagonised both the Sotho and Basutoland Administration and wanting his post vacant, transferred him against his wishes to a magisterial post in the Cape Colony, and replaced him with James Rose Innes, related to Sprigg by marriage. His transfer was much criticised by Sprigg's political opponents.[9]

A second result of the smallness of the staff was that the men on the spot were perforce allowed a great deal of discretion in their actions. The departmental staff was soon unable to keep up with the inflow of letters, which were dealt with according to strict civil service procedure and replies hand-copied into record books.[10] According to Bright's successor as Under-Secretary, by the early 1880s there was ample work for nine clerks to do.[11] Improvements in the postal service to outlying areas were therefore outweighed by the growing departmental delays in answering letters. General Charles Gordon, when he visited the country in 1882, found magistrates complaining that their questions were not being answered.[12]

All these circumstances resulted in the men appointed to magistracies in Basutoland enjoying a great deal of freedom in adapting their administration to local conditions, unfettered, at least until 1879, by inappropriate directives from Cape Town. Basutoland was divided into four districts, as Barkly had earlier proposed,[13] and Inspector William Henry Surmon, Bowker's deputy, was appointed to act as Magistrate in charge of the Berea District.[14] This was formed by amalgamating the northern part of the central district with the southern part of Molapo's country, in an arrangement which left Molapo with considerable influence in that district. He, however, resided in the northern part of his territory, now called the Leribe District after his village, where Major Charles Harland Bell assumed duty as Magistrate on 13 May 1871.[15] A retired officer from the British Army who had served in South Africa and been recommended for his post by Currie, Bell was described by Barkly as 'a gentleman of much experience in dealing with the Kaffir Tribes of the Eastern Frontier'.[16] The local doctor wrote a fuller and less official description some years later:

> Though of rather a 'stand off' manner, he was a thorough gentleman, and a type of the old-time British officer, very dignified, but of a most kindly and generous disposition. He had served with distinction in India, and in the old Cape Colony wars, and was held in the highest respect, alike by the officials who served under him, and by chiefs and natives. Many of the latter named their children after him, so that the Leribe district had a big crop of toddling 'Major Bells' in the native villages.[17]

The reduced central district was named after Thaba-Bosiu which was situated in it, and was served by both the Governor's Agent performing the duties of Magistrate from the newly created 'capital' of Maseru,[18] and an Assistant Magistrate who was later to be based at Mafeteng. This was the Reverend Emile Rolland, whose memorandum on the Sotho had been so influential in the establishment of Basutoland's legal system and who resigned from the mission to become a magistrate.[19] The son of a Basutoland missionary,[20] he was brother-in-law to J. M. Orpen and the only magistrate to speak, read and write Sotho fluently, though the other magistrates gradually acquired a working knowledge of it. Bowker, when suggesting him for the post, wrote of him: 'he is a first rate man and well liked by the Sotho'.[21] John Austen continued as Magistrate in the south, now called the Cornet Spruit District. Tylden describes him as 'a very dark-skinned man'[22] and a French missionary referred to him as '*un homme de couleur*', which in a race-conscious country may explain his touchy, defensive attitude thoughout his term as a magistrate in Basutoland. He persistently reminded his superiors of his expertise gained from ten years of missionary experience and sixteen years living among Africans on the banks of the Orange River before taking up his latest appointment.[23] However, his knowledge of Sotho law was rather uncertain.[24] He had originally been transferred to Basutoland to save the Cape Government from criticism for his trading activities in the Wittebergen Reserve, which he had pursued while acting as Superintendent. The rough justice he had administered by means of an illegal mixture of African and colonial law had also had parliamentary repercussions.[25] His arbitrary actions and the fact that his son had fought with the Orange Free State in the last war had made him unpopular with the Sotho, but he was also respected, or at least feared.[26]

Charles Duncan Griffith, the leader of this team and the man who in practice for at least the next eight years was to exercise the most influence in deciding how Basutoland should be ruled, was an experienced and dedicated district officer. Born in 1830, he had served with the Frontier Armed and Mounted Police and had been a magistrate in the Cape for nearly fifteen years in Albert, Queenstown, Grahamstown and King William's Town. While he was fully aware of the advantages of playing the chiefs off against each other,[27] he was rigidly upright in his adherence to the regulations. On his arrival in Basutoland, for example, Masopha sent him an ox, the traditional mark of respect for a chief. Griffith's reply was that he thanked Masopha very much if he had intended to show respect and submission to the Queen's Government 'but at the same time with no wish to hurt your feelings or in any way treat you with disrespect I am obliged to decline your kind present and send the ox back to you because as an officer holding the responsible position which I do I am not allowed by the Queen's Regulations to accept any present or gift from any person'.[28] A man of commanding presence, his consistently firm and just handling of both subordinates and Sotho won him their respect, but it could only have been his own respect and liking for the Sotho[29] which gained him such trust and affection as are evident in the Sotho chiefs' unprompted plea to the Governor when faced with Griffith's (temporary, as it turned out) removal to command the police and then the Cape forces in the 1877–8 frontier war:

To the Chief Bartle Frere!
Dear Sir,
    By this letter I desire to speak with you, and to question you; but not I only, likewise the men of Lesuto. What we wish to say to you is simply this:– We hear that the Chief Griffith is about to leave us, and return to the Colony. Now we say to you Sir, this news confounds us, we cannot rightly understand it. Also we say therefore how is it that our Chief is taken from us? Because as for this our shepherd, we have become intimate with him and we understand each other in all that we do. We also greatly love him as our shepherd. And now we humbly pray to you and say, Oh Sir, this shepherd of ours, we do not wish that he should leave us alone in the wilderness.
    As for our desire and our prayer to you, Sir, it is that you should leave us our shepherd that he may remain with us. This is truly what we ask, from you, Sir, by this letter. Again, Sir, you must not think that we could slight him who may come in the room of this our shepherd: but it is only because we have seen how he has worked in guiding this nation of the Lesuto. During all the years which he has lived with us we can say that he has guided us well, until now.
    This is why we address you on this matter of Mr. Griffith's leaving us.
                    I remain, Yours,
                    I Letsie, and the men of the Lesuto.[30]

Griffith's influence with the aged Paramount Chief can be gauged from the Acting Governor's Agent report:

The Chief Letsie upon hearing that Mr. Griffith would shortly leave Basutoland was so deeply affected as to be immediately seized with violent pain and sickness and was seriously ill for some days. I do not exaggerate in saying that Mr. Griffith's departure has deeply affected the whole Basuto tribe.[31]

All the magistrates in Basutoland had heavy work-loads and several complained of the impossibility of adequately administering the large areas and difficult terrain which comprised their districts, although this was later partly remedied by subdividing some districts. However, the Governor's Agent was particularly over-worked.[32] The magistrates had administrative as well as judicial duties, such as issuing trading licences, collecting hut tax, and making roads; the Governor's Agent had all the duties of a resident magistrate in the District of Thaba-Bosiu until 1877, and in addition, he was from mid-1872 also Accounting Officer for Basutoland.[33] This entailed such a vast amount of complicated paperwork that in 1877 he eventually persuaded the Native Affairs Department in Cape Town to appoint his Chief Clerk, Henry Lee Davies, as an Assistant Magistrate at Maseru to do some of the work, and in 1878 to appoint a full-time Accountant.[34] As Governor's Agent he also governed Basutoland, dealing with all decisions and correspondence of a political character, since he believed the magistrates' duties to be of a purely judicial and administrative nature.[35] It remains a mystery where he also found the time to act as Chief Magistrate with duties which included hearing appeals from the courts of other magistrates, reviewing their decisions, and acting as judge of the divorce and insolvency courts. He certainly discouraged magistrates from seeking his advice on points of African laws,[36] leaving them to settle matters as best they could. Nor were conditions conducive to the long hours of office and court work these duties required. In 1878 Bowker, temporarily acting as Governor's Agent, described them to the Secretary for Native Affairs:

The Governor's Agent's and Magistrate's offices are in adjoining rooms, very small and stuffy, and very inadequate,—hot in summer and icy cold in winter. No privacy is attainable and things are apt to get inextricably jumbled. The clerks' offices, two in number, are at a distance in separate buildings. When the Governor's Agent or the Resident Magistrate wishes to communicate with his clerk, he has to go out in sun or rain or cold or wind—or else shout in an undignified manner unless the orderly happens to be at hand . . . the present buildings are . . . falling into disrepair and quite unworthy of being the head offices of Government. They were originally the premises of a Kaffir trader built in the first year of our occupation, and are shabby and paltry beyond description. The court room is very insufficient[,] dark and close,—and when densely crowded as it is three or four times a week is something like a second 'Black Hole of Calcutta'.[37]

A further problem for magistrates in Basutoland was that to be an effective magistrate a man required not only a good knowledge of the Sotho, judgement and tact, but the ability to withstand years of isolation from his own culture; often his family, his clerk (if he had one), and possibly any nearby trader or missionary would be the only regular personal contacts he would have with it, even when not cut off from the nearest village by flooded rivers; and if he did not speak the local language he would have very little opportunity for spontaneous conversation with anyone else. As land was 'leased' only to officials, traders and missionaries, no settler community developed, and the number of whites in Basutoland throughout the period remained very small. The 1875 census,[38] the only one taken in Basutoland by the Cape Government, showed a total of 378 Europeans.

Under these conditions there was a strong possibility that the local white community would have a disproportionate influence in relation to its size on the kinds of changes which magistrates sought to introduce into Sotho society. Traders, as the most numerous group, might have been expected to have had the greater effect: until the 1880 Gun War depleted their numbers,[39] they easily outnumbered both missionaries and officials. The first trader settled in Basutoland in 1834;[40] by mid-1872 there were twenty fixed trading stations, thirty by 1873, fifty by 1874, and approximately seventy by 1877, many of them doing a great deal of business.[41] These men represented the interests for which the Cape had annexed Basutoland, and they were soon adding considerably to the Cape revenues;[42] but the Governor's Agent was directly opposed to the policy of exploitation presupposed by the annexation,[43] and no doubt firmly discouraged any attempts to capitalise on Cape greed at the expense of the Sotho. Nor were any efforts made to appeal over his head to the Cape Government: traders were scattered throughout the country and the records show them uniting only twice to form a pressure group—in 1878-9 to press for changes in the trading regulations of 1877[44] and in 1879 to impress upon the visiting Prime Minister the dangers of applying the disarmament policy to Basutoland.[45] On what appears to be the only other occasion on which a trader made direct representation to the Cape Government, by protesting at the ban on the sale of red ochre, the regulation remained in force and was subsequently approved by the traders' meeting held in 1878.

The missionaries were far better organised to exert pressure and were no doubt more aware of the exact changes which they wished to see made in Sotho society. Although there is little evidence on the question, presumably changes in Sotho law were discussed on the occasions when missionaries and magistrates met, and the French Protestant missionaries certainly campaigned vigorously, if not successfully, in both official letters and in their monthly news-paper.[46] From 1872 to 1877 *Leselinyana la Lesotho*, as it was called, published a smaller English counterpart, *The Little Light of Basutoland*, three copies of which were promptly requested for the Colonial Office in Cape Town every month; it was also sent regularly to the Governor, Governor's Agent and magistrates in Basutoland.[47] It is not clear whether it was ever opened by anyone in the government offices in Cape Town, but there is evidence that it was read at least occasionally by the Governor and the Cape officials in Basutoland.[48] Probably as the only locally published English newspaper in the country it would have been read by most of the white community, especially as it carried government notices (and both as the only newspaper in the vernacular, and as the place where description of impounded cattle were published, *Leselinyana* would have had a growing readership among the increasingly literate Sotho).[49]

Given these factors and the backgrounds of the magistrates, it seems at first surprising that the missionaries were not more successful in obtaining their desired changes in the law through their pressure on officials at least. Rolland, the man who was Assistant Magistrate in Griffith's district and later acted as Governor's Agent for more than a year, was the son of a Basutoland missionary, an ordained minister himself, and had resigned from the mission to enter the Administration.[50] Austen had ten years of missionary experience behind him. Griffith himself was obviously highly thought of by the missionaries and took a keen interest in their work, both educational and religious.[51] Yet, despite all missionary arguments, polygamy, *bohali* and circumcision continued to be recognised, if discouraged. The reason can probably be found partly in the Sotho reaction against the extreme nature of the Paris Missionary Society's views,[52] partly in the opinions and characters of Griffith and his magistrates. Sympathy for the arbitrary abolition of the most basic Sotho customs was unlikely to come from a man who could quote approvingly, as Griffith did, the words of Sir Arthur Gordon:

> If we follow the example of those great masters in the art of Government, the Citizens of ancient Rome, and permit those who have come under our sway to develop in their own way and after their own fashion, the civilization that suits them, we shall do wisely and well.[53]

Not that Griffith was averse to guiding that development towards the goal of a European way of life and values, but both his temperament and commonsense, not to mention his instructions from Cape Town,[54] led him to disagree with the missionaries as to the correct speed and method for achieving this. As early as 1873 he attacked the missionaries in his annual report for 1872 for checking religious and educational progress by overzealously introducing certain uncalled-for measures.[55] Nor was he alone in this opinion. That year both Austen and Rolland voiced the same criticism in their annual reports, though these were tactfully censored by the Cape Government before publication.[56] Rolland went so far as to make it quite clear that in such matters he supported the Government against what he characterised as 'one of the narrowest sects in Europe'. In his 1877 annual report yet another magistrate, Major Bell, joined the attack; he suggested that the separation from unconverted Sotho enforced by the missionaries was responsible for the number of renegade converts in the country; 'There is at the station too much of the exclusiveness of a religious community, this becomes irksome to the converts, and at the same time causes the people to stand aloof.'[57] With so many magistrates sceptical of the missionaries' claim that only good could come from the rapid abolition of Sotho customs, it is not surprising that missionary influence on Basutoland's Sotho law policy was not strong.

However, in essence the missionaries and magistrates differed only on the question of the desirable speed and method of abolishing Sotho customs, not on the ultimate aim in this respect. Faced with a two-pronged attack by missionaries and Government on their customary means of influence, the chiefs not unnaturally did all they could to counteract the threat wherever they would detect it; and this in turn reinforced the Administration's determination to undermine the chiefs' power.

5 Neutralising the Chiefs

In the early days of the Cape Administration, the magistrates were very aware of the hostility of the Sotho chiefs, and feared that, given the right conditions, they might attempt to lead a revolt against the Cape Government. It seemed likely that any large-scale revolt would most easily be led by one of the major chiefs, who could automatically command the allegiance of the largest numbers. However, the Paramount Chief, Letsie, did not seem a likely candidate. As a young man he was tall and well-built, but had been blinded in one eye. A reputation for cowardice and, according to oral tradition today, a marked streak of cruelty, did not enhance his popularity: in 1847, for example, against the advice of his counsellors, he had a man stoned to death for refusing to acknowledge the jurisdiction of his court, an act for which he was publicly reprimanded by his father.[1] However, by the time the Cape Government took over the country, he was in his early sixties[2] and had mellowed considerably. In 1878 the Acting Governor's Agent described him as 'about 70—In character he is timourous [sic], indolent, mild, suspicious, and peaceably inclined. He is very stout and unwieldy, and suffers from gout, is fond of his ease and hardly ever stirs from his village.'[3] As he was very much under Griffith's influence and was supported in his position by the Government against his more popular and vigorous younger brothers, he had neither the will nor the incentive to lead a revolt.

His next brother, Molapo, about three years his junior, at first seemed more threatening. The most powerful chief in the country after the Paramount, he was highly intelligent, generous, and a fine warrior. He was also, according to Bell, capricious, arbitrary, and jealous of his prerogative.[4] Letsie's long-standing jealousy of his good relations with their father had soured relations between them,[5] and he would probably have seceded from Letsie when Moshoeshoe died, had the imposition of British rule not prevented him from doing so. His large and remote northern district was described by his harassed magistrate as having least felt 'the white-man's power';[6] or, it seemed, that of anyone else:

> It has been a common thing when a Chief has on account of some crime sent to a village to seize the cattle of a villager, that the inhabitants have turned out in arms and resisted; the village communities have it would seem always considered themselves bound to protect the persons and property of the individuals composing such communities without in every case asking whether such individuals have or have not transgressed the law; a stranger is murdered in a village and the community band together to prevent the murderer being found out—and Molapo's country appears to have been for years a sort of Alsatia, a refuge for murderers and other transgressors.[7]

However, Molapo and his sub-chiefs had quite enough control over their Sotho subjects to prevent anyone from entering the African police force established by Griffith in 1872 and, after six 'Zulu' were recruited (Bell's entire police force), so incited their people against them that the police asked to be armed.[8] In August 1873 Molapo caused Bell some anxious hours by arriving with about 150 armed and drunken men to attend the trial of some of the chief's followers for assaulting Bell's Chief Constable in Molapo's presence.[9] Bell informed them that although they saw only three or four constables, the whole of the forces of the Queen were at his back, a statement which he ruefully pointed out to Griffith was true in theory but unfortunately not in practice.[10] He himself advocated that an armed white police force be established in his district, and wrote a number of letters to the Governor's Agent pressing for the magistracy to be moved to a position which could be fortified and where Molapo could not see which of his men were disobedient enough to take their cases to the magistrate's rather than the chief's court or seek refuge at the magistracy.[11] Eventually, after a delay caused by the Governor's Agent's doubts about the expense involved in fortifying the new magistracy,[12] Bell moved in 1876 to Hlotse Heights, a craggy, flat-topped hill half surrounded by the Hlotse and Caledon Rivers.

But by then Griffith had taken full advantage of an unexpected event which effectively converted Molapo willy-nilly into a Government supporter. Langalibalele, a Hlubi chief living in Natal, defied a Government order to register his guns and, when an armed Government force was sent to enforce obedience, fled with his warriors and cattle over the Drakensberg towards Basutoland. He had already contacted Molapo, in whose territory many Hlubi were living, and expected at least shelter, if not active aid, despite the Cape Government's warning to Molapo and Masopha not to receive his cattle for safekeeping.[13] The armed party which pursued Langalibalele was routed by his rearguard, which killed five men including the son of the Natal Colonial Secretary. Colonists throughout South Africa suddenly realised that unless the errant Hlubi clan was immediately and publicly subdued, South Africa faced the possibility of a full-scale rebellion by an unknown number of tribes, especially in view of Langalibalele's wide contacts.[14] Offers of help came from as far away as the Diamond Fields, and soon a Natal force was in pursuit while Cape forces advanced from Basutoland and Griqualand East. The Natal authorities offered a reward of 150 head of cattle for the capture of Langalibalele alive, 100 head if dead,[15] and Griffith on his own initiative promised Molapo and Letsie any cattle belonging to the rebels which they might capture. This latter offer, according to Lagden, a subsequent British administrator of Basutoland, was probably the major factor in deciding the loyal response of Molapo and his sons;[16] but in addition there was the fear that the Zulu would allow their cattle to overrun the Sotho cornfields if they got that far,[17] and the greater fear engendered by the prompt appearance of a contingent of the Frontier Armed and Mounted Police.[18]

Despite all the colonial forces searching the mountains, it was Jonathan, Molapo's heir, who first found the exhausted Hlubi clan. By pretending friendship, he induced Langalibalele and his bodyguard of eighty-four men (including five of the chief's sons) to surrender to Griffith and Bell on 11 December 1873 without a fight.[19] The next day 200 more surrendered, but the main body of the clan was compelled to disperse only after being attacked by the police. Joel, another son of Molapo, meanwhile attacked the rear of the rebels on his own initiative and captured 500 head of cattle, which he was allowed to keep.[20] After a travesty of a trial, Langalibalele, his sons and some of his followers, were sentenced, Langalibalele himself to life imprisonment and banishment. He spent the next twelve years on Robben Island and the Cape mainland, until in mid-1885 his physical and mental debility induced the Natal Government to agree to his return to Natal, although not as a chief.

Molapo realised that this betrayal of Langalibalele would earn him the distrust of other sections of his nation, as well as of the Zulu,[21] so there was a strong incentive to ensure his safety by the obvious means open to him—Government support. In reply to a Government letter of thanks for his part in Langalibalele's capture, he admitted that he had objected to Major Bell's presence at first, but declared that he was now very thankful to the Government for sending him a magistrate.[22] His thankfulness was probably reinforced by the maltreatment of his ambassador to the Zulu Paramount in September 1874,[23] which left him nervous enough to send to Bell in alarm in the middle of the following year when rumours began to circulate that Cetshwayo was preparing for war.[24]

Although Molapo's opposition to Government did not therefore remain a problem for long, that of his brother Masopha, the third of the triumvirate of leading chiefs, never abated and increasingly became a focus for dissatisfaction with the Government. A man who had obtained great influence with the Sotho by his bravery in the war against the Orange Free State,[25] he was about nine years Letsie's junior and the son who most closely resembled Moshoeshoe. In his father's declining years he was the old chief's right-hand man and was already defying the Government when Griffith took over. On Moshoeshoe's death Letsie had stayed at his village of Matsieng, and it was Masopha who had moved to the back of Thaba-Bosiu, the original citadel of the Basuto nation. As the mountain was already established as the customary home of the Paramount, on the division of Basutoland into districts, Masopha was allocated the Berea District and ordered by Bowker to move from Thaba-Bosiu. He did not move however, and on Barkly's first visit to Basutoland the Governor informed him that he was unlikely to receive his percentage of the hut tax unless he did so.[26] But Masopha, strong in the knowledge that the Government could not enforce its will, stubbornly remained, and Griffith on his arrival tentatively suggested that it was a pity to make an enemy of him over a trifle such as whether he lived at Thaba-Bosiu or seventy miles away. However, he added that in view of Bowker's and Barkly's warnings, 'it will not do to let him feel that he has got the better of us'.[27] Barkly believed it was imperative to move Masopha for other reasons:

his bravery during the late war, and his great influence over the 'Tribe', render it all the less desirable that he should be allowed to enjoy the prestige of residing at a stronghold—for which especially since it became the burial place of 'Moshesh', the Basutos entertain a superstitious reverence which might easily be turned to account by an ambitious man desirous of subverting the authority, or disturbing the peace of the country of his more peacefully disposed elder brother.[28]

There followed a tussle of wills between Masopha and Griffith: Masopha refused to move and in 1872 Griffith withheld his hut tax percentage until he did so. Masopha retaliated by forbidding his people to pay further hut tax, an order which he only countermanded after Letsie agreed to ask the Government to alter the boundary lines of the two districts so as to cut Masopha's village into the Berea District. Letsie's role in this, as in other disputes, was dubious. At the 1873 *pitso* Masopha declared he would move if ordered to do so by Letsie—but Letsie never gave the order, whether because he feared disobedience or because he found it convenient to have a focus of disaffection apparently unconnected with himself is uncertain.[29] The Sotho were past masters at keeping all their options open, as their pre-1870 negotiations had shown. Meanwhile neither did Letsie make the promised request for a redefinition of the boundaries, Griffith continued to withhold the hut tax percentage, and Masopha ordered his people not to pay their 1874 hut tax.[30]

Faced with this deadlock, afraid of a serious loss of Government prestige, and in need of the 1874 Berea hut tax, the Government was about to adopt a face-saving formula to allow Masopha to remain at his village,[31] when he unexpectedly consented to move as soon as the grass and reeds were fit to use for building new huts.[32] In May he was persuaded to plough land in the Berea District preparatory to moving, whereupon Griffith, 'knowing the fickle and changeable character of the man, and the possibility of his still changing his mind again at any moment', hastily called a meeting of Letsie, Masopha, and their people and announced that the boundary had been redrawn to include Masopha's present village within the Berea District, as an act of clemency by the Government.[33]

It is questionable how far Masopha had ulterior motives in insisting on remaining near Thaba-Bosiu—Griffith throughout obviously thought it could not benefit him strategically—but the five-year struggle built up a reservoir of bad feeling between him and the Government and he became the obvious champion to whom Sotho could look whenever anti-Government agitation arose, a situation little altered by his subsequent behaviour. At the 1873 *pitso* he publicly advocated that chiefs should be given the means to enforce summonses[34] and Surmon's annual report of 1874 noted: 'the Chief Masupha, while professing loyalty before any one favourable towards the Government, does, I regret to say, all he dares to keep his followers from becoming acquainted with, and obeying the instructions and laws of the Government, and to uphold the continuance of their heathenish customs'.[35] At the 1875 national *pitso* Masopha declared that the people should bring all their cases to the chief in the first instance,[36] and later in the year he and Surmon, his Magistrate, clashed openly over a number of Surmon's legal decisions to which Masopha objected. Masopha complained to Griffith, who, after investigation, confirmed all Surmon's decisions; he also warned Masopha against his present course of obstructing his Magistrate and doing his best to make the people dissatisfied with the Government.[37] But this warning did not have the desired effect. Surmon and Griffith went out of their way to avoid a confrontation with Masopha. Surmon even sentenced a man caught committing adultery with one of Masopha's wives to imprisonment with hard labour, and Griffith allowed the sentence to stand since adultery was still nominally a crime in the Cape, although never prosecuted. As he explained to the Secretary for Native Affairs, 'upon grounds of policy I allowed the conviction to stand—the Chief "Masupha" being much enraged . . . I was afraid might take the law into his own hands'.[38] But Masopha continued to oppose the Government's policy of discouraging certain Sotho customs. In 1877 the missionary newspaper, reporting that he had refused to sign a memorial for the abolition of circumcision, sighed: 'although he received some education in Cape Town, and was for a time a member of the church of Thaba Basigo, he is now one of the worst heathen in the country'.[39] As late as 1880 his Magistrate wrote to Griffith that it was not unusual for Masopha, when an important measure was being carried out by Government or when the country was unsettled, to get up a scare in his district and have a difference of opinion with his Magistrate 'evidently for the purpose of distracting the Government and if possible gaining back some of his gradually waning power'.[40]

It was obvious therefore that his influence had to be permanently neutralised if the Government was to be safe to enforce and extend its policy of breaking down Sotho laws and customs. The measures the Government adopted fell into two categories—those aimed at preventing Masopha from forming an alliance with other chiefs, and those aimed at weaning the people from their allegiance to the chiefs and attaching them instead to the Government. In preventing Masopha from forming alliances, certain facts of Basuto life worked in favour of the Government. Polygamy ensured that every chief had a large number of sons who survived childhood, and though Sotho law prescribed inheritance by the eldest son of the first wife, the ruling was not rigid and was subject to confirmation by a lineage council after his father's death. Thus sons of minor wives, and even more so younger sons by the first wife, were all potential challengers to an heir, who was obviously very aware of this. Letsie's only surviving child by his first wife was a daughter, and although this girl had a son who by family agreement and possibly Sotho law ranked as part of Letsie's family[41] and whom Moshoeshoe had expressly declared to be the heir to the paramountcy, he had done so without consulting his people and in violation of the normal Sotho law of succession passing only through the male line. The boy had no hope of inheriting instead of Letsie's established and powerful eldest son, Lerotholi, who was generally regarded as the heir. Rolland, who had been Magistrate with Lerotholi for several years, described him in 1878 at the age of 41:

> He possesses much energy and activity, is courageous and hot-tempered, very wily and plausible, but is not much liked—he is quite uneducated and is proud and ambitious—professes great loyalty to the Gov[ernmen]t, speaks well and has always acted loyally and supported the Government. He is very intelligent, and recognises that it is in his interest to be loyal. He is a heathen and dislikes Christianity, but does not oppose it openly. His residence is near Mafeteng (Mr. Surmon's magistracy)[42] and has a district of about 5000 souls who recognise him as chief. Letsie is very jealous of him but uses him largely as a messenger and generally listens to his advice. He is poor and more or less dependent on his father. A large proportion of the people near him are Christians, and becoming civilised.[43]

Lerotholi was therefore unlikely to join his uncle Masopha in an anti-Government plot unless he felt very sure of its success and of the support of the people.

Moshoeshoe's influential sons by his next five wives presented a different problem. Unlike the sons of his first wife, they had not been 'placed' at an early age in charge of large districts, and were relatively poor men. In an earlier period they would have moved off with their followers to new land and set about improving their fortunes by means of cattle raids on their neighbours. The encircling settlement of Boers and British, and the imposition of British rule, made this impossible. Not surprisingly, in January 1871 three of these sons who had received some education in Cape Town, Nehemiah, George, and Sofonia,[44] provoked by the newly revealed regulations, began to say publicly that the Sotho should have a parliament of their own to make laws for the government of the country, and that the chiefs should have control of the tax revenue.[45]

Nonetheless, after the Annexation Act became law, the new regulations, complete with their taxation provisions and other unwelcome innovations, were reproclaimed as the 'Governor's Code', and came into force on 1 December 1871.[46] With such confirmation of the ineffectiveness of their letter of objection,[47] the Sotho chiefs decided that representations to the Governor were obviously an inadequate means of expressing their dislike of the regulations; they therefore submitted a petition for the vote so that they could air their grievances and also have some say in the way their taxes were spent.[48] Orpen certainly and Buchanan possibly had a hand in the petition.[49] Mabille, a P.M.S. missionary, later claimed that it was written mainly on Orpen's advice,[50] but the ideas expressed in it, if not the timing, probably originated with the Sotho themselves, as shown above.

Since the Government was unwilling to grant the franchise to the Sotho, the petition put it in an embarrassing position. It replied through the Governor that a necessary correlative of the franchise would be that Cape laws would supersede Sotho customary law and the land could then no longer be reserved for Sotho communal tenure.[51] This was a fallacious argument, as Orpen subsequently pointed out to Parliament,[52] but for some years no more was heard from the chiefs about the vote.[53] Possibly they were not willing to risk their position, for the Governor had been careful to remind them in his answer that at present the Government protected at least some of their customary law privileges: he had recently instructed Griffith to entertain complaints against those men who would not perform agricultural labour traditionally done for the chiefs, although his motives were actually further to destroy the chief's powers.[54] Eight years later the Governor's reply was to be denounced as having misled the Sotho about the very real change in status brought about by the annexation of Basutoland to the Cape. No doubt even at the time when it was given, it was vehemently denounced in private by Moshoeshoe's sons, especially those who had inspired the petition.

It was therefore necessary to neutralise these junior chiefs, and all but two of those still alive were given appointments in the police force[55] (to Letsie's and Masopha's great disquiet[56]), thus firmly tying their interests to those of the Government. Some of them provided invaluable assistance to the Administration; in 1881 for example, Griffith was to write of George Moshoeshoe: 'I don't know what I should have done without him when we first commenced our rule in Basutoland'.[57] Public service regulations were stretched to allow them to speak publicly at *pitsos* as chiefs rather than Government employees.[58] Several of their sons and those of other chiefs and counsellors, some already in their twenties, were sent to school in Cape Town by the Government in the hope that, away from the influence of friends and relatives, they would there acquire a liking for the white man's ways and presumably a healthy respect for the white man's power.[59] Griffith even took Lerotholi and four other important chiefs to Cape Town with him when he went on a visit, and reported them much impressed by the experience.[60] In addition, allowances were paid to various chiefs who demonstrated their loyalty to the Government by their good behaviour.[61]

The magistrates did their best not to give the chiefs any unnecessary cause for grievance against the Government that might, despite other interests, drive them into Masopha's arms. Griffith, for example, agreed with Bell that his district was too large to be administered efficiently by one person, but felt that a sub-magistrate or clerk should be appointed rather than another magistrate of equal responsibility, as the division of the district into two separate jurisdictions 'would give dissatisfaction to the Chief Molapo'.[62] When in 1873 Letsie caused a national sensation by surrendering his nephew, the Chief Sekake, to the Government on a charge of homicide, the Government informed Letsie that it was willing to release the chief from imprisonment on payment of a fine of £75 'in consideration of your loyal conduct in delivering "Sekake" up to justice'.[63] When allaying fears or issuing orders to chiefs, Griffith often worked through Letsie,[64] thereby using traditional allegiance to ensure obedience and prevent an unpleasant confrontation with chiefs. Similarly the use of Moshoeshoe's younger sons as policemen had the additional advantage of adding their authority to that of the Government when sending them to cajole and, if necessary, force recalcitrant chiefs to obey the law.[65]

It is possible, too, that other factors were at work reconciling the chiefs to the activities of government officials, despite the loss of revenue and political power that the Administration's interference entailed. The files, for example, are silent on the methods used to collect hut tax, beyond letters sanctioning payment to those chiefs and headmen who assisted in its collection;[66] there is no indication of what form that assistance would have taken. However, given the small number of magistrates and police, their many duties, the scattered placing of homesteads (frequently objected to by Griffith), and the distances and ruggedness of the districts, it seems virtually certain that the Administration must have relied heavily on the chiefs for both assessment of what was owed and for collection of the tax. Hut tax was paid on the number of huts—and therefore principally the number of wives—in a kraal,[67] so the number would obviously have varied from year to year and been difficult for the Administration to ascertain without seeing the kraal or hearing evidence on the status of its various members. Research on how a system operates elsewhere in Africa where local chiefs are responsible for assessment as well as collecting tax and paying it to the central authorities[68] suggests some interesting possibilities in the Basutoland situation. The principal chiefs received a percentage of the hut tax and lesser chiefs and headmen were, on the recommendation of the magistrates, paid for their assistance in collecting it, so at first sight it would seem to have been in their interest to have collected as much as possible. However, they may well have considered that the possibilities for obtaining political power offered by manipulation of the tax system were worth some financial sacrifice. The favour of under-assessment and the threat of a full assessment in the future would have provided chiefs and headmen with a new form of patronage unknown before the advent of the Administration. In addition, in 1871 at least, magistrates were instructed to refuse passes (necessary for Cape or Orange Free State travel) to anyone unable to produce a tax receipt *unless guaranteed by his chief or headman to be in need of a pass to the Orange Free State to earn the tax money*.[69] As in modern Niger, such opportunities for manipulation could have been utilised to give an indirect but still quite effective sanction to encourage compliance with chiefs' judicial decisions and administrative commands. There need not even necessarily have been loss of revenue for the chiefs involved, since at best they received only one shilling in every ten that the Administration collected, and this—or more—could easily have been levied for the favour of under-assessment, while still leaving the tax evader in a better position financially than on a full assessment.

It is true that there would have been a danger of missionaries and Christians learning of such practices and informing the Administration, but the risk was doubtless minimised by the fact that Christians lived in separate villages on mission stations and that tax evasion could be organised relatively privately compared with most other forms of opposition to the Administration. The more likely limitations in Basutoland to use by the chiefs of this form of patronage were, first, that the senior chiefs may have objected to such practices since, depending how the system worked, control of it could easily have escaped them, depriving them of both revenue and the advantages of tax manipulation. The second likely limitation would have been the fact that the majority of commoners had only one wife and therefore offered less scope for under-assessment. That the chiefs did not or could not use this form of leverage to a great extent would seem to be borne out by the way in which the people increasingly resorted to the magistrates' courts.[70] Judging by such evidence, while hidden forms of adaptation by the chiefs to their new situation probably existed, these would have been far from fully reconciling the chiefs to their changing circumstances.

However, some causes of dissatisfaction amongst both chiefs and commoners could often be nipped in the bud by the Administration, for there was a constant circulation of information between a chief and his magistrate. Magistrates notified the chiefs of events of importance within southern Africa and consulted them over such matters as land allocation within their districts;[71] chiefs in return were required to inform their magistrates if they held a public meeting, fortified a position, sent or received ambassadors or messengers from inside or outside the country, and any other matter of importance that they deemed fit for their magistrate's ears.[72] For those matters not reported, there were other sources of information. Messengers and many other Africans would usually make a courtesy stop at the magistrate's office when passing, even if not required to do so by Government orders,[73] thus enabling the magistrate to form a shrewd idea of whatever was afoot. Converts, missionaries and even traders[74] acted as a fifth column, and a corps of African detectives was supplemented by a systematic use of payment for information from agents whose identity was not revealed in public.[75]

Nevertheless, these methods of keeping the magistrate in control of the situation could occasionally be turned against the Government, as in the case of Tsekelo, one of Moshoeshoe's sons by his sixth wife. To acquire power, Moshoeshoe's younger sons had two choices: either to collaborate with the Administration, or to become indispensable to the senior chiefs. Or the more devious could even try both courses simultaneously. The educated Tsekelo had been quick to offer his services to the new Government. A month after Basutoland was annexed to the Crown, he and his brother George had written as much to Wodehouse, adding:

> we shall be pleased with all the laws which may be introduced in our country . . . Your Excellency can therefore trust us, not looking to the colour of our skin, but believing that we are real Englishmen at heart.[76]

It is true that Tsekelo was subsequently one of the delegates who went to London to object to the Aliwal North Convention, and that he probably inspired both the opposition to the regulations promulated in December 1870[77] and also Letsie's first objection to the exclusion of Nomansland from Basutoland.[78] However when the new magistrates took office under Griffith, he initially acted as a collaborator with the Government, making a loyal speech at Griffith's first public meeting,[79] acting with George as a sub-collector of taxes,[80] and volunteering letters warning against the disaffection of the three principal chiefs and various other anti-Government developments.[81] Griffith thought highly of his intelligence[82] and appointed him as Sub-Inspector in the Basutoland Police, a rather surprising move in view of Barkly's warning against employing him[83] and his past record.

> Intelligent and plausible, handsome, and utterly without principle, Tsekelo seduced several of his brothers' wives, excusing himself on the ground that he was so attractive that the women were unable to keep away from him.[84] At the beginning of 1861, after he had deprived Masopha of one of the widows of Majara,[85] he was obliged to flee to the Colony, where he then humiliated his father by spreading the most damaging reports about him. He

was received back, but in 1862 fled once again. This time there were rumours, apparently well founded, that he had twice attempted to murder Moshoeshoe, once with a poisoned cup of coffee, and once by blowing him up with gunpowder.[86] Claiming his father's approval, however, he spun such a convincing tale to President Pretorius that he was given a post in the Orange Free State police, and in October or November he was suspected of leading a night raid on Thaba Bosiu in an attempt to spike his father's new cannon. In spite of this he was again received back into favour, and in 1865 he was similarly reinstated after he had been caught stealing horses from the Free State. Perhaps some of the allegations against him were false, but even so he had clearly done enough to forfeit his father's indulgence time and time again.[87]

Presumably the charm or protestations of complete reform which had repeatedly won over his father worked on Griffith too.

In 1875 he accompanied Griffith to Griqualand East (originally Nomansland) and was given leave to attend to some personal matters before returning to Basutoland. He proceeded to overstay his leave by several months,[88] teaching the followers of his discontented brother, Nehemiah, the skills he had learned in the police. Griffith dismissed him from the service and in 1876 wrote in disillusioned tones to Brownlee: 'with regard to "Nehemiah" and "Tsekelo" I am well aware that they are both restless scheming fellows who cannot exist without some sort of Excitement'.[89] Yet Tsekelo must have been a remarkable man, for in 1877, after he had served a three month prison sentence for being an accessory to a theft, the Acting Governor's Agent wrote to Brownlee on his behalf. He reported that Tsekelo now deeply repented and suggested, in view of his undoubted ability and good conduct since leaving prison, that he be given a post in the Transkei, away from the scene of his previous folly. 'This plan would also possess the advantage of removing Tsekelo from Basutoland where he would always be tempted by the influence his words possess with the other chiefs to intrigue.'[90] His influence by this date could not be doubted; the Magistrate of the Berea District had just reported that Tsekelo appeared to have considerable influence in the district, especially with Masopha,[91] and at the previous annual *pitso* the chiefs had chosen him as their mouthpiece, impressed probably by his knowledge of the white men's world gained largely in their schools and service. Unfortunately, however, Brownlee was against employing him in the Transkei,[92] and Tsekelo continued to create excitement for himself.

This took the form of stirring up trouble among the chiefs. In 1878 he united Letsie with Masopha in a petition for a number of changes in the regulations,[93] basically aimed at removing all power from headmen, who tended to support the Government, and giving the senior chiefs completely untraditional despotic powers. Nor had Tsekelo forgotten himself: the Government was asked to place itself under the direction of an African council under the presidency of Tsekelo, who was to receive a salary of a guinea *per diem*! The petition purported to come from the whole nation, but the indignant Acting Governor's Agent pointed out that not only was the petition in Tsekelo's style and handwriting, but was signed only by Letsie and Masopha and two confidential servants of each, that not another chief or headman knew of it, and that there had been no meeting at which it was submitted to the people. He concluded that since neither Letsie nor Masopha would dare to mention it to their headmen or people, the only value of the petition was in 'showing the nature of the schemes which it is Tsekelo's life-business to promote in his mysterious itinerations from one chief's place to another. I firmly believe that in this instance the chiefs are merely his puppets.'[94]

Thus, although Tsekelo's efforts to unite the chiefs had to be carefully watched, the Government's policy towards the chiefs of 'divide and rule' appeared to be working.

6 Winning over the People

Closely associated with the Government's policy of dividing the chiefs was that of weaning their people away from them. So long as this policy proceded successfully, the danger of a revolt led by the chiefs continued to diminish. It was, however, a policy which required careful handling, for loyalty to one's chief was a basic virtue in Sotho society, although counterbalanced by a man's ultimate sanction of withdrawing his allegiance and joining another chiefdom. Unlike the missionaries, the Government did not ask the Sotho to abandon their chiefs physically and move into Government-controlled villages, but the magistrates nonetheless quite consciously tried to undermine the authority of the chiefs. As they were also simultaneously attempting, by enforcing the regulations, to introduce a number of unwelcome changes into the daily life of the Sotho, they required a nice judgement of what changes in Sotho law would be tolerated by the people in return for such advantages as Government protection from unwelcome impositions by their chiefs. Simultaneously, the magistrates had to prevent the chiefs from becoming so discontented at their loss of power over their people that they united against the Government. An initial salutary lesson assisted Griffith to strike a suitable balance in future.

He had started off briskly with a circular to his magistrates on 30 January 1872:

> With reference to Native Customs in Basutoland, and the attitude which Officers of the Government should assume with regard to them, I shall from time to time have occasion to communicate with you my views and instructions.
>
> Some of these customs will be found not only harmless but useful and beneficial to the people at large, and in that case they should be encouraged and supported. Others will be found hurtful and illegal, both in the general tendency and practical results, and these should be discountenanced and done away with at once.[1]

He then proceeded to recommend the encouragement of *maboella* (the custom of setting aside and protecting winter grazing lands from animals during the summer to ensure some grass survived the severe winter frosts) unless proved to have been used by chiefs or others 'as a means of oppression, injustice, or petty annoyance'. He also ordered the discouragement of *letsema*, which he regarded as 'pernicious in its tendencies' and described in terms which clarify his objection to it:

> It consists in the compulsory cultivation of the Chiefs' gardens by the enforced labour of any of the common people whom they may call upon, from time to time, to work for them without wages, without compensation, and without their being allowed to plead any excuse, however reasonable, for noncompliance with the requisition to labour thus arbitrarily (often most oppressively and injuriously) inflicted upon them by their chiefs.[2]

In addition, as he subsequently pointed out to Southey:

> when the custom of Letsima [sic], which is one of long standing, was originally adopted by the Basuto Chiefs, it applied only to the cultivation of one garden in each case, namely that belonging to the Great Wife of each Chief. Gradually however the application of the custom has been extended to the cultivation of *all* the garden lands of the Chiefs, which have consequently greatly increased in number and extent, the produce being sold by the Chief for his own benefit. Thus have the Chiefs established a traffic, to their own advantage, upon the forced labour of the people; claiming for the whole of their arable lands the benefits of a custom which, arbitrary as it was when applied to a limited area, became well nigh intolerable when extended to an almost indefinite because ever increasing number of gardens.[3]

Magistrates, Griffith ordered in his circular, were to protect Africans refusing to take part in this custom.

The circular was partly the result of a case which had come before Griffith that month—*Motube* v. *Makhebe and others*—for assault committed on Motube by order of Masopha for not attending Masopha's gardening session. In giving judgement for Motube, Griffith had been careful not to speak out against the *letsema* system as such but only against the practice—a recent development since

Moshoeshoe's death[4]—of using personal violence to enforce it. But he promptly sent out the above confidential circular to the magistrates. There is no indication whether Griffith and the other magistrates realised that the *letsema* system was also used to cultivate *lira* lands, the produce of which was not the chief's private property but was given to the poor and widows.[5] Nor is it clear whether they knew that the fields of the senior wives were regarded as the property of the chiefdom and that the chief would use their produce to entertain guests and feed the men when they were conscripted for military purposes.[6] An attack on the institution of *letsema* was therefore an attack on more than the chief's income and power.

In these circumstances it is not surprising that although he had not publicly attacked the custom, the case aroused great interest throughout Basutoland. Letsie and Molapo both immediately objected (although, surprisingly, not Masopha, who caused the fines imposed on Makhebe and the others to be paid).[7] Molapo went so far as to let it be known in his district that he would fine any person who did not attend his gardening session and punish anyone who complained to the Magistrate about such a fine.[8] This alarmed Griffith sufficiently for him to write to the Governor for instructions.[9] The reply took the form of a rebuke for acting 'somewhat precipitately in endeavouring to set aside suddenly and without reference to the several native chiefs, a custom of long standing in the country, such as Letsima [sic]'.[10] It would, Barkly suggested, have been more judicious to have announced at the hearing:

> that, while bound to protect every one from violence, you were quite prepared to hear what Masupha might have to urge in defence of his claim to Motube's labour on the occasion. This would have afforded you an opportunity for showing that the sons of Moshesh had encroached on the liberty of the people, and the result would probably have been to establish a right of commuting whatever feudal service was really due into a trifling money payment, if the defendant preferred making such payment to working.[11]

These instructions set a model for the Administration in their neat combination of attaching the people to the Administration without too greatly annoying the chiefs, and at the same time of drawing the people more into the money economy. They resulted in Griffith directing his magistrates to proceed with caution in discouraging the custom and to inform him of the views of the chiefs in their districts before taking any decided measures to suppress customs sanctioned by long usage.[12]

This setback caused Griffith and his magistrates to tread more carefully thereafter. In November 1872, for example, special permission was obtained from the Governor to allow Bell to fine rather than execute some Nguni murderers in the Leribe District, ostensibly because Molapo had made special representations on their behalf that they had been left in ignorance of the nature and force throughout Basutoland of the new regulations, but also because the execution of the murderers would probably have resulted in a riot.[13] It was this case which prompted Griffith to issue a circular on the subject to the Sotho on 17 December 1872, explaining the new capital punishment regulations. Significantly, it was a verbatim copy of a circular issued in 1850 by Theophilus Shepstone, then the Diplomatic Agent to the Natal tribes, in which he had carefully made use of African law concepts to explain the alien provision to the Zulu.[14]

Much was done to decrease the people's feeling of unfamiliarity with the new court procedure too. Griffith, in 1873 when writing to Rolland, stated that 'in Civil Cases, all the Rules of Court apply, at the discretion of the Magistrate, and with due regard to the circumstances of the country',[15] which left the magistrates with plenty of discretion as to how they would try cases. Griffith, for example, always invited chiefs and counsellors who were present at trials to speak in court,[16] and there is evidence that in other districts African rather than Cape rules of evidence were observed. A new magistrate appointed to the Berea District in 1877, for example, remarked in a private letter to his father

> The system here of allowing any number of witnesses to talk as much irrelevant nonsense as they like, makes the proceedings very tedious. They declare, however, that the only way with Basutos is to let them talk, and that if prevented from doing so, they will give no information whatever.[17]

Despite this rather unsympathetic attitude, it is probable that, from hearing all the issues involved in a dispute and the historical background of each case, magistrates would not have been either able or willing to take the narrowly legalistic approach to cases that strict adherence to the English or Roman-Dutch law tradition dictated. As a result of the war in 1880, detailed case records from this period are scarce, but the impression gained from surviving material is that the magistrates tried to give judgements that took account of the need to preserve an ongoing relationship between the disputing parties, and in their settlements attempted to find a solution to underlying causes of friction as much as to the immediate issue in dispute. In this they approximated far more to traditional adjudicators in Sotho dispute resolution than the judges of the Cape legal system, a factor that would have been of crucial importance in increasing the people's feeling of familiarity with the Administration's courts, even if indigenous categories and modes of argument were not always catered for.

The Administration was keenly aware of the importance of close and reliable communication with the Sotho in such settings, as well as in negotiations with chiefs, and therefore attached great importance to obtaining interpreters who were both competent and trustworthy. This they found difficult, however, since not only had the missionaries given all instruction in the vernacular until the British took over the country,[18] but Sotho interpreters were also thought to favour their friends.[19] Eventually in 1877 it was decided to give clerks £50 extra if they became sufficiently proficient in the notoriously difficult language to act as interpreters—a necessary incentive to members of the Administration since no officer other than those who had grown up in the country had at that stage succeeded in acquiring more than a very imperfect knowledge of the vernacular.[20]

To further improve communication with the Sotho and dissolve the feeling that the Administration was a strange and unfriendly foreign import imposing inexplicable laws, Griffith also took over the Sotho custom of holding national meetings to discuss the laws, at which every male member of the nation was free to speak irrespective of rank. Molteno was rather dubious of this move, disliking the idea of large gatherings of Africans, but Griffith's reply listing the advantages to be gained from such meetings overwhelmed all argument.[21] He pointed out that according to national custom whatever was said or done at *pitsos* acquired the stamp of authority; that attendance at these meetings by the chiefs was regarded as their acknowledgement of their subordination to the Government, and 'as the common people are allowed to speak, they also are enabled to assert their position as subjects of the Queen, having equal rights with the Chiefs to protection and other benefits conferred upon the country by the Government'; that by holding all such meetings, the Government acquired prestige as being able to summon the only real national meeting in Basutoland, while at the same time making the Sotho feel that they had a say in how the country was run and that the Government cared about their welfare; that it thereby acted as a safety valve, enabling men to communicate their grievances publicly to the Government, and generated an infectious spirit of loyalty which could be used by the Government to influence the people in favour of desired projects. Molteno gave way.

Some features changed, of course. Victorian decorum prevailed and meetings no longer began as in the days of Moshoeshoe, when proceedings 'started as a festival: the king's servants provided ample supplies of *joala* [a locally brewed, alcoholic drink], distinguished warriors sang their praise songs, and everyone indulged in war-dances'.[22] Under the Cape Government's Administration these activities, which had lasted for several hours before business commenced, were replaced by a prayer offered by a missionary. But in essence the meetings remained the same: a general debate, lasting all day, on proposed measures, at which everyone had a right to criticise the authorities. At each of the first few annual *pitsos* the regulations were read aloud and objections to them and the Governor's Agent's rulings were expressed, answered, and occasionally noted with a view to alterations in the matter.[23] Griffith would then, as Moshoeshoe had done, sum up, answer criticisms, and announce his decisions on the matters raised. Under Moshoeshoe, Casalis wrote:

> When the assembly are satisfied, they give vent to a sort of prolonged shout, dwelling upon the monosyllable: 'E! . . . Yes! Yes!' Then each one jumps up and waves his shield, shouting with all his might, '*Pula! Pula!*' (Rain! Rain!) an invocation signifying we are satisfied, and only thinking of cultivating our ground.[24]

Under the Cape Government the invocations for rain continued but proceedings would terminate rather more decorously, with 'three hearty cheers for the Queen'. By 1874 Griffith could report that the annual *pitso* was attended by all the principal and other chiefs, headmen, and common people from even the remotest parts of the country.[25]

Pitsos were also held to discuss special issues, which ensured that commoners' views were known on such matters and that information was not withheld from the people by dissatisfied chiefs: aims likewise achieved by the Magistrate visiting the villages or sending policemen to tell the people of controversial matters.[26] For the same reason there was also, for commoners as well as chiefs, free access to the Governor's Agent and magistrates, a right which was liberally exercised.[27]

Whether it was the result of deliberate policy or not, the Sotho's feeling of familiarity and identification with the Administration would have been further increased by the gradual appearance in its ranks of young men whose families were known to the Sotho and some of whom they had known as children. In 1871 Bell's son, Charles George Harland Bell, was appointed Clerk to his father, and in 1873 his brother, Fitzwilliam Bell, was appointed Clerk in the District of Berea. Both young men spoke Sotho. Shortly thereafter Charles Maitin, who had been born in Lesotho, the son of one of the French Protestant missionaries,[28] was appointed Clerk to the Assistant Resident Magistrate of the Thaba-Bosiu District. He not only spoke the language perfectly, but could both read and write it.[29] In 1877 Surmon's brother, James Surmon, was appointed Clerk to the Magistrate at Mohale's Hoek (Cornet Spruit District). In the same year Arthur Barkly, the son of Sir Henry Barkly, the ex-Governor of the Cape, was appointed as Magistrate for the Berea District, a fact which Masopha announced with some pride, or possibly irony, at the 1877 *pitso* after Sir Henry Barkly's farewell letter had been read to the nation:

> I thank the Government for my new magistrate (Mr. Barkly). He is the son of 'Ramabekebeke' (glittering uniform), the author of this letter, and the Government has given him to me.[30]

By 1878 Charles Bell had been promoted to the rank of magistrate, and both he and the clerks mentioned above each served in a number of districts throughout the country, often as Acting Resident Magistrates.

An increasing number of Africans were being brought into contact with the Administration by the creation of new magistracies: the Assistant Magistrate of Thaba-Bosiu District was moved to Mafeteng soon after the Administration was established, and in 1877 the post of Magistrate of Thaba-Bosiu District was separated from that of Governor's Agent, to relieve the Governor's Agent of that responsibility. In the same year an Assistant Magistrate was appointed to the Cornet Spruit District, based at Quthing, as Austen had found his district too big for him to be able to exercise more than a nominal control over part of it.[31] Simultaneously, as the magistrates were extending their control, the great chiefs were losing theirs. As each of the great chiefs was assigned a district, he ceased to be a national figure to a large extent and lost much of his power in districts other than his own. This had the unfortunate effect, so Letsie claimed, of undermining his control over his more rebellious brothers,[32] but it also undermined the chiefs' ability to unite the whole nation in rebellion.

On the other hand, the prestige and power of the magistrates continued to increase. Although sheer weight of numbers meant that magistrates still exercised control only by virtue of African consent, they had acquired the means to enforce their decisions where enforcement would not arouse large scale public defiance. In 1872 Griffith had established the Basutoland Mounted Police Force,[33] paid for from the steadily rising hut tax, to replace the sixteen privates of the Frontier Armed and Mounted Police who had formed the entire police force in Basutoland after Griffith took charge.[34] The new police force gave greater weight to magisterial arguments that the Government provided a more effective way of settling disputes than did the chiefs, forbidden as the latter were to enforce their judgements. It also enabled the Administration to enforce its decisions on the chiefs, although such direct action was not always necessary since, where a chief's cooperation was not forthcoming, magistrates had the often effective threat of withholding any hut tax percentage owed. As mentioned above,[35] after Griffith took charge all chiefs, petty chiefs and headmen or others who made themselves useful to the magistrate in each district in collecting hut tax were paid according to the magistrate's recommendations—another Government measure that incidentally helped to pacify Moshoeshoe's junior sons. However, where this means of obtaining compliance was not available to the Administration, or proved ineffective, the regulations provided that not only lesser chiefs, but Moshoeshoe's sons and the Paramount himself could be charged in court and fined, or even whipped and imprisoned, and with the new police force available to assist with enforcement, such cases did occur. By February 1879 Letsie counted eight of Moshoeshoe's sons who had been in prison.[36] Commoners also benefited from these provisions and the Government's power to enforce them, finding that they were able to defy their chiefs on certain issues with effective Government support; in civil suits as early as 1872 chiefs were being summonsed for debt by commoners.[37] Government enforcement was also popular for extending to areas where the chiefs had never had any authority without resorting to raids, notably for obtaining redress against Orange Free State and Cape settlers.[38]

Nor was the Government slow to realise the active assistance which the forces of European civilisation were rendering in drawing the people away from their chiefs. The effect of trade became particularly obvious in this period, for with the spectacular discoveries of diamonds in the arid regions of nearby Griqualand West, traders flooded into Basutoland. By buying Sotho grain and meat at the high prices generated by the demand for food at the new diamond fields, they drew more and more Sotho into the money economy and helped to develop a class of peasant producers. Even within the period of the Cape Administration, the impact of the market economy was felt throughout the society. By 1873, for example, the attitude to *bohali* was becoming commercialised already,[39] and as early as 1872 the hut tax was paid entirely in cash, not kind.[40] A steady stream of migrant labourers moved between Basutoland and both the diamond fields and Cape railway works, attracted by the high wages and easy availability of guns;[41] others went for shorter periods as reapers, shearers, or labourers on farms, while even boys hired themselves out to white farmers to herd livestock. By 1877 Rolland estimated that of the able-bodied adult male population of 25,000, at least 15,000 went out to service each year,[42] which incidentally must have further affected the women's role within the family and village. Moreover, already a small number of Africans, supporting themselves by trades or as transport drivers, postmen and policemen, depended on their waggons and labour as much as their land for their livelihood, and the Sotho chiefs soon realised, as Moshoeshoe had done, that dependence on the white man's economy rather than the chiefs' largess loosened traditional controls.[43] They did not try to prevent their men going off to work in the Cape Colony or Griqualand West, since these men brought back both weapons and wealth—an official in the Leribe District recorded, for example, that it was customary for every man from there returning to Basutoland after a spell of work to present Molapo with a minimum sum of £1 out of his earnings,[44]—but repeatedly in the early years of Cape rule there is evidence of the chiefs objecting to traders once they had seen the effect on their people of money obtained from selling goods.[45] However, the Administration continued to protect traders and the Sotho were soon dependent on them for many items.

Similarly, the Administration continued to protect and encourage the missionaries and their converts, whose numbers were growing steadily. By 1875 the census showed 6,399 Christians out of a population of 127,707,[46] but this figure did not include catechumen. Perhaps a more accurate reflection of church adherents would be that provided by Rolland the preceding year, when he reported that approximately one tenth of the Sotho were Christianised.[47] The chiefs, realising that church teaching against polygamy, *bohali* and initiation undermined their position, reacted by sporadically oppressing converts by whatever means came to hand. This fact was not lost on Rolland, who wrote:

> The Christians naturally look to the Government for protection and get it, and are thus strong partisans of our rule as opposed to that of the chiefs. In any outbreak they would side with us to a man, and their example would be followed by their friends and relations and by all those who have learned to look up to their superior intelligence and experience for guidance and advice. The chiefs know this and know that no intrigues could be carried out without some Christian hearing of it and warning us, and thus a great moral check is established upon them, far beyond that which would be exercised by a mere political minority of the tribe.[48]

The French Protestant missionaries had originally converted not only some of the more important chiefs outside Moshoeshoe's family, but even a number of Moshoeshoe's own family, including Molapo and Masopha in their youth. Even Letsie himself, ever since the days of Arbousset, had impulses towards conversion, and was for some time a catechumen. Mrs Mabille, wife of his missionary and daughter of Casalis, wrote that 'he could quote the Bible as no other'.[49] But disillusionment with the white man, the missionaries' attitude in certain political matters during Moshoeshoe's time,[50] and the effect of missionary teachings on their powers as chiefs, had led to nearly all the converts in Moshoeshoe's family breaking away from the Church. Many of these chiefs proceeded to lead a revival of

Sotho customs condemned by the missionaries, and enthusiastically supported such practices as circumcision and polygamy, which bolstered their powers.[51] They usually remained on fairly good terms with their missionaries, appreciative of their educational and other skills—Mabille became an influential adviser to Letsie on the country's external affairs—and Letsie at least would give a divorce to any of his wives who truly converted. He even on at least one occasion, after soundly thrashing her, allowed a converted daughter to marry a Christian without the payment of *bohali*.[52] But neither he nor his brothers ever reverted to the Church. Even had they wanted to, there were strong political pressures to prevent any such move. When Molapo, for example, at missionary prompting, attempted to abolish circumcision among his people, he yielded when challenged by his heir, Jonathan.[53] With Letsie the missionaries had even less hope of success. He was, as the missionaries themselves admitted, 'still less strong than his brother Molapo'[54] and would have faced powerful opposition to any such step from his strong-willed, anti-Christian eldest son, Lerotholi. And the requirement of monogamy remained a major deterrent even in old age. As Molapo, complaining of his seventy wives to the Leribe doctor, once remarked, 'What do I want with all these girls? I am an old man now, and yet I have to go on marrying fresh wives to keep up my position in the eyes of my people, though they are a terrible nuisance to me.'[55]

Faced with the hostility of the chiefs to Church teachings and the fear of pagans that if children were sent to mission schools, they would be converted, the Administration decided that more must be done to bring the benefits of a European education and way of life to the Sotho. In 1871 it had agreed to subsidise mission schools, and in the next few years, after initial hesitations, an attempt was made to institute a Governmental system of education; but the new Inspector of Schools on his initial tour of the country showed himself to be strongly in favour of religious education even in Government schools, and aroused such overwhelming opposition, from the magistrates as well as the pagans, that he resigned and the whole scheme collapsed.[56] Thereafter the Administration contented itself with encouraging mission education and especially women's education: educating women was regarded as a means of attacking polygamy, the levirate, the sororate, women's status in Sotho law as perpetual minors, and various other customs that were thought by the missionaries and Administration to be degrading, and that bolstered the chiefs' powers.[57] By 1877 there were approximately

3,000 pupils at some seventy flourishing schools in the country, over half of which were subsidised and supervised by the Government and many of which were staffed by locally trained Sotho who had passed the Cape Government's elementary teachers' examination at the training college in Maseru.[58]

Similarly, Griffith successfully advocated the appointment of district medical officers on the grounds both that the Sotho had requested them and also that the 'barbarous superstitions' of the Sotho could best be destroyed by teaching the people 'the absurdity of the modes of cure resorted to by their witch-doctors'.[59] By the end of 1876 the appointment of three district surgeons had been authorised, the surgeons to be stationed at Leribe, Maseru and Mohale's Hoek so as to have as wide an influence as possible.[60] These district surgeons would, incidentally, have been another source of information to the magistrates on local opinion. Their work brought them into close contact with people from even remote villages, and the evidence shows them to have been in touch with the magistrates. One, Dr Henry Taylor, married a daughter of Major Bell, the Magistrate in his district. Where there was no doctor in an area, the Sotho desire for medical treatment soon brought them to the magistracies. Fanny Barkly, the wife of a magistrate, described how people sought her assistance. Having brought to Basutoland medical books and a good medical chest, she was able to provide simple medicines, and word of this spread: ' . . . when I came out in the morning I always found rows of natives sitting on the ground, dressed in skins, and each holding a fowl to offer me in exchange for my doctoring as my fee. . . . My husband rather encouraged these doctoring performances, and we got acquainted with the Basutos in that way, continuing thus to pick up a fair sprinkling of Dutch and Sesuto, of which we were both, at first, profoundly ignorant.'[61]

Despite what the missionaries bitterly described as the Sotho's servile respect for their chiefs, almost bordering on superstition,[62] it seems clear that in a surprisingly short time the Government had successfully won support from the people, for its challenge to the chiefs' authority to settle all cases proved increasingly effective. Griffith in his 1873 report in the Cape Native Blue Book gave some indication of the opposition the magistrates faced in 1871 and how they were able to overcome it:

At first very few Basutos brought their cases before the magistrates, most of them being deterred by fear of the chiefs, who foresaw the loss of their power. The people were taught to believe that the magistrates had come to subvert all their cherished laws and customs. They were told that although the white man might be clever enough in many ways, he never could understand and grasp the merits of a native case as these chiefs could.

Gradually, however by dint of perseverance and firmness, and by a judicious mixture of forbearance and severity, the magistrates succeeded in winning the confidence of the common people. These began to find out that the Government was their true friend and protector against the arbitrary and unjust acts of their chiefs. Every case which was decided by the magistrates was duly canvassed, and increased the prestige of the Government. Prejudices bagan to disappear, and many people openly supported the Government; those who did so prominently being jeered at by the chiefs as 'rebels and turncoats'.[63]

The magistrates were no doubt greatly assisted by the fact that they took up their duties immediately after a period of great social disruption. The chiefs' credibility as leaders and protectors had suffered greatly in the face of Free State military successes, and their demands for contributions from their followers had become increasingly onerous and therefore resented. Although the chiefs had at least partially reasserted their control over their people after Wodehouse's intervention, there would not have been time for old doubts and resentments to have vanished before the Administration began to undermine the chiefs' status and powers of enforcement.

The statistics for a magistracy give some idea of the increase in Government strength: in the Sub-District of Thaba-Bosiu some thirty civil cases were heard in 1872; in 1873 sixty-six. 'A much larger number of cases, principally of a petty character, were settled amicably out of court, on the recommendation of the magistrate.'[64] And the numbers continued to grow. In his report for 1876 the magistrate for the district reported that 'the judicial, and other work at this office during the past year has greatly increased'.[65] The following year it was reported that twenty-eight more criminal and thirty-three more civil cases had been tried than in 1876. The report continued: 'The growing confidence of the people in the Government is manifested by their daily appearing in this office in great numbers, either to have their cases settled, or else to ask some friendly advice, and has a decided tendency to increase the work of this department'.[66] By 1878 the Acting Governor's Agent was able to write in his report on the whole of Basutoland that the Africans brought most or all of their cases to the magistrates,[67] while Rolland could add a few months later: 'most if not all the headmen are loyal supporters of the Government, and would refuse to join the great chiefs in any movement hostile to the Government'.[68] Altogether, the Government's divide and rule policy with regard to both chiefs and people had been extremely well managed. After some initial wavering, the Sotho had loyally assisted the Government in the face of the Langalibalele revolt; had remained quiet in 1876 when Nehemiah, Moshoeshoe's influential son in Griqualand East, was charged with inciting rebellion there and faced a delayed and lengthy trial;[69] and, apart from the Quthing District, had not become even restive when the Africans on the eastern frontier of the Cape Colony rose in revolt in the 1877–8 war.[70] Asked by the Government in 1878 for his opinion as to why Letsie had remained loyal then, Rolland gave as the first three reasons Letsie's realisation that it was not in his self-interest to rebel, the friendly and confidential relations between him and the Government officers, and 'the conviction that the large majority of the people were loyal and satisfied with our rule and w[oul]d not support a rebellion'.[71] (The remaining reasons he suggested were fear of the Orange Free State, the Sotho's own nature natural disposition coupled with widespread missionary and civilising influences, and the lucrative state of the grain trade.) In discussing the possibility of a general Sotho uprising, he added that:

> no such combination could be found or carried out except through gross mismanagement on our part, preceded by mis-government and consequent unpopularity. As long as the *personnel* of the Government commands respect and is duly supported by the indispensable display of material force, so long will we possess the confidence and respect of the people.[72]

It is interesting in this context to note J. H. Bowker's comments of 18 April 1878 on his return to Basutoland as Governor's Agent to relieve Rolland after an absence of seven or eight years:

> There is one point upon which I think the public have formed an erroneous opinion, and that is that the Basuto chiefs have lost their power and influence. It is true that our plan works well, and

the chiefs do not discourage the introduction of law, or their people resorting to the magistrate's courts, as it releases them from a large amount of work, and the percentage paid them out of the hut-tax is equivalent in money. But in every other way their attachment to the chiefs is quite as strong as when I took over the country from Moshesh in 1868. There are a few time-serving vagabonds, who will betray their chiefs to-day and their magistrates tomorrow, but the mass of the people are in all matters of state, as much devoted to their chiefs as in the days of the old chief; consequently the introduction of any new system must be most cautiously done, and every preparation for a united opposition seen to.[73]

This opinion appears directly to contradict all the other evidence available, so the question must be asked whether Bowker was likely to have been able to form a clearer view of the situation than the magistrates on the spot. This seems improbable. He had been in charge of the country for only two years some seven years earlier when conditions were very different, and when he wrote this letter had been back in Basutoland just over a month, most of which he had spent campaigning in the wildest and most recently controlled area of the country, the isolated Quthing district. Griffith, when he wrote his detailed account of how cases were gradually drawn away from the chiefs' courts, had already been Governor's Agent for over two years and was describing a process in which he had actually participated.[74] The only indication in the early annual reports of the magistrates that the increasing number of cases brought to the magistrates were taken there with the consent of the chiefs comes from Bell's report for 1874,[75] by which stage Molapo was anxious to stand well with the Cape authorities. All other reports for the early years speak of the chiefs opposing their loss of jurisdiction. The judicial situation Bowker described in 1878 was almost certainly the result of the chiefs being worsted in the earlier struggle to win over the people, and not an indication that they were more than resigned to their loss of jurisdiction. If this is correct, it seems that Bowker was probably misled by his short and superficial observation in an unrepresentative corner of Basutoland into overemphasising the degree of attachment of the people to the chiefs.

That there was attachment cannot be denied. Traditional loyalty to the chiefs was deeply ingrained, and in 1878 Arthur Barkly could still write of 'the slowness with which some among the natives have emancipated themselves from the control of their chiefs, though aware that their power to enforce obedience has long passed away'.[76] That same year Rolland and Davies, faced with a riotous and seditious village meeting held by three chiefs,[77] decided they would have to hold a public enquiry rather than a trial: 'We knew that however loyal the people might be they would shrink if called upon to incriminate these chiefs.' And Canon Widdicombe, the Church of England missionary at Leribe, has left evidence of the flourishing state of the institution of *letsema* despite official disapproval.[78] But all the magistrates, including Rolland with his long and intimate acquaintance with the Sotho, were unanimous throughout their reports on the slackening of the chiefs' influence and the preference of the people for Cape rule. Unless the entire Administration was guilty of consistently closing its eyes to the true state of affairs, it would seem that Bowker was mistaken. Masopha's angry conclusion to his speech at the *pitso* in November 1875 carried more than a grain of truth: 'We are of no use as chiefs. We have no more power. The people despise us.'[79]

7 Changing the Law

So successful a challenge to Sotho custom in such a short period of time gives rise to the suspicion that the magistrates were perhaps not enforcing those aspects of the regulations most unpopular with either the chiefs or people. But sufficient records survive to show that this was not the case. As mentioned above,[1] chiefs were tried in court, and on the even more sensitive question of land allocation, Griffith acted firmly despite periodic protests and attempts at obstruction from the chiefs. He did not claim the exclusive right to allocate land, but insisted on ultimate control. As he explained to a complaining Letsie,

> the Government has never interfered with any old kraals and in the allotment of land the Chiefs are expected to consult the Government first; and the Government reserves its right to interfere where a Chief is acting unjustly to the people, or trying to cause disputes between people, as is often the case.[2]

He and his successors duly interfered in various cases where chiefs tried to drive men off land allocated to them,[3] and adjudicated in disputes over land rights.[4] There is also evidence that on at least one occasion Griffith used his power to locate people himself.[5] Furthermore, he obtained a ruling from the Secretary for Native Affairs that the wood, reeds and grasses highly valued by the Sotho for such uses as thatching and basket-making should be considered as transferred with the land to the Queen; patronage in distributing them was no longer a right of the chiefs but a privilege delegated to them by the Government, which would be removed if abused.[6] At the 1874 annual *pitso* this was announced to the people, presumably much to the irritation of the chiefs, who had been able to exercise a great deal of power through their patronage and had, according to Griffith, recently used it unfairly to oppress certain Government supporters.[7]

Surviving evidence, though scanty, also shows that a blind eye was not turned to regulations as galling to commoners as to chiefs. In 1876 the *Little Light of Basutoland* was able to report of circumcision:

> We are happy to state that the Magistrates connected with the British Government in this country, do their utmost to put it down. They seize every opportunity to help the Christians whose children are sometimes enticed away to be circumcised. They commend the parents who forbid their children to go to the rite, as there is a law giving the guardian such authority.[8]

The right of a widow to custody of her children,[9] and of a girl to freedom to marry against her father's wishes once she had reached the age of majority[10] were enforced; infanticide and concealment of birth was punished,[11] and imprisonment was frequently used as a punishment. The wide discretion left to the magistrates in their enforcement of the regulations was in practice of particular importance for the magisterial use of coercion. Despite objections from the Legal Adviser to the British Colonial Office who had vetted Wodehouse's regulations before handing them and the Sotho over to the Cape in 1871, the Colonial Office attitude had been that the man on the spot knew best how far to push changes. As Sir Frederick Rogers, the Under-Secretary for State in the Colonial Office commented:

> These kind of rough rules for rough circumstances will seldom bear close legal inspection: and I am inclined to think that it is better that the authorities sh[oul]d be left without notice to exceed their powers when there is nobody to call them to account, than that they should be hampered by objections—on points of strict law—or that the Colonial Office should be called on to sanction especially that which is not [legal] in strict law.[12]

How effective the application of these 'rough rules' were in obtaining compliance is demonstrated by an incident during this period described by the Leribe District doctor.

> Some thirty miles from Thlotsi there was a large bed of reeds, and when the time came for cutting them, a dispute arose between the men of two chiefs, who both claimed ownership of them. As neither party would give way, they brought out their guns and

fought for a day, a number of men being killed and wounded. This was duly reported to the Magistrate at Thlotsi, and a single native policeman was sent up to the scene of events, with an order that every man who had taken out his gun to fight was to report himself at the Magistrate's office the next morning, bringing his gun with him. We had no knowledge whatever as to who had been out fighting, or how many, and I was a bit curious to see what would happen. The next morning over 200 men rode in to the court-house, each carrying a rifle; they filled the small court-house to overflowing. When the charge of fighting was read out to them, they all pleaded 'Guilty' in a unanimous shout; they were fined £2 each for the offence, and every man's rifle was confiscated for three months. The whole 200 deposited their guns on the floor of the court-room without a word, each gun was labelled with the owner's name, and they were told they could come and fetch them in three months' time. The fines were duly paid, some in money and some in cattle, and the incident ended.[13]

So successful were the magistrates in exercising their discretion during this period that the Administration was able not only to enforce the 1871 changes in Sotho law and custom, but also to extend their scope. In June 1872, as a result of the Sotho chiefs' petition for the vote, the Cape House of Assembly appointed a Select Committee to consider and report on the Basutoland regulations.[14] It recommended a number of changes, but J. M. Orpen, the Chairman, persuaded it and the House of Assembly that a more thorough knowledge of Sotho law and custom was required before the regulations could be altered. As a result, in August 1872 the Governor appointed Griffith as Chairman of a Special Commission consisting of the magistrates of Basutoland, to inquire into and report upon the laws and customs of the Sotho, and on the operation of the regulations established for their Government.[15] The Commission sat from only 3 to 10 December 1872, probably because it was considered unwise for the magistrates to leave their districts for more than a week, and took evidence from two missionaries (Mabille and Jousse) and nine Africans, including a brother of Moshoeshoe, the Paramount Chief Letsie, and three of his half-brothers, two of whom had received part of their education in Cape Town. Of the nine, three were Christians (including Moshoeshoe's brother) and one a church attender although not formally converted. Only two of the nine were not chiefs, one being a counsellor sent by the semi-independent chief of the Taung, Moletsane. There was no representative of Chief Moorosi[16] of the Phuthi, a group originally of Nguni origin whose customs differed slightly from other groups in Basutoland, and the predominance of Moshoeshoe's family—five of the nine African witnesses—makes it even more dubious that all variations in the law throughout Basutoland were noted. The Swazi resident in Molapo's district, for example, had retained many features of Swazi law, but the regulations recommended by the Commission were to be applied to all Africans living in Basutoland.

Of the main institutions involved, although opinions on the value of cattle marriages and polygamy varied, there was unanimity on the lack of value of circumcision schools. However, closer investigation shows that of the seven men who were asked their opinion of the matter, two had not been circumcised and another was the Paramount Chief, whose father had temporarily abolished the custom; two others were Christians, one a church attender, and one a counsellor of the Christian chief, Moletsane, who had abolished circumcision for his people. Luckily the magistrates knew their districts and although in its report the Commission recommended that circumcision ought to be abolished as soon as possible, it added the warning that

> at the same time your Commissioners consider it to be their duty to point out the inadvisability of dealing roughly with this custom, bad as it is, for in the districts of Leribe, Berea, and Cornetspruit very large numbers of the chiefs and people are staunch supporters of it, and would probably strongly resent its suppression. Therefore great caution will be necessary in any steps which are taken for abolishing it.[17]

Together with *lebollo* or initiation, the Commission classified polygamy and 'marriage with cattle' as the customs that appeared to be 'most injurious to the people, morally, socially, and politically, and to retard them in the progress of civilisation'.[18] It believed the latter two to be too firmly established to be abolished easily, but that over a long period Government and missionary influence would lead to their disappearance. In this it explicitly disagreed with the missionaries who gave evidence[19] and who, according to the Commission, wished to make Christians of the Africans by legislation; in contrast the Commission believed this must result from conviction, although the Government should at every possible opportunity indicate to the Sotho that it did not approve of 'these heathenish and barbarous customs'. It was fortunate for Basutoland's tranquility that the 'expert evidence' of the missionaries was given before men with some claim to expert knowledge themselves, and who also had the responsibility of enforcing their recommendations.

On a more detailed level, the Commission recommended a number of changes in the regulations, as a result of the magistrates' eighteen months experience with them. To make magisterial justice less arbitrary, they suggested various amendments in the review and appeal procedures that would accord more nearly with the indigenous law position and so appear more just to the Sotho.[20] These still did not meet Orpen's criticism in his appendix to the Select Committee's report:

> In Basutoland, with its scant European population, the magistrates have little society, save with each other. The few Europeans there are on terms of perfect social equality and intimate intercourse—a few gentlemen constantly at each other's houses. An appeal from one to the other of them is not, on constitutional grounds, a sufficient thing, though I believe Mr. Griffith to be one of the best constituted minds I know to bear the strain.[21]

But the legal obstacles in the way of the Cape courts administering African law left very little alternative.

Of the other innovations suggested, the most important were those dealing with the marriage regulations. The Commissioners found it necessary to draft an entirely new set of regulations for various reasons. They wished to make several important innovations safeguarding Christian marriages from the effects of Sotho law marriages. At the same time they bowed to the need to abolish the obligatory registration of marriages and the compulsory removal of a widow's children from her custody if she remarried. The innovations in the draft marriage regulations were all designed to ease the path of the Sotho who wished to follow in the white man's ways. Civil marriage, as opposed to marriage by a Christian minister, was made legal 'in order to meet the case of many people who are unable to get married by a Christian minister, either because they are heathens or under church discipline'.[22] Both civil and Christian marriages were to confer on the parties and their children the same rights as marriages contracted under the marriage laws of the Cape Colony—a move recommended by Mabille to prevent the children of converts being claimed by heathen relatives. For the same reason, where a couple were converted and remarried by Christian rites the children of their Sotho law marriage were brought under Cape marriage law. However, some provision was made to prevent the children of Christian and civil law marriages claiming to be the only legal heirs, to the exclusion of children of earlier marriages by Sotho law to other wives, in the event of their father dying intestate: such estates were to be administered according to the relevant Cape ordinance 'in so far as it shall be deemed applicable to the circumstances of the country'.[23] The Commissioners also believed the Sotho should be given the right to make wills, a feature virtually unknown in Sotho law.[24] Presumably to prevent complications when applying Cape law, the age of majority for all Sotho, men and women, was fixed at twenty-one years of age.[25]

Provision was also made for granting divorces in cases of people married either according to Sotho law or in civil law or Christian ceremonies, a point which had been overlooked in the earlier regulations, to the distress of the missionaries. Moreover, section 10 provided:

> That in the event of any person after having contracted a marriage according to the rites of the Christian religion or the civil marriage law of the Cape Colony taking another wife according to the custom of the Basutos, he shall be considered to be guilty of bigamy, and after due proof and conviction shall be liable to the pains and penalties attached to that crime by the law courts of the Cape Colony.

Mabille had shown that many men regarded a Christian marriage as 'something like a joke',[26] a way of acquiring a wife without having to pay *bohali*, until a more valued wife could be afforded. Despite promises not to marry any additional wives by Sotho law, many men did, and the second wife was then regarded as the principal one. The missionaries were naturally anxious to prevent this.

On the other hand, the Commission conceded the need for increased access to the courts in disputes arising out of marriages by

Sotho law: as recommended by the Select Committee, it abolished the missionary-instigated obligatory registration of marriages. The pagan majority of the population had never registered theirs; 'the consequence', the Commissioners reported, 'is that those people are now obliged to go to their chiefs with their cases of disputed dowry, our courts being closed to them'.[27] As this directly conflicted with the policy of weaning the people from the chiefs' courts, the Commissioners recommended that registration should be optional. But since they offered no new incentive to register a marriage, the new provision was unlikely to have any effect beyond legalising the existing situation. However, it was felt necessary to retain obligatory registration for Christian and civil law marriages, so the minister or officer performing the ceremony was given the power to register the marriage, to save the parties involved what was often a long journey to the magistrate's office. And the provision was to apply retrospectively to legitimise some earlier registrations by missionaries.[28]

Another suggestion of the Select Committee was also adopted by the Commissioners: they recommended that it should no longer be obligatory to remove a widow's children from her custody on her remarriage. The redrafted regulations provided that in Sotho law marriages not only guardianship but also custody should in future be regulated according to Sotho law and custom. This is the first positive indication that anyone drafting a set of regulations for Basutoland was aware of the difference between these concepts, and even here the wording is slightly unclear. The overall effect of the recommended changes in the marriage regulations was to give the magistrates' courts power to hear virtually all recent cases arising out of marriages in Basutoland; by far the greatest cause of litigation in the country had been brought within the scope of the Administration's control.

In the section on land and hut tax the commission again recommended various innovations as well as changes. The changes were relatively minor, but in addition, freedom of movement was partially curtailed by making it obligatory to obtain a pass when leaving Basutoland and to report to the magistrate of the district within ten days the arrival and property of anyone entering the country. Failure to report could be punished by a fine on the local chief or headman. Passes were already demanded by the Cape, but this was the first time such a limitation on freedom was to be imposed within Basutoland; and chiefs were already expected to report the arrival of ambassadors from foreign chiefs, but not of every visitor. Both controls were probably introduced in an attempt to check stock theft, but would also have given the magistrates a greater check on what was going on in the country. On the other hand, such requirements were bound to be unpopular, which would possibly explain the Governor's earlier veto on Griffith's suggestion that a provision for passes be included in the 1871 'Governor's Code'.[29]

The second major innovation in this section dealt with a matter to which the chiefs had always objected, and would continue to do so when this new section came into operation:[30] provision was made for the establishment of Government pounds for stray stock. The position in Sotho law was that all strays were reported to the principal chiefs and eventually became their property if unclaimed.[31] According to Rolland, 'a good deal of petty stealing was thus carried on by them'.[32] Griffith had in fact soon after his arrival in the country forbidden the chiefs from claiming strays[33] and the following year had established a pound in Maseru for all stray cattle found in Basutoland, with Sofonia Moshoeshoe as pound master.[34] This prevented the chiefs from augmenting their herds by what they regarded as their lawful right, and the perpetuation and extension of Government interference could not fail to be unpopular with them.[35]

However, although from the start the Commission's report was in practice to act as a handbook on Sotho customs for the magistrates in Basutoland[36] in the same way as Maclean's 1858 *Compendium of Kaffir Laws and Customs* was used in the Ciskei and Transkei, there followed an interval of over four years before the changes recommended by the Commission were implemented, much to the irritation of the magistrates.[37] After consideration by Brownlee and much drafting and redrafting by Griffith and the Attorney General, the amended regulations were eventually proclaimed on 1 July 1877.[38] Although there were numerous changes beyond those recommended by the Select Committee and Special Commission, many were merely to close loopholes in the wording of the laws or clarify the intentions of the original legislators.[39] Slight alterations were made in some punishments and some changes were made in sentencing policy. Although the trading regulations were extended, they did not introduce any new principles that affected Sotho law.

But one radical change was made in the regulations as originally drafted by the Commission: for the first time provision was made to apply Cape law to the white section of the Basutoland population, and in doing so the whole legal policy on the conflict of laws shifted against the Sotho. It is true that some alteration was required to make legal the application of Cape law in cases between whites in Basutoland: it was inconceivable that African law should have been applied, and Bowker in his evidence before the Select Committee had admitted that he would have applied Cape law illegally in such cases.[40] However, the new regulations provided that Cape law was to apply except where all parties in the case 'are what are commonly called Natives, in which case it may be dealt with according to Native law'.[41] This meant that in all disputes between white men and Sotho, Cape law would apply. And the section went on to provide that 'the proceedings shall, as near as may be, and so far as circumstances will permit, be the same as those in the Courts of Resident Magistrates in the Cape Colony'. While this allowed a fair amount of discretion to the magistrate in how rigidly he applied colonial procedure, the attitude to Sotho law and procedure was changed at a stroke from regarding it as the normal law of the country to regarding it as a concession made to the Africans.

The regulations in general bear the marks of more professional drafting than any earlier Basutoland code, and undoubtedly strengthened the Administration by meeting several complaints of the Sotho, notably the compulsory registration of marriages. Also, by bringing marriage cases within the scope of the magistrates' courts, they further undermined the rapidly dwindling power of the chiefs' courts. But they introduced several new grounds for complaint, especially the interference in the Sotho law of inheritance, the legal sanction on Christians marrying by Sotho law while still married by Christian rites to another wife, and the application of Colonial law in disputes with white men. Even more serious, by the introduction of Cape law as the basic law of the country, they posed a long-term, though unrealised, challenge to the Sotho's own legal system.

8 Prophesies

The Sotho apparently accepted the new code, as they had the old. At the *pitso* at which it was read to the nation, no objections were voiced except to the one pound deposit required when lodging an appeal.[1] Yet despite such acquiescence, there were indications that not only the chiefs but the people were deeply disturbed by the changes introduced by the white man. They might swallow their grievances for the other advantages the new order gave them, but in a few years their traditional way of life was being altered before their eyes in ways that were no doubt deeply disturbing. Missionary influence was especially insidious and all-pervasive; in his 1874 report, for example, Griffith could write:

> so deeply has the leaven of Christianity penetrated amongst the Basutos that, at least in some of its outward observances, it affects even the raw heathen population to such an extent that none of them are to be found working in their gardens, or travelling the roads, on the sabbath day; a remarkable circumstance, unparalleled (as far as I am aware), amongst the heathen in any other tribe under British rule.[2]

By 1877 Rolland estimated that 'the number of natives brought directly and indirectly under the influence of Christianity is very considerable amounting to about one half of the tribe'.[3] To add to the conservatives' disquiet, most Sotho probably overestimated the degree of collaboration between the missionaries and Administration: after the uncompromisingly severe resolutions of the 1872 Paris Missionary Society Synod at Thaba-Bosiu became known, so many rumours began to circulate that the Government would support and carry out the resolutions, that Griffith had to write to Letsie asking him to make it generally known that the Government was no party to them.[4] Griffith also did his best to reconcile the Sotho to the changes imposed by the regulations. Of the 1874 *pitso* he demanded:

I ask you whose subjects are you? (The people answer 'the Queen's'.) When Moshesh annexed any tribe to his own people, did he learn their customs and laws, or did they learn his? (The people answer 'They learnt his.') Well, then, do you want to teach us how to govern you? We come to teach you, not to learn from you![5]

But though such tactics might have convinced the Sotho that they should accept the regulations, they would hardly have reconciled them to the unavoidable injustices generated either by the clash of Sotho and European values or by the different policies towards African law observed on each side of the Cape/Basutoland border. And injustices could also occasionally result from mistakes being made by Basutoland magistrates as to the content of Sotho law.[6] Altogether it seems inevitable that such conditions should have generated strong if often subconscious unease among the Sotho.

The result, as in so many other places in Africa, was the rise of a prophetess movement. There had, according to the *Little Light*, been one in Basutoland some thirty years before,[7] and a variety of 'prophets' and 'prophetesses' had appeared since then, some more than others in the tradition of the diviner of pre-*lifaqane* Sotho society.[8] The reaction to the increasing influence of foreigners after the Cape annexation appears to have produced another batch.[9] By 1873 Tsekelo Moshoeshoe ended a letter to the Government with the ominous warning:

The eighth matter which I wish to explain to you clearly is one hidden to those who are foreigners (i.e. not Basutos). It relates to Basuto customs, and consists in designs enforced by commands from the dead, and which are transmitted by diviners who dream dreams. It is said that Moshesh has said that his children are to blame for having allowed the white men to make a plaything of his residence (or tribe). He says they must only enter into the Queen's Government with one foot, for his ultimate design is to release them from the dominion of the white man.

This is a matter to which you ought to pay especial attention above others, for it surpasses all the rest in stupidity, and also in being believed and honoured.

It is said that Moshesh is exceedingly angry, and that he commands in the strongest manner that his people should have no fellowship with the white men. That a certain specified ox must be immolated, with which Moshesh's sons must purify themselves, and then also purify the nation . . . There is also already another message which comes through a prophet in Morosi's country commanding people to hate the Queen's Government by order of Moshesh, and threatening that if they do not obey his commands he will smite the tribe a second time with the white men, and further that he will command the white men to introduce new laws into the country, that those laws may oppress and afflict us, and drive us out of this country and cause us to go into the land of the stranger to perish there.[10]

However, the Administration could do nothing about the movement, and there is no further mention of it until the last edition of the *Little Light of Basutoland* for 1875 reported:

A few weeks ago, the rumour went like lightning through a great part of Basutoland that the gods had made special revelations. Many women and girls were said to be under the influence of the gods, and began to prophesy all kinds of things. There was a great shaking of the head whilst prophesying. The message was as follows: The God of the white man does not exist; therefore all that has been brought into the country by the white man must be cast away: merino sheep, angora goats, horses, ploughs, pots, pipes, woolen and cotton blankets and all kinds of European clothing. Messages were sent here and there, to get the people to obey the order; two or three villages consented to give up the pipe, but nothing else, they and all other people declaring they could not live without the other things . . . The villages where such prophets lived were for some time shut against the people who Sunday after Sunday go into the different villages to try and instruct the poor heathen. Messages were sent to Christians that, if they did not throw their religion away, they would be cast into fire, etc. Some members and candidates were so frightened that they listened to these lying messages and have gone back to the orgies of the heathen dances and of the circumcision. But the influence of these prophecies has already much diminished.[11]

The missionaries were being rather over-optimistic, although in the same issue they reported a revival of the rite of circumcision for girls throughout the country, which should have warned them that anti-Christian feeling was increasing. But they merely blamed it on feminine superstition prevalent even among converts that an uncircumcised girl was unfit to become a mother. Ironically, it seems that under the influence of the national return to paganism, the British change in the African law of guardianship was having the opposite to the desired effect: women were encouraging girls to run away from missionary classes to initiation schools, but the widows among them were now protected in their custody of their children even if Christian relatives objected.[12]

Throughout 1876 the prophecy movement grew in strength. Almost every issue of the *Little Light* bemoans its effects. In March a missionary went to see several of the prophetesses with their attendants, about forty in all; his account of his interview with them and of their beliefs demonstrates how much Christian beliefs had affected even this movement:

He had much opposition to overcome before being allowed to go near them and to see them at their antics. They were old and young women, covered with grease and red ochre; some were sitting still, but at moments there would be a jerk of the neck backwards, enough to break the neck of any body else; others were dancing, others again running backwards very swiftly, some times stumbling and falling on the ground, some times running until exhausted. The missionary had a long conversation with them. They say they are under the power of a spirit, which tells them to do all [t]hat they do; they maintain that they pray [to] the one living God and they speak a little of the Saviour. They are afraid of all white clothing. They say, the spirit has told them to hate sin; but as to drinking, polygamy, cattle marriages, circumcision, and even worse things they have as yet received no instructions. Neither have they received any advice about joing [sic] to church.

What is rather singular, is that they say their God is not the same as the God of the white man; but yet he has created everything and every one. They insist very strongly on the fact that they have one God only, and not many Gods.

This is one of the songs, much in favour among them just now: 'We pray unto thee, God, the father of the Saviour with the pierced hands, who has created men and beasts and the gnus of the field. We have met together to pray unto thee.'[13]

Their leader was possibly inspired by other considerations too:

The great prophetess, 'Manthunya, is much sought after, so much so that the people who come to consult her bring as many as 30, or 50, or even 60 sheep or goats to her every day as fees; each animal must be accompanied with one shilling.'[14]

From late March the *Little Light* claimed that the novelty of the prophets was wearing off and that fewer people were going to see them[15] but in October there was a revival of their power.[16] The missionaries suspected that the movement was created by the chiefs or other dissatisfied parties,[17] but the Administration obviously did not share this opinion: to judge by the Cape files, Griffith did not discuss the matter with either the Secretary for Native Affairs or the Governor. Nor, although Governor Barkly knew of it,[18] did Griffith make more than a passing reference to it in his report on 1876.[19] None of the other magistrates mentioned it either, except Rolland, who gave a light-hearted account of it, and Austen, who merely remarked in his report of December 1875 that 'rumours of absurd false prophets' were circulating,[20] and the following year that 'that absurd phenomenon' had gradually died away.[21] The official attitude was obviously expressed by Barkly when he wrote in his farewell letter to the Sotho:

> I deemed it unwise to take notice of this delusion, and thus give it importance, believing that if left to itself it would die out. I have not been mistaken in this expectation.[22]

On the other hand, if the missionaries' suspicions are ignored, it is difficult to explain why the movement should have revived from late 1875 to March 1876 and again in October.

One suggestion is that it was caused by the shock to national prestige of Molapo's submission to the Government,[23] but Molapo's submission had come in 1873, two years before. Another possibility is the strong unrest caused by the rumours that Carnarvon, the British Secretary for the Colonies, had offered the Orange Free State a piece of Basutoland as inducement to join Carnarvon's proposed South African confederation, but the rumours were only publicly discussed by the *Eastern Star* and the *Friend of the Free State* in April 1876,[24] and could hardly have been circulating for some six months before being mentioned by the irresponsible and rumour-prone press; while the denial of the rumour took place in the Cape Parliament in July.[25] Drought did not affect Basutoland in 1876, and although the diamond boom began to tail off from that year, the effects were only just beginning to be felt by the date in question. But in November 1875 Masopha was in the middle of his dispute with Surmon, and in December was reprimanded for his actions; it may be that the missionaries were at least partially right in thinking that the chiefs were behind the prophecies. As had happened in the past, they no doubt encouraged movements hostile to the white man, even if they did not instigate them.

This links up with a second suggestion by Tylden[26] that the movement was the result of public indignation at the arrest of Sekhonyana Moshoeshoe in the adjoining territory of Griqualand East. Nehemiah, as he was known after his conversion in 1843 or 1844,[27] was the only son of Moshoeshoe's third house and the first of Moshoeshoe's children not to be circumcised. He was an able, ambitious man who wished to become a chief in his own right. As a result, in 1859 he and his followers moved into the relatively unoccupied land below the Drakensberg, known as Nomansland, with the consent of all possible claimants to the area: Moshoeshoe, the Mpondo chief, Faku and the British Government. In 1862, however, some 3,000 Griqua under Adam Kok were also allowed by the High Commissioner to settle there and rapidly evinced ambitions to dominate the area. Early in 1865 they chased Nehemiah and his Sotho out of Nomansland,[28] allegedly on account of their cattle-stealing activities, and when another group of Sotho, who had lost land to the Free State, settled round Nehemiah's old lands in the vicinity of modern Matatiele, the Griqua obtained the acknowledgement of their chief, Makoai, that Kok was their overlord. Subsequently yet another group of Sotho from Basuto-land, under their chief, Lebenya, settled in the area west of Makoai, and it was to this location that Nehemiah returned after the wars with the Free State. By this time the area was known as Griqualand East and was being ruled, albeit without formal authority, by the Cape Government. From there Nehemiah continued the fight to reclaim his original lands around Matatiele, and strongly objected to the assumption by the Cape Government of a right to exercise authority in the area by virtue of an informal cession of land by Faku to the British in 1861. Commissions in 1872 and 1875 enquired into and rejected his land claim, but by the end of 1875 many of his followers had returned to Matatiele and his influence in the area was increasing. When Cumming, the Resident Magistrate, ordered him to surrender some cattle allegedly stolen by his people, he refused to do so on the grounds that Cumming had no authority in the territory until such time as it was annexed. He and Tsekelo (the latter on his unauthorised leave from the Basutoland Police) then proceeded to travel around the northern Transkeian territory seeking support for Nehemiah's claim and urging resistance to Cape encroachment.[29] Blyth, the newly appointed Chief Magistrate of Griqualand East, had them arrested and forbade Nehemiah to cross into the northern area again, without a pass. But six months later he and Nehemiah clashed once more, this time over Nehemiah's followers' refusal to obey Blyth's orders: a group of Sotho at Matatiele refused to obey a summons to the magistrate's office, and, when Blyth went to arrest them, put up an armed resistance before fleeing into the Drakensberg. Nehemiah, although he had been away in Lebenya's location at the time, was nevertheless held responsible; Blyth was a highly emotional man[30] and had obviously been exasperated by Nehemiah's activities. Nehemiah was arrested and, in April 1877, charged with inciting his people to rebellion. The trial, which was held in the Cape Colony, caused much excitement. As some of the men involved in the disturbance had already been fined and released, the trial appeared most unjust according to African law principles. As the *Little Light of Basutoland* explained:

> According to native custom, if it can be proved that they acted on Nehemia's [sic] orders, they are not guilty; the guilty one would be their chief; if they acted on their own responsibility, then they have been judged, and found guilty; then what can Nehemia's guilt be?[31]

Although Nehemiah was acquitted on a technicality, the Chief Justice pointed out that the evidence did not incriminate him anyway. There was certainly a number of features of the case to excite public indignation in Basutoland,[32] but not the revival of the prophetess movement from late 1875 to March 1876 and again in October: Nehemiah's arrest took place only after October 1876.[33] However, his and Tsekelo's earlier agitation against the Cape Government did coincide with the revival of the movement, and may well have fed discontent being nurtured by the chiefs in Basutoland itself.

After 1876 the movement did not die but merely subsided. At the 1878 annual *pitso* someone mentioned that the prophetesses were still prophesying and that a number of people consulted them to learn what was going on at the war front, but it seems from the reaction of others present at the *pitso* that he had breeched an unspoken conspiracy of silence.[34] Though the prophetesses were lying low for the moment, by 1879 they would be influencing Masopha with their prophesies that he was to be the future Paramount Chief.[35] Whether consciously or not, the prophetesses spoke for the Sotho in their denunciation of the white man, his way of life, his religion and his laws.

9 Moorosi Rebels

Meanwhile, a far greater reaction to Cape rule was fermenting in the far south of Basutoland. Moorosi, the veteran chief of the Phuthi (or BaPhuti), had been Moshoeshoe's subject ever since his people had been conquered by Moshoeshoe's brother in about 1825; but he had been left a great deal of independence after early efforts by Moshoeshoe to bring him under closer control had merely resulted in Moorosi migrating further south across the Orange River in 1846. There he built up a large chiefdom of Sotho, Nguni and San. In 1850, however, the British annexed the area to which he had moved—later to become known as the Wittebergen Native Reserve and, thereafter, the Herschel Reserve—without obtaining his consent or even consulting him. Moorosi subsequently moved further east beyond the Tele River and, although he continued to claim that his territory included the Wittebergen Reserve, the Cape colonial authorities insisted that his land ended at the Tele River, which formed the eastern boundary of the Reserve.[1] It was during this period that Moorosi and John Austen, then Superintendent of the Wittebergen Reserve, developed their strong distrust of each other.

In 1869, after negotiating the Convention of Aliwal North, Wodehouse met Moorosi and agreed to his request that his territory should be joined to Basutoland. However, owing to the delay in ratifying the convention, this did not actually take place until June 1870, when Bowker and Austen arranged a meeting with Moorosi and his headmen to find out whether Moorosi was still of the same mind, by which time he appears to have been having second thoughts. What arguments were used by Bowker and Austen are unknown but Austen reported:

> After a very long argument Moorosi plainly and formally declared 'that he was a subject of the late paramount chief Moshesh, and that he would follow in the footsteps of his master; that he had acted the part of a dog lingering behind at the old

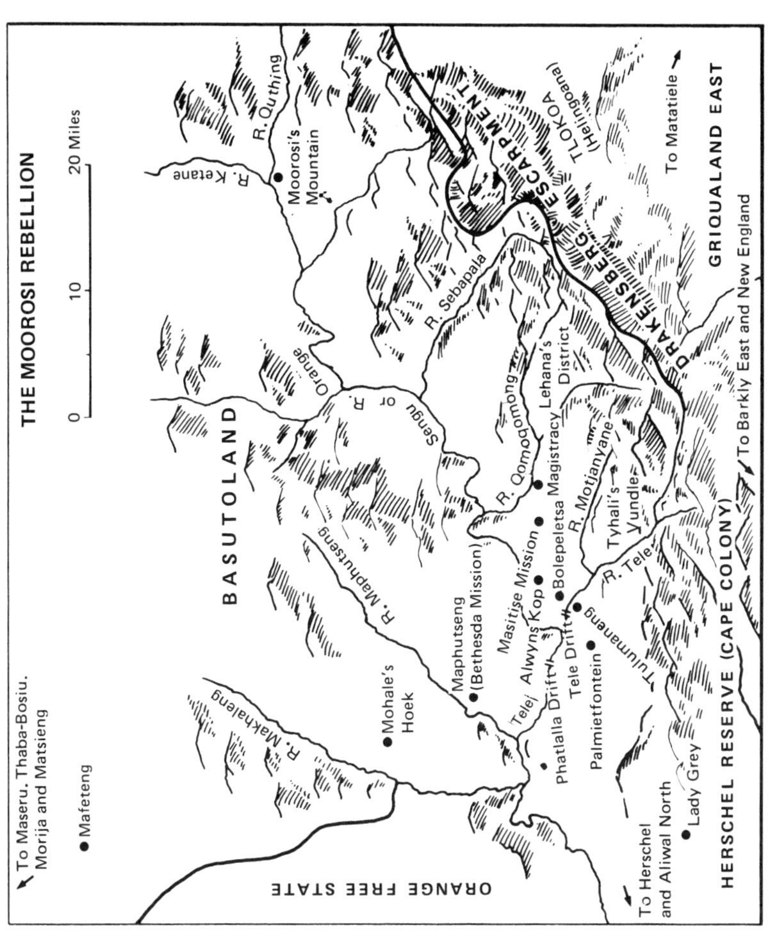

Map 5   The Moorosi Rebellion

kraal, eating the bones after his master had left, and that followed up the trail of its master.'[2]

He also agreed to pay hut tax and to submit to the proposed regulations.[3]

At the time he could not have known that the man who would be appointed as Magistrate of his district would be his old enemy, John Austen, but nonethless, even after Austen's appointment, he was content enough for the next few years while left alone in his rugged southern corner of the country, secured by distance and the periodically impassable Orange River from too much interference by the District Magistrate at Mohale's Hoek. The people on his side of the Orange included not only Phuthi, but also other Nguni, some Sotho, and San—Moorosi himself probably had some San ancestry[4]—and according to Griffith were 'about the wildest and most uncivilised of any in this Territory'.[5] On Griffith's recommendation a separate sub-district was created over this area in 1877 with a Magistrate based at Quthing. Moorosi was by then over eighty[6] but retained his early shrewdness, self-possession and objection to control by any authority. He also had a reputation for obstinacy.[7] The young Clerk at Mafeteng, Hamilton Hope, who was promoted to magisterial rank to fill the new post and keep an eye on Moorosi, was far too inexperienced for the task. He was duly introduced to the chief and his people by Griffith, who reported that they received the new Magistrate 'most cordially, the old chief Moorosi expressing his thanks to the Government for the interest taken in him and his people by kissing my hand and saying that he received the Magistrate with his whole heart'.[8] Griffith did not mention in his report that this took place only after Moorosi had opposed the subdivision for a full day, saying that he did not want a magistrate and was quite satisfied with the seat of magistracy being situated at Mohale's Hoek.[9] However, Hope was left twelve African policemen[10] and it was arranged that Moorosi, as the principal chief and a man of great influence in the new district, should be paid an allowance of £50 per annum 'to retain his influence on the side of the Government'.[11] The Clerk assigned to Hope, Charles Maitin, had been born and bred in Lesotho and spoke Sotho fluently. All looked set for another peaceful take-over of a chief's powers.

Hope, however, demonstrated a lack of judgement from the start. Shortly after his arrival he precipitated a confrontation by unwisely exceeding his powers. A complaint was made to him that Raisa, an influential headman under Moorosi's son, Lehana (known to the whites as Doda) had destroyed a widow's cornfield. The widow had refused to go to Raisa under the levirate system,[12] and although the regulations prohibited the enforcement of the levirate against the wishes of a widow, they did not in that case safeguard her land. She held the land by virtue of being a man's wife, not his widow, and if she refused to cooperate with his family after his death, she lost the use of the land if the family claimed it back. Raisa therefore felt he was fully within his rights, and refused to appear before Hope when summonsed to answer the charge. Hope fined him for contempt of court and Raisa turned to Lehana and Moorosi as his superiors to right this wrong.

The next development is best described by Hope himself in his report to Griffith, which illustrates the pressure that a chief could bring to bear on an isolated magistrate without taking any illegal action. It also shows the crucial gulf between Hope's and Moorosi's views of the situation.

> Resident Magistrate's Office,
> Quthing, 23rd June, 1877.

The Governor's Agent Basutoland.

Sir,—I have the honour to inform you that yesterday the chief Morosi came here with a very large following of about (500) five hundred men. He said he had come to greet me as his Magistrate.

He and all his sons came here, and after sitting for some time he said that he would ride over to Mission Station at Masitisi, where he intended to sleep. I sent over an ox to the chief to slaughter, which he seemed very pleased to receive. This morning a larger number of men assembled here than yesterday with the chief. Every man amongst them was armed either with a gun or a bundle of assegais.

Morosi asked me to meet all the people at a *pitso*, which I consented to do; and when they were all assembled I told them as they had come to see me I was very glad of it, and I greeted them, but if they had anything to say they must, one and all, put away their different weapons, such as guns and assegais, or else I should not talk to them at all; after considerable fencing on the part of Morosi, they went and piled their arms and re-assembled.

Morosi said that he had brought all his people to hear the laws read, that they may obey them. I then asked Mr. Maitin to read each clause of the regulations headed, 'Courts of Law', and to tell them that amended regulations would soon be promulgated, which would be read to them also, but that they did not differ very materially from the ones they had heard. Morosi then repeated all the speeches made at my installation, and said that he was much displeased with me, as I had not asked his consent for everything I did, that I had fined Raisa for contempt of court, which he said was illegal, and a great deal more in the same strain; and at last said, that nothing could be done by me without his consent, and called upon the people to say whose people they were. He said are you my people, or are you the Government people? If you are Government people you are fools. Do you obey this man (pointing to me) or do you obey me? They all with one voice cried out, we obey Morosi. I at once got up and left the meeting with Mr. Maitin, and the police and constables.

About two or three hours afterwards Morosi sent to me to ask if I wanted to speak to him. I consented, and he came to my office, where we had a long conversation, the substance of which I shall have the honour of reporting to you; but at this point of the proceedings a diversion was created by a war-dance being got up by some of Tyali's Tembookies,[13] who, in common with all the other people, had resumed their arms.

Several shots were fired, and dancing and singing war songs going on, when it was reported to me by the chief constable that a man had been shot dead in the crowd.

I left the office and ordered the corporal of police and two men to go down, unarmed, to see if the report was correct, and if so, to arrest the man who had fired the fatal shot, and bring him to the Court. Seeing some delay in bringing up the man, and fearing that the policemen had been mobbed, as they had to make their way through a closely packed and excited crowd of 500 or 600 armed men, I thought it advisable to go myself to the spot. The chief Morosi and his principal followers were already there, and I found that the corporal had arrested the man who had killed the other, but that he had been forbidden by Morosi to touch him under pain of being beaten; but as he was determined to carry out my orders literally he was threatened in different directions by Morosi and others with sticks and other weapons, and there appeared to be an intention to mob him and his men; when fortunately a man named Rakhoahei, who came with me from

Mafeting [sic] interposed and at this critical moment Mr. Maitin and myself arrived on the spot.

I at once took charge of the prisoner in the name of the Government and handed him over to the corporal. After having, with the assistance of Mr. Maitin, examined the body of the dead man, whom we found lying on his right side with a small punctured wound in the region of the heart, I returned to the office and had the prisoner brought forward. I spoke strongly to the people against bringing guns and assegais to a friendly meeting, and reminded them of what I had said in the morning upon this subject.

I forbade anyone to approach me then unless unarmed, and after they had put their arms away, I held an inquiry into the incidents connected with the fatal occurrence, at the close of which I was convinced that the deceased had been shot through the heart with an iron ram rod, fired from a flint musket by the prisoner, but whether accidently [sic] or not I found it impossible to decide, as the crowd was too great, and at this time too excited to admit of any order being established without a larger force of police, than I have, being at my command.

I handed over the prisoner to the representative of the chief Tyali, who became security for him, and promised to produce him here at any time, to answer any charge made against him in this matter.

After this having been settled I returned to the office, and the conversation I have referred to between Morosi and myself was resumed.

He said that he blamed me for having left the meeting in the morning, and asked me why I had done so. I said that he had come with other subjects of Her Majesty to greet me as the chief Government officer in this District; and I had been delighted to see them, that though I had not summoned a *pitso*, I did not object to meet them when so assembled, and at their request I had read them the regulations, but as immediately after I had done so, they chose at his (Morosi's) instigation to behave in unseemly manner, and make a public display of their preference for Morosi, as opposed to the Government, and, in answer to a direct question from him, declared their intention of obeying him instead of me, I could not, consistently with my duty as a Government officer, remain any longer.

Believing it to be expedient to overlook many other marks of their want of respect for the Government, I listened patiently to all that Morosi had to say, which occupied the time until sunset, when I answered him, and explained everything with the utmost care; but he still keeps firmly to his text, that you and Mr. Austen said, that I was in all cases subordinate to him, and upon my asking him plainly what he wanted, adding that my most earnest wish was to govern this district well and to deal kindly and justly to everybody, he said he would never give in until I consented, in all cases, whether Civil or Criminal, first to report to him, and, upon receiving his permission, commence proceedings, but if I adjudicated in any cases before doing this he would complain, and justly too, that I was killing him.

He further said that I had exceeded my authority in adjudication in Raisa's case, for that, although I had been shown to him by you and Mr. Austen, my authority as Magistrate had not commenced and that, not till he gave me authority to act, could I do so; he, therefore, wished me to restore Raisa's fine.

Notwithstanding the preposterous impertinance of all this, and his refusing to listen to or take heed of any arguments which I made use of, although he was advised to do so by 'Mofetodi and others',[14] I patiently bore with him, but as I did not yield an inch of ground to him, he gave up the discussion, saying that Mr. Austen has never decided any case without asking first if it had been taken to him (Morosi), and, if not, sending it back to him. Of course I replied that as Mr. Austen was not present I could not discuss any of his proceedings.

Morosi expressed his intention of returning home to-morrow, but I told him I should be glad of another conversation with him on Monday, which he consented to.

If the opportunity offers I will make another effort to convince him of the impossibility of my complying with his absurd request.

I have the honour respectfully to request your early reply in the event of your having any instructions to give me in this matter. In the meantime I will maintain the stand I have taken, but as I expect open resistance to be offered to the constables should they be ordered to arrest any person, as Morosi was at no pains to hide the fact that such would be the case, I beg you to take into consideration the incalculable advantage of crushing any such resistance at once, and to strengthen my hands by augmenting my police force, at any rate for the present, which could be done by the temporary transfer of men from the other Magistracies.

I have, &c.,

(Signed)   HAMILTON HOPE,

Resident Magistrate.[15]

The following Monday Moorosi returned with about a hundred men, still armed but mainly with assegais, not guns. Hope duly reported:

We sat down outside the office and the men all assembled. I told them that the language they had used at our last meeting was disloyal to the Government, warned them all, chiefs and common people, that I should not allow such disrespect to pass unnoticed if repeated, and told them plainly that they were liable to be treated as rebels.

The chiefs seemed impressed with what I had said, and Morosi appeared to have seen his mistake.

I sat for the whole day (as Morosi had asked me again to explain the laws to him and to tell him what his duty was to the Government) explaining the laws, and the duty of Morosi and every other faithful subject of the Queen, but at every turn Morosi came round to his original starting point, that he was the supreme chief here and that the Magistrate was his subordinate.

I explained to him that he had a perfect right to act as arbitrator in civil cases if both suitors requested him to do so, but that he could not enforce his decisions by attaching property or by seizure, and that in criminal cases he had no right to fine any one, telling him at the same time that he received a stipend from Government which had been generously increased from £20 to £50 per annum, with which amount he must be satisfied.

He most ungraciously grumbled at the amount, and said it should have been £100, but after I had talked to him on the subject for some time, he seemed more satisfied.

A great deal of time was occupied in discussing various other matters, all of which he brought round to the same point, viz., his paramount authority; and at last he asked for a few minutes' private conversation with only Mr. Maitin as interpreter, and his son Lituka [sic] as a witness.

I agreed to this, and we adjourned to the office, where Morosi said that a village near here was to be fined for making a practice of selling 'Juala'[16] as he would not allow such a thing in his district.

I said he was quite right, and that as a practice it could not be allowed, that I could put it down at once, and asked him to give me the names of the delinquents, and I should enquire into the matter. He immediately got excited, and said he had already made the enquiry and ordered the people to pay a fine.

I said 'to whom are they to pay a fine?' He replied, 'To me of course.' I replied that this was just a case in point in which he had no jurisdiction, but he insisted, and in spite of my reasoning with him, he said he would never submit to this.[17]

He would preserve his independence and adjudicate in any cases he chose, and that in this case he would enforce the fine.

I told him it was too late to talk of his independence, that he should have said this to Moshesh before Basutoland was given over to the Government, but he only replied that he had never given *his* country to the Government.

Even at this point I preserved my composure, and warned him that his language was rebellious. He said, you may kill me but I will not submit or resign any of my privileges.

I then said, 'Very well Morosi, I have been patient with you and borne a great deal from you. Now you openly defy the Government, be warned before it is too late, for if you openly resist me as a Magistrate, in the execution of my duty, you will repent it, and the responsibility will be on you.' He replied, 'So be it, I am now going to decide this case and enforce the fine in spite of you.'[18]

After this confrontation two of Moorosi's advisers apparently roundly condemned Moorosi to the white officials. Mafetoli, Moorosi's official messenger, went so far as to tell Maitin that on his return home he intended to resign his office, so strongly did he disapprove of his chief's conduct.[19] No doubt it was as a result of their representations that Hope was able to report the following day that 'after a final struggle', Moorosi had 'come to a complete understanding'. Moorosi apparently had soon regretted his challenge of the day before, and had put out peace feelers:

He sent two or three messages to me this morning to know if I was coming over to meet him; and let him point out to me a plot of garden ground for my policemen, but knowing that he only wished to entrap me, I steadily refused until he had retracted what he had said yesterday, and made an ample apology.

So eventually he came over at 2 p.m. and entered the office [;] all his chief sons were present and one or two other men.

Mr. Maitin was my interpreter, and I had the two constables, and the corporal of police in the room, the latter I placed at my side, and in three arms' length of the chief, to await instruction.

Morosi tried to fence the question again, but at last I saw I must take the risk of bringing matter [sic] to a crisis, so I asked him plainly whether he would submit to my authority or not; that if he did I would shake his hands as a faithful British subject, but that if not, he was a rebel, and I must treat him accordingly.

The situation had now become one of intense excitement as shown by the faces of his men, but I am thankful to say the chief made a most manly and complete apology, and promised never to oppose me again.

We shook hands and went in front of the office where, with Morosi's consent and his wish, his son Letuka called all his escort, and they gave three hearty chears for the Queen.[20]

The experienced Griffith realised that this was not necessarily the end of the matter. He wrote advising Hope

to be most careful and judicious in carrying out the judgements and orders of your Court to see that they are not carried out by your policemen &c with too high a hand—every possible care must be taken to prevent any of 'Morosi's' supporters being forced into open resistance or bringing on a crisis, as, I am not in a position to say that you would receive any physical support if such an unfortunate result should happen.[21]

But Griffith's advice came too late. Raisa had obviously been persuaded by Moorosi and Lehana to submit to Hope's court, for the records show Hope giving judgement against Raisa for 'three sacks of Kafir corn' as damages to the widow. Whether Moorosi considered this an unreasonable amount in the circumstances or whether he had by then had second thoughts on the matter is uncertain, but he informed Hope—probably while Griffith's warning letter was still on its way—that he had ordered Raisa not to pay until the matter had first been reported to Letsie and the Paramount's advice received on the matter. Hope's reply was yet another challenge to the chief's authority: Hope sent back a message with Moorosi's messenger that if the complainant in the case sent to say that the judgement had not been satisfied, he would enforce it, for while Moorosi was at liberty to send any message in the matter to Letsie, the Magistrate was not responsible to either of them.[22]

Griffith, on being informed of this, at once despatched Inspector George Moshoeshoe and Sub-Inspector Sofonia Moshoeshoe to Letsie to recommend that if Moorosi applied to him, he should advise compliance with the Magistrate's rulings. He also requested Letsie to send an official messenger with George and Sofonia to explain to Moorosi his present position under the Government. To Hope he wrote advising that he should not act hastily but should try to persuade Raisa to comply with the judgement without his having to enforce it.[23] This diplomatic handling of the case averted a crisis: Raisa satisfied the judgement of the court and George and Sofonia returned with a long letter from Moorósi claiming that all the trouble to date had been due to misunderstandings—which Griffith clearly believed to be an attempt by the old chief to save face.[24]

Despite this outward submission, however, Moorosi remained unreconciled to magisterial rule. In August 1877 war between the Cape Colony and the Africans on the Cape's eastern frontier resulted in Rolland temporarily replacing Griffith as Governor's Agent. It also resulted in the withdrawal of the police stationed at Palmietfontein, which was about ten miles from the magistracy and was the camp in the Cape nearest to Moorosi's border with the Colony. In November Moorosi seized this opportunity to challenge Hope's powers: he informed Hope that he was coming 'on a friendly visit', at which he was evidently to be attended by all his followers, fully armed.[25] Hope found the district to be buzzing with rumours of Moorosi's intentions 'such as, a plan to extort from me a promise to acknowledge his authority as superior to mine, or else to expel me from the district by force'; but whatever else Hope's faults, he did not lack courage, and replied that he would meet Moorosi on 3 December. He did, however, try to dissuade him from bringing his followers armed.[26] In this he was unsuccessful. Moorosi expressed himself vehemently to Hope's Chief Constable in words that were to have even more significance the following year.

> I will not leave my weapons at home when I go to a 'pitso' to speak with a chief. I cannot leave my weapons. Intercede for me to this effect with the magistrate. Ever since I was born it has been our custom; I have not invented it, it is so from ancient times.

Even when I go to my lands I take my assegais; all these people here can tell you so, it is our national law. . . . If the magistrate says I must leave my arms then it is that he refuses to see me; we shall then not meet, and the magistrate will prove that he does not wish to speak with me. See you, I do not want to walk stark naked, this is my nature. Even to pay hut-tax I go with these arms; they do not prevent me from paying Tax, I pay it all right.[27]

Hope, with the events of the previous armed meeting still vividly before him, not only made a report to Rolland of what was transpiring, but even sent a telegram to the Secretary for Native Affairs, asking for instructions. It was Rolland, however, who had immediate responsibility for Hope. He at once wrote reprovingly to Moorosi, cancelling the meeting,[28] and also arranged for Letsie to send a messenger to remind Moorosi of his subordinate position.[29] This obviously proved successful, for by early December he was able to inform Brownlee that everything had quietened down[30] and in January that Moorosi's 'conduct and professions ever since have been of the most loyal and satisfactory description'.[31]

But with the following month came a new crisis. On 29 January Hope gave judgement against a headman, Maikela, and four other men, all from Lehana's district, for hut tax due by their widowed mothers, who had never paid hut tax before. Although the regulations did not provide for exemption for widows from liability to pay hut tax, the magistrates normally issued certificates of exemption where a woman was 'too old or infirm to support herself'.[32] The widows in this case were still quite active and cultivated lands, so the male heads of their families were liable to pay hut tax for them, but they claimed that Austen had exempted them. Hope gave them fourteen days in which to get proof in the form of certificates of exemption from Austen, and no doubt the men immediately reported to Lehana, for a few days later he visited Hope to ask about the case. Hope 'explained the matter to him, adding that every one had the right to appeal'[33] but on 14 February, when Hope sent to tell the men that the fourteen days had expired, they returned no answer. Two days later one of Hope's policemen informed Hope that for the preceding week all Lehana's men had been assembled, armed with guns and assegais, with instructions to shoot any constables sent to arrest anyone or attach any stock.

It is not clear why Hope's ruling engendered this reaction. Possibly the men could not easily reach Austen at Mohale's Hoek, since it was the rainy season and the Orange was impassable except by boat for seven or eight months every year.[34] But there is no mention in all the correspondence of this being a possible explanation or excuse offered. Bowker, (shortly to become Governor's Agent) ascribed Lehana's actions to a war-spirit generated by the Thembu in Moorosi's district, who were in contact with the rebellious Thembu in the Transkei.[35] Hope suspected Moorosi of fermenting trouble, but in the light of subsequent developments, it seems far more likely that Lehana was indeed the moving spirit, rather than his father. It is noteworthy that on 15 January Captain Blyth, as Chief Magistrate of Griqualand East, wrote to Brownlee on behalf of Letuka, Moorosi's eldest son, who had been allowed to settle with his followers in Griqualand East.[36] Letuka asked permission to assume the chieftainship of the Phuthi in place of his father. No prior indication of this request had been received from Moorosi, and the Government was still considering the matter when Lehana precipitated the next crisis. Lehana was not the next son in seniority to Letuka, but he was influential with Moorosi and the old chief obviously had difficulty restraining him. It is possible that Letuka, anxious that his inheritance might be endangered or even challenged by his younger brother sooner or later defying the Magistrate, was anxious to be in a position to restrain him; Letuka was subsequently to work with the Government to try to prevent a Phuthi rebellion.

Whatever the reason, when a constable and four men, all unarmed, were sent to serve a writ on Maikela, they found him at Lehana's village. Hope reported that

> Doda [Lehana] said he should not allow the money to be paid; and when asked why they had not appealed if they did not think the judgement just, said, 'I have nothing to do with Makhoa [white men], I only know Morosi.'
>
> The chief constable then said he had not been sent to argue but to serve a writ, and returned to Maëkela's [Maikela's] village.
>
> A crowd, armed with assegais, followed, and one man rode on ahead, and when they got to the kraal the cattle were all in it, and the rocks above swarming with armed men, of whom there appears to have been seventy or eighty.
>
> The chief constable drove out two cattle that he believed belonged to Maëkela, and all the men then ran down and

flourished their sticks and assegais, and threatened the constable, who, as I had ordered them to prevent any disturbance, abandoned the cattle, telling the men that they were rendering themselves liable to punishment, and came and reported the matter to me.[37]

When a criminal summons was issued against Lehana and his men, most of them fled with their stock to the mountains. Moorosi, called upon to arrest Lehana, pleaded that he could not find him and twice offered money to pay Lehana's obligations. It therefore seems unlikely that he had actually instigated the incident, even if, as Rolland suspected, he subsequently sanctioned it. Hope, however, refused the money and informed Lehana's people that he would not receive their hut tax nor grant them passes till the matter was settled.[38] But neither Hope, Letsie nor Ellenberger, the local missionary, were able to persuade Moorosi or Lehana to surrender.[39]

It was this deadlock which faced the man who replaced Brownlee as Secretary for Native Affairs when the Cape Government was dismissed in February 1878. William Ayliff lacked Brownlee's strong personality but was knowledgeable about a number of different African communities. His opinion after reviewing the correspondence was that Hope had again acted unwisely: firstly in not following Austen's more experienced lead in exempting the widows from hut tax under his discretionary powers; secondly in refusing the money Moorosi had offered, which could have been interpreted as a token of submission; and thirdly in antagonising Lehana's people by refusing to grant passes, since the evidence showed many of them were against Lehana's actions.[40] To make matters worse, not only was Hope antagonising the people, but Moorosi was simultaneously doing his best to ensure that they were on his side. As Hope bitterly reported:

Latterly in every case, whether civil or criminal, that Morosi has been able to hear of, he has pointedly taken the part of the defendant or the accused as the case may be, and has done his best to prevent the case coming to court, by sending for the defendant the very day he was summoned for, and sending me a message to tell me he had done so.

Rather than have any disturbance at present, I have postponed cases as often as three times to try to get them settled quietly; in most instances I have been successful but in some not.[41]

Matters were only resolved on the arrival in Basutoland of James Henry Bowker to replace Rolland as Governor's Agent. As the Cape was still engaged in mopping up rebels on the Colony's eastern frontier, white troops could not be spared for Basutoland. Bowker therefore persuaded Letsie to organise a force to act against Moorosi—tradition has it that he threatened him with the confiscation of the Quthing District to pay for Cape colonial troops if they were required[42]—and an expedition was sent down to the Orange River, consisting of about 700 Sotho, some 80 African police, Bowker and five officials to command them, and the Medical Officer from Leribe. There they waited several days for a wagon-load of cartridges to arrive, during which time the Sotho levies rapidly dwindled away. By the time the cartridges appeared, Bowker was in no position to attack the mountain with his remaining reluctant troops. There followed several tense days of negotiation, with Bowker determined not to fight if he could help it but Moorosi afraid to come out, suspecting treachery.[43]

Hope meanwhile remained alone at the magistracy about ten or twelve miles away, with some of Bowker's six white companions going over every afternoon and spending the night with him in case the magistracy was attacked. The magistracy was close to Moorosi's mountain[44] and Taylor, the Medical Officer, had left a vivid picture of riding over one afternoon 'to keep Hope company' and arriving just before dark.

> I found him at the door of the house, listening to the horrid threats of fire and torture hurled down at him by masses of the Baphuti, collected on the rocks just above the house; these were of a bloodcurdling nature, as they described with no omission of detail what they would do to us that night. . . . When darkness fell, someone proposed we should barricade the doors and windows, so that we could not be rushed without warning, but Hope knew better. He flung the door wide open, put lights in the rooms, and opened the windows, remarking that our only chance of safety was to show them we were not afraid of them. . . . He was one of the pluckiest, coolest men I have ever known.[45]

Bowker eventually ordered Hope to abandon the magistracy and retreat to the camp. The magistracy was sacked and looted the following night.[46]

At last, with assistance from Lerotholi, a meeting was arranged at Bowker's camp. Moorosi insisted on coming armed, saying that 'he was afraid he would be caught like Langalebalele'. Bowker agreed, for 'Lorothodi [sic] was almost crying at the time for fear I would not agree; he said it was the only way of saving the country from a war'.[47] Moorosi therefore arrived on the scene with 800 horsemen fully armed, and again Taylor provides an eye witness account of what followed:

The meeting was held in the space outside our mess hall. Colonel Bowker and his staff sat on a bench placed against the wall: our police were drawn up in two sections, to right and left of us, and what was left of the Basuto levy stood some distance off in the foreground. An ammunition box was placed some three yards in front of us, for Moorosi to sit on. Presently he emerged from the crowd, and seated himself alone on the ammunition box, an old man with an impassive face and quiet manner, quaintly dressed in an old silk hat, and a cloak. Immediately behind him were ranged a double row of his sons, grandsons and head men, about eighty in number, all having superior rifles. Just behind them congregated the rest of his people, and near Moorosi stood Doda, a black-browed, sullen-looking ruffian, with a deep scowl on his face.

After the formal official greetings, there was a deep silence, Moorosi sitting still on the box. I was sitting next to Colonel Bowker, an experienced old warrior in native wars, who knew their ways and customs as few others did. He turned to me and said: 'As long as that old man sits on that box, we are safe, but if he retires from it and goes among his people, there will be one rush, and we shall all be pinned to the wall behind us, like so many cockchafers.' . . .

Presently Moorosi rose to his feet, and, addressing Colonel Bowker in quiet tones, said: 'By the order of the Government I have brought Doda here; there he is.'

A dead silence prevailed, broken only by a clicking sound, as the eighty men just behind Moorosi brought their rifles to the full-cock. The tension was tremendous, and unbearable for long: one felt that the slenderest thread held things together, and that the smallest incident, the accidental discharge of a gun, the falling of anything on the ground, would break it, and there would be a rush and a massacre. 'There is Doda,' continued Moorosi, 'take him!'

But eighty rifles brought to the 'ready' said 'No! Touch him if you dare!' All, both whites and natives, were feeling intensely the terrible strain on their nerves.

As I looked at the gleaming eyes of the eighty, just behind Moorosi, kneeling on one knee, clutching their rifles, holding them ready to put to their shoulders and fire, I felt that the crisis had come and could not last many seconds longer. Colonel Bowker saw it too, and rising from his seat, he spoke as follows:

'Moorosi, I am glad to see that you have listened to the word of the Government, and have brought Doda here today to be judged. I shall not put Doda back in prison, out of consideration for you, his father, but he must be punished for what he has done, so I fine him twenty head of cattle.[48] Now the matter is finished, go home in peace.'

As soon as these words were spoken, the situation was relieved. Loud cries of 'Pula! Pula!' ('Rain! Rain!') broke from the ranks of the Baphuti, rifles were lowered, the ranks broke up into a confused crowd and the affair was over.[49]

Bowker decided that Hope had shown bad judgement in his handling of Moorosi and replaced him with Austen, despite Hope's protests.[50] Moorosi also promptly protested, an action which Rolland subsequently explained as the result of Moorosi's belief that 'he could manage more easily with Mr. Hope, Mr. Hope being a young man. He knew Mr. Austen of old, and was afraid of him'.[51] There seemed at last every reason to hope that Moorosi would subside into submission: he had publicly surrendered his son, been placed under an experienced magistrate, and had the example of the Cape's victories in the war on the other side of the Drakensberg to remind him of the forces he would be facing if he gave too much trouble.

Nor was this hope at first disappointed. In September Moorosi readily surrendered two other sons who had organised a stock theft,[52] but in November Austen made the serious mistake of unnecessarily pushing the old chief too far. Legally but unwisely he arrested Lehana/Doda for horse-stealing which had been committed by Lehana's men while they were hiding in the caves some nine months before. As Rolland subsequently explained:

> He was not personally concerned in the stealing as far as I could understand. He was in command of some men who left the cave during the time that Mr. Bowker was in Basutoland and went and stole horses. He was an accomplice after the act, or it was stated to have been done by his orders. . . . One or two of the thieves, I think grandsons or sons of Morosi, were apprehended and lodged in gaol. Some stolen cattle had been traced to them, and afterwards one of their mothers, some old woman, came and gave information, saying, that she did not see why her son should suffer and Dodo [sic] and the others escape. The matter on her information, was traced home to two or three men of Dodo's.[53]

Lehana was a favourite younger son, a fact that Austen would have known even before he reported that 'the Chief Moorosi appeared with the two accused natives[54] on the day set down for their trial—and remained in Court the whole of the three days occupied on the trial—that he came with a large following all without arms of any kind—and all behaved in a most orderly manner'.[55] Austen further added that he had given the chief and principal men full scope to put any questions they pleased to the prisoners and witnesses, and that Moorosi had stuck most tenaciously to the defence of Lehana, whom he held to be innocent. But nearly all the influential men agreed with Austen's assessment of Lehana's guilt—including, interestingly, Letuka and Motsapi, who as Moorosi's heir and second son respectively would have had a vested interest in seeing a favoured challenger behind bars.[56] Austen convicted Lehana and Thlali of being accessories before and after an act of theft, and sentenced them to four and two years' imprisonment with hard labour respectively. In reporting to Griffith, who had by this time reassumed the office of Governor's Agent, Austen added:

> It came out during the investigation that Doda was ripe for rebellion while in that cave—I therefore think that if you uphold my judgement, it would be highly desirable in the interests of the Government, and good order of the people, if 'Doda' and 'Thladi' [sic] were both removed from this territory to undergo

their punishment at the Breakwater, or some such other place as you may be pleased to recommend to the Government.[57]

The sentence was a harsh one, particularly in view of the great fear among the Sotho of transportation; knowing of Moorosi's feelings, Austen showed further lack of judgement in not placing a proper guard on the ramshackle lock-up where the prisoners were awaiting transportation to the Cape. This resulted in the door of the lock-up being forced one night at the beginning of January at Moorosi's instigation and the men inside being freed.[58] Suspecting Moorosi of being responsible, Austen called upon him to help capture the prisoners,[59] and Letsie was persuaded to exert pressure on Moorosi when it became fairly certain, from statements made by a number of men from the district, the Lehana was being hidden on Moorosi's mountain.[60] Whether such measures would eventually have had any effect is uncertain, for at that point the Cape Government, to support its demands for Lehana's surrender, ordered reinforcements to move to the Cape military camp at Palmietfontein. Griffith was not told of the troop movement in advance and prophetically pointed out that it might frighten Moorosi and his followers into rebellion—for fear of invasion and punishment.[61]

It was Austen, however, who made the final and crucial mistakes that alienated most of the people who had remained loyal and stampeded Moorosi into action. As the more inexperienced Hope had done, he took fright at rumours that Moorosi was about to attack the magistracy and, without referring to Griffith, on 21 February sent his wife and children to Palmietfontein over the border in the Cape. At the same time he called upon the Commanding Officer there to march up every available man to defend the magistracy, a move which Griffith condemned unequivocally:

I entirely disapprove of this action on the part of Mr. Austen, who appears to have been more alarmed, I think, than the occasion absolutely required; and even if there was no doubt as to the intention of Morosi, I consider it to be a false move to march an armed force into this territory for no other reason than to defend a few buildings which it would be impossible to defend with any hope of success if attacked by any force. And then again the mere fact of moving an armed force into this territory is likely to precipitate matters as far as Morosi is concerned, but also to cause great confusion and excitement in the Quthing District, as well as in this territory generally.[62]

As evidence later showed, Moorosi was certainly preparing for war,[63] but whether he would have attacked the magistracy before his territory was invaded is unknown; even at this late date Letuka prevented a raid the day after the troops arrived at Palmietfontein.[64] But the following day Austen clinched matters by abandoning the magistracy as a result of further statements made to him that an attacking party was forming. His little group of himself, Maitin, the magistracy police, and some local traders, were allowed to leave unmolested, though watched, Austen stressed in his report, by scouts on all the surrounding hills. An irate Griffith, on hearing from Austen in Palmietfontein, pointed out that only the preceding day Austen had reported Moorosi to be anticipating an attack by the newly arrived Government force at Palmietfontein, and that the scouts were probably on the lookout for this.[65] 'Had they been preparing for an attack upon Mr. Austen, it would have been easy for them to have closed in upon him, and cut off his retreat altogether. In fact all the evidence that has been adduced goes more to show that Morosi's people were acting, more on the defensive, than the aggressive'.[66] However, presented with this victory before they had even fired a shot, the Phuthi sacked the magistracy and looted the Africans loyal to the Government who had stayed behind.[67] And left without protection from the Government, even the hitherto cooperative Letuka joined his father.[68]

The Cape Government was faced for the first time in Basutoland with a full-scale revolt, brought on almost entirely by a chief objecting to the application of the regulations, and subsequent ill-judged actions by his Magistrate and the Government. Nor could the Administration be sure that Moorosi would be regarded unsympathetically by other chiefs in Basutoland. As shown above, none of the major chiefs was happy with the regulations, and there were other factors prompting general unease among the Sotho at that time. At the 1878 national *pitso* Griffith, on instructions from the Cape Government, had announced that the Government planned to disarm the Sotho.[69] Subsequently, both he and Bowker reassured the Sotho, telling them that only rebels would be disarmed;[70] but the damage was done. Disarmament was discussed everywhere, a growing rumble underlying all other complaints. In

January rumour was fed by the outbreak of the Zulu war. On 22 January came the stunning defeat by the Zulu of a British Force at Isandhlwana; nearly a whole battalion of infantry with guns was annihilated. It was unprecedented in South Africa and the shock waves ran through every tribe. In Griqualand West there had been sporadic acts of violence by the Khoikhoi and Tswana since 1877 and volunteer forces had recently been sent in to suppress these 'rebellions', while to the north in the Transvaal both the Pedi (Northern Sotho) under Sekhukune and the burghers were giving trouble to the British Administration there. Not surprisingly one of Austen's men, after a visit to Moorosi's mountain on 21 February, reported that the men there were being encouraged by reports of all these troubles for the white man and were saying that the Government was quite powerless.[71] Moorosi could therefore have hoped for sympathy at the very least from the other major chiefs, and a repetition of the desertions which had been such a feature of the first 'Doda disturbance'. He would probably not have revolted had he not expected active assistance from Molapo, Masopha, and possibly Letsie.[72]

However, other factors came into play which enabled Griffith not only to prevent such an alliance, but even to use Sotho troops to attack Moorosi.[73] The Phuthi were separated from the rest of the Sotho by differences in language, descent and customs,[74] for having always been more an ally than a subject of Moshoeshoe, Moorosi and his people were never fully absorbed into the Sotho nation. Moorosi's independence had extended to preventing Letsie from placing some of his sons high up the Orange River,[75] an interference which would have annoyed the Paramount's family even more than Moorosi's subsequent rescue of his son from jail. And this latter piece of presumption provoked Letsie to demand of him:

> how is it, if Moorosi be a servant of Moshesh's, that his sons should be held so much more precious than the sons of Moshesh—for eight of Moshesh's sons have been in prison and yet no man opened the prison for them?[76]

As Hope had pointed out earlier, it would benefit Letsie in a number of ways if Moorosi defied the authorities and were attacked with Letsie's help: Letsie could avenge his grudge, seize Moorosi's cattle as loot, and obtain his land for Letsie's younger sons, which would also substantially increase Letsie's hut-tax percentage.[77] But whether these incentives alone would have led Letsie and his brothers to assist the Government, or at least stay neutral, is an academic point; Griffith clinched the question in favour of Sotho assistance by warning Letsie and the Sotho that if they did not turn out to assist the Government in suppressing the rebellion, he feared that the Quthing District would be confiscated to pay for the expenses of the Cape troops used. Letsie subsequently claimed— though admittedly while trying to prevent the confiscation of the Quthing District—that this threat alone induced him to fight.[78] But the relevant praise-poems of his two most senior sons, composed shortly after the Moorosi campaign, also indicate that both they and Letsie fought Moorosi with extreme reluctance. Maama, for example, described riding to the war:

When I came to the home of the chief of the Hounds[79]
Even my father asked me no questions:
I saw that his eyes were full of tears.[80]

Moorosi's original plan seems to have been to try to prevent an invasion of the Quthing District by stopping the Cape forces from crossing the rivers which marked its boundaries. Ellenberger wrote of him and his followers riding towards the border after a false report that the invasion had started and 'passing the mission in full battle array, chanting their war cries'.[81] (Moorosi was by then in his mid-eighties.) But an unsuccessful skirmish between some of his younger sons and the Cape forces obviously led him to fall back on diplomacy, for he made a last-minute appeal to Lerotholi to intervene with Griffith on behalf of the Phuthi, and warned that if the Cape forces crossed into his country he would fight to the death.[82] His appeal was unsuccessful; Griffith invaded the Quthing District in mid-March and rapidly drove the Phuthi back to Moorosi's mountain.

The mountain was a formidable fortress to capture, between 750 and 800 feet high with sheer rock faces, all fortified, on three sides, and only a narrow footpath leading to the top of the heavily fortified and steep fourth side. It had several springs and a number of caves.[83] The defences had been prepared over many years and a large amount of ammunition accumulated. As a result, the siege that followed lasted from late March until 20 November, with the Phuthi repulsing several attacks and even launching some of their own. They managed to take up fresh supplies at night throughout the siege, and inflicted what, for a colonial war, were heavy casualties on the colonial forces. Griffith returned to his duties at the end of May, handing over the command to Colonel Brabant, who had brought reinforcements and a more powerful field gun but had equally little success. The winter was bitterly cold and morale was low.[84] Moorosi made several attempts to sue for peace, hoisting a white flag and meeting the Cape's representatives on the mountain; but every time unconditional surrender was demanded. In mid-July Ellenberger reported that 'after considering the matter for three days, he replied that he preferred to die on his mountain',[85] and his reply was the same to both Brabant in September and Prime Minister Sprigg in October when they met him; 'You talk of peace, yes, peace for the Whites, but not for my people; you would not even let me die in my country, where I wish to end my days.'[86] Colonel Bayley then replaced Brabant and, using Cape Mounted Riflemen to climb one of the less strongly fortified rock faces, took the mountain on 20 November. There were only about sixty or seventy defenders on it by then,[87] not enough to defend it properly, and one of the attackers wrote afterwards:

> From the moment of our gaining a footing on the top of the mountain, the Maphutis [sic] never had a chance. There was no escape for them anywhere. They stood their ground splendidly to the last.[88]

The old chief and all his principal sons were killed. About twenty defenders escaped (although several later died of their wounds, were captured or surrendered) and only two or three prisoners were taken; the rest were killed.[89] Lehana himself escaped, but subsequently surrendered himself in December 1881.[90]

Today the Phuthi are scattered, for the majority that survived, men, women and children, were sent to work on Cape farms after the rebellion. Only those groups of Moorosi's subjects that had remained loyal to the Government were left undisturbed. They mainly comprised Christians at the mission station and Tyhali's Vundle, the latter having only just avoided being drawn into the rebellion.[91] It was a terrible retribution for an old chief's unwillingness to surrender his son to a dreaded fate. But had Moorosi's revolt been caused by that alone, it is unlikely his people would have fought for him, endured an eight-month siege to which there could be only one outcome, and in the end, died for him. Only extreme desperation could have driven them to such a stand—fear of execution or deportation, the loss of their families and country, once the first shots had been fired. But before that, before there was no turning back, there was fear of disarmament, fear of strange and unacceptable laws, and fear of all that the white man did in changing a known and predictable world into one of unexpected pitfalls and humiliating confrontations. For exacerbating those fears, the two magistrates who served in the district were largely responsible; they were for Moorosi, his sons and his people the daily, tangible expression of the far-away Administration, and they were most unfortunate choices. Yet the Administration was not peopled by vindictive, unfeeling men bent on destroying the Phuthi. The officials in charge in Maseru, with ultimate control of decisions during the two years of clashes—Griffith, Rolland and Bowker— were all experienced men with a deep interest in and sympathy for the people of Basutoland. But they too were afraid—afraid in the crises that erupted of revolt by the entire Sotho nation, or even perhaps by all the Africans in and to the north of the Cape Colony; and, continuously, afraid of rejection of the values, law, and way of life for which they stood and to which they were entirely committed. And so incompetence, intractability, conflicting interests, and above all, fear, make the outcome seem, in retrospect, inescapable. Yet there were many points in the course of events where men who were a little more flexible, a little less hostile, might have made the crucial difference. For Moorosi, all his struggles with the Administration, even the last, hinged on the issue of how far the Magistrate was to be allowed to interfere with his actual power to control and protect his people. Had either Magistrate or chief been more willing to compromise, the Phuthi might still exist as an important chiefdom today.

The story of Moorosi's revolt highlights how delicate was the balance which enabled the Cape to impose its system of direct rule on Basutoland, and should have ensured even more careful handling of affairs there in the future. But this was reckoning without the Government in Cape Town 600 miles away. Ignoring all warnings, it proceeded with blind obstinacy to create throughout Basutoland the very conditions that Griffith and his magistrates had spent the preceding nine years working to make impossible.

10 The Collapse of Magisterial Rule

The Sprigg ministry, which had come to power in the middle of the first confrontation over Lehana, appeared at first sight to have a policy on 'Native Affairs' very similar to that of its predecessor: to undermine the power of the chiefs and replace African institutions with colonial ones. But the new ministry visualised so different a time scale for this process that it became in practice a totally different policy. Under Brownlee, the Molteno ministry's approach had been extremely pragmatic: chiefs and institutions were to be undermined how and where the chance arose, within very broad guidelines. It was envisaged as a gradual process which would take many decades of slow, steady loosening of traditional bonds. In contrast, under Sprigg a new policy of 'vigour' was introduced. Changes were to be introduced immediately when ordered by the ministry in Cape Town, not achieved by a combination of patient whittling away of chiefly powers and improvising on opportunities.

The man who was to implement this policy was William Ayliff, the new Secretary for Native Affairs. He was knowledgeable enough about African customs—as the third son of a missionary, the Reverend John Ayliff, he had grown up on mission stations mostly among the Mfengu, though also on one for displaced Thembu, Tswana and Mfengu. However, he seems to have been a singularly colourless man and practically no writer on the period, whether contemporary or historian, mentions more than the fact that he was appointed. In day to day matters the Under-Secretary for Native Affairs actually controlled decisions—Ayliff told De Wet, the Secretary for Native Affairs in the 1884 Government, that he himself saw every letter but did not read all: 'they were sent to him with marginal notes describing contents—the routine letters he did not interfere with but no letter of importance was answered without his seeing the reply'.[1] However, the policies of the ministry, including those of the Native Affairs Department, were obviously all Sprigg's.

For Basutoland, the most important of these policies, which was introduced in 1878, was brought before the Cape Parliament in a measure ironically entitled the Peace Preservation Bill. It enabled the executive to issue proclamations ordering Cape Africans to hand in their arms, for which compensation would be paid. It was on hearing of this that Griffith had warned the 1878 *pitso* that Sotho disarmament would be called for. The act as it stood did not apply to Basutoland but unfortunately Sprigg, visiting Basutoland in the middle of the Moorosi trouble, saw a force of 7,000 Sotho cavalry perform manoeuvres and decided that for colonial protection the policy must be applied there too.[2] In his subsequent obstinate insistence on this policy he was supported by Sir Bartle Frere, the Cape Governor since 1877, who was bent on achieving his own pet scheme of a South African confederation and believed that disarmament was essential if this policy was to succeed.[3]

To the Sotho, such an idea was anathema. Over at least the preceding six years there had been a great increase in gun buying. These guns were often purchased out of wages earned at the diamond fields,[4] and each gun represented hours of labour for the buyer. Guns might also become necessary to defend their land once more were the white man ever to abandon Basutoland, as had happened in 1854;[5] the magistrates had, after all, been in the country for less than eight years. Most important, guns were considered a sign of manhood: to be disarmed was regarded by the Sotho as equivalent to being reduced to the status of children. Moorosi had spoken for all Sotho when he had declared that he would not attend a *pitso* unarmed, for 'when a bull goes to pasture, he does not leave his horns in the kraal, he goes out with them, that he may defend himself by them from his assailant and gore it also'.[6] Finally, the Sotho interpreted the disarmament policy as a sign that the Administration distrusted them. No argument advanced by the Government or missionaries could overcome the combined force of these considerations, and no advantages of the still relatively new Cape rule could outweigh this disadvantage. If any issue could unite the whole nation behind any available Sotho leader in opposition to colonial rule, this was it.[7]

Sprigg decided to visit Basutoland to explain the law personally to the Sotho chiefs and people at the national *pitso* for 1879. The meeting, held in Maseru in mid-October, was attended by most of the magistrates, missionaries and traders as well as a large number of farmers from the Free State and between 6,000 and 10,000 Sotho.

The following day Sprigg met the principal chiefs and their representatives in the schoolroom in Maseru.[8] Significantly, Letsie, Molapo and Masopha all pleaded that they were too ill to attend in person on the second day, and with Moorosi still successfully withstanding the siege of his mountain in the south, Sprigg's self-opinionated manner appeared ludicrous.

> Being of insignificant stature, having a short staccato manner of speech, and dressed in a tweed suit and a straw-hat furnished with a long puggaree,[9] he looked anything but an important and powerful personage, while his general manner was fussy and wanting in dignity, and in no way impressed the people. He . . . made speeches to them full of trite platitudes, which they pushed contemptuously on one side. He talked of the necessity of their surrendering their arms, so that they could devote all their energies to going forward on the path of progress, civilisation, and education, and thus become prosperous and happy in this life, and be fitted for that higher and better life that is to come, and so forth, and so on.
>
> The chiefs indignantly replied that though they had guns they had never done any harm with them, but on the contrary, when called upon by the Government to use their weapons to keep order in Basutoland, they had always obeyed: they instanced the war against Moorosi, when nearly 2,000 Basuto had taken part in the siege of his mountain. How, they asked, were they in future to preserve law and order in the country, if they were turned into women by being deprived of their arms? They challenged the Government to name any case in which they had used their guns improperly, and cited many cases in which, on the other hand, they had rendered good service in putting down disturbances. No! They saw that the Government wanted first to emasculate them, and then, when they were powerless, to make slaves of them and their wives and children. They had always obeyed the Government in all things before, but they could not, and would not, consent to give up their guns. They said that when their late great Chief, Moshesh, handed over the country, he gave it to the Great White Queen, and not to the little man who had been making speeches to them, and that no word about their guns had come from the Great Queen, to whom the country belonged. Floods of oratory on both sides were expended, but to no purpose.[10]

To make matters worse, the Cape Government also announced a number of other measures, each of which alone would probably have aroused only dissatisfaction; combined with the disarmament legislation and the Government's mishandling of its implementation, they could hardly been worse timed. Moorosi's mountain was taken a month after the 1879 national *pitso* and, having decided to punish Moorosi's rebels, Sprigg produced a plan for dividing the Quthing District into white farms. This scheme was to produce repeated protests from both Griffith and Letsie[11] on the grounds that this was entirely contrary to the undertakings of the British Governor to Moshoeshoe never to alienate any portion of Basutoland, and that the nation, having loyally supported the Government against Moorosi, had done nothing to deserve such treatment. To understand the strength of the Sotho reaction to the confiscation of Quthing, it should be borne in mind that the Sotho felt they had already been unjustly deprived by the British and the Cape Governments of much of their national patrimony since 1844, the latest deprivation being the Matatiele District. Although the Sotho claim to Matatiele was based on a grant by Faku to Moshoeshoe which the Cape Government regarded as invalid, the Sotho naturally regarded the Quthing confiscation as further evidence that the Cape Government desired to gobble up Sotho land for white men's farms.[12] Nevertheless, in December a commission was appointed to inspect the country with a view to dividing it up for white settlement and, to add insult to injury, without consulting Griffith the Government appointed Austen to serve on it.[13] Furthermore, the ministry decided to double the hut tax to £1.[14] This was a completely unjustifiable move in view of its already announced intention of appropriating £12,500 from the Basutoland account to pay for Cape expenses,[15] despite the original undertaking that all money raised in taxes in Basutoland would be spent on Sotho needs.[16] As the missionary newspaper had complained about this breach of faith in more than one issue,[17] it seems reasonable to assume that a large number of Sotho would have been aware of the full injustice of the tax increase.

Both Rolland, in giving evidence before the Select Committee on the Basutoland Hostilities,[18] and Griffith in a letter to the Secretary for Native Affairs, unmistakably warned of the cumulative effect of these measures on Sotho goodwill. Griffith added that by obliging him to enforce them the Government had placed him in an equivocal position 'which must naturally create a wide gap in that good feeling which has hitherto existed between the whole nation and myself as their "Father" and the Government representative'.[19] But the ministry remained set on its course, except for agreeing to return the £12,500 taken from the Basutoland Treasury 'as a contribution to the expenses of suppressing the rebellion'. The reason Sprigg gave for its return was that the revenue paid for auctioning the Quthing lands would pay for this instead.[20] In March it confirmed its intention to auction the land in the Quthing District[21] and a month later formally doubled the hut tax by a proclamation amending the Basutoland regulations.[22] In addition the same proclamation provided for quit-rent grants of land round the magistracies and to 'traders residing at isolated stations', which was a further violation of Wodehouse's agreement with Moshoeshoe and as such a further grievance on the Sotho's rapidly lengthening list. Its inspiration was probably a request from the traders' meeting of 1878 to which Griffith had been sympathetic,[23] but it was almost certainly illegal in view of past parliamentary recognition of Sotho land as being inalienable. Even in quieter times comment would have been difficult to avoid, but to have introduced the measure at such a time was an open invitation to trouble. With thirty-two years of service behind him,[24] Griffith had his pension to consider, but he was deeply attached to the Sotho and aware of the inevitable result of the policies he would be forced to implement. Placed in this impossible position, he asked for long leave, but was too valuable for the Government to spare at such a time.[25]

The unfortunate magistrates, who objected to disarmament as strongly as Griffith, found themselves expected to disarm the Sotho by the exercise of moral suasion alone. The Peace Preservation Act was not extended to Basutoland, as a number of Cape Parliamentarians had from the start supported the act on the understanding that only clearly disaffected frontier areas would be disarmed, and Sprigg no doubt feared opposition if he officially extended the act to a Basutoland that had just assisted the Cape Government to quell Moorosi's revolt.[26] However, as the Sotho knew their magistrates' opinion of disarmament, moral suasion alone was not successful. Through Griffith, the Sotho sent two petitions against disarmament to Cape Town—one to the Governor and the other to the Queen. Letsie, on being informed on Sprigg's orders that the Government was resolute in insisting on disarmament, replied with dignity that he was awaiting the results of the petitions, that the act was not yet proclaimed, 'and therefore hitherto we have not refused obedience to any order. Therefore I still pray the Hon. Colonial Secretary and yourself, Sir, that you would treat me as a man possessing some rights as a British subject, as I have hitherto considered myself as such.'[27] In March 1880 Sprigg bowed to necessity and sent Griffith the proclamation extending the act to Basutoland, much to the relief of the magistrates. However little they might wish for disarmament, they were obliged to implement the policy and had realised that the inevitable failure to disarm the Sotho by moral pressure alone would lead the Sotho to regard the Government as weak; but they had reckoned without the Reverend Adolph Mabille.

The French Protestant missionaries, as the original advisors of the Sotho, had already been drawn into the mounting protests. Initially, however, they had little effect. The Morija missionary, Mabille, had been the agent through whom Griffith had received the two petitions against disarmament from Letsie,[28] but these were unsympathetically received by both Frere and Hicks Beach, the British Secretary for the Colonies.[29] The Quthing missionary, the Reverend Frederic Ellenberger, wrote to Griffith to object to the boundaries to the lands it was proposed to allot to his mission station, and to point out that the confiscation of Quthing was contrary to Moshoeshoe's original arrangement with the British; but without effect.[30] Missionary appeals to Frere merely annoyed the Governor,[31] and although at missionary prompting the Aborigines Protection Society espoused the cause,[32] the Colonial Office in England was unsympathetic to pressure from it or from the missionaries themselves for fear of being drawn into the looming revolt.[33] For this same reason, representations from Basutoland traders were equally ineffective.[34] In the British Parliament Gladstone refused to intervene,[35] and when the English ministry did finally make representations to Frere, they were too weak to be effective.[36] Pressure within the Cape Parliament was equally useless, as the matter had become a party issue once the Opposition had realised that it was a good platform on which to attack the Government,[37] but it did not have the support to effect a change of policy. The only effective blow was achieved by Mabille, and had the unfortunate effect of weakening the authority of the local Administration. Mabille refused to translate or print the proclamation extending the Peace Preservation Act to Basutoland, since he felt that the Sotho should first receive an answer to their petitions to the Queen and to Parliament.[38] As the Morija press was the only one in the country, he succeeded in delaying the date on which the proclamation was to take effect. With subsequent delays, it eventually came into force only on 12 July.[39]

With the Administration hamstrung and most Sotho antagonised by the new measures, the chiefs found themselves in an unexpectedly strong position. Their long-standing grievances over the effects of the regulations on their customary powers made them the natural leaders to spearhead Sotho opposition, now that at last they had the people behind them. But Letsie was old, obese, sick and vacillating, much under the influence of Griffith and the missionaries, and unwilling to lead a revolt which, if successful, would have disastrous results for Basutoland. As Moshoeshoe's heir, his experience fitted him to understand better than most the inevitability of aggression by the land-hungry Orange Free State should Basutoland completely shake off colonial rule—and protection. He therefore set out to do all in his power to avert the armed resistance that he foresaw would follow if the Government tried forcibly to disarm the Sotho. Upon the failure of the petition against disarmament which had been sent to the Governor (in effect the Cape Government),[40] he arranged for a delegation of chiefs and a missionary to take petitions against disarmament and the alienation of Quthing to the Cape Parliament in April.[41] The Sotho willingly subscribed £3,000 towards the expenses of the trip and, with Griffith's help, Letsie successfully besought the Government to suspend the Peace Preservation Act from coming into effect until an answer was received to the petition to the Queen and the delegation in Cape Town.[42]

This moderate opposition had the effect of further strengthening the chiefs, as Arthur Barkly pointed out in May 1880. Support for their rapidly reviving power was not, he wrote,

> as heretofore, confined to the ignorant and barbarous alone; for, as the chiefs have, thus far, carried on their opposition with a fair show of adherence to constitutional means, and, ostensibly at any rate, repudiated the idea of any appeal to physical force, they find followers now amongst the more moderate and intelligent natives in the country.[43]

But despite their moderation, the Sotho chiefs were not allowed to argue their own case before Parliament. Their old friend, J. M. Orpen, and Thomas Fuller, one of the members for Cape

Town, led the fight in a debate which lasted from 20 May to 1 June 1880 on Fuller's motion to alter the disarmament policy in Basutoland.[44] From the public gallery above, the Reverend Mr Cochet and the six-man Sotho deputation watched the Cape Assembly divide on largely party lines[45] and defeat the motion by nine votes.

Even after this, Letsie advised submission rather than violence, but was in the uncomfortable position of advocating a policy to which the vast majority of his people and fellow chiefs were opposed, and from which there now seemed no escape short of armed revolt. Griffith became seriously alarmed that the Paramount Chief, who had neither the energy nor the power over his people to grapple successfully with the current state of affairs, might be drawn into the anti-Government movement.[46] Such action was Letsie's only hope of undermining Masopha, who was daily strengthening his position as leader of the majority view and whom the prophetesses had begun to predict would be the next Paramount Chief. It must have been obvious to Lerotholi that if he was to retain the paramountcy, he must join his powerful uncle in leading the opposition to disarmament.

Molapo counselled obedience to the Government but had not been much involved in the dispute, as he had been stricken with paralysis since mid-1879.[47] His death on 28 June was to bring his branch of the family back into the limelight. Joseph, his eldest son by his first wife, was insane and his heir was therefore his second son by that wife, Jonathan.[48] However, Joel, Molapo's eldest son but by his second wife, proceeded to contest the inheritance.[49] The two brothers were very different personalities and cordially hated each other. Jonathan, partially educated in Cape Town, was something of a dandy and had great charm. Taylor, who knew them both well, described Joel as 'uneducated and illiterate, but a man of considerable force of character—not so smooth in his manners as Jonathan, but perhaps none the worse for that'.[50] Faced with this challenge from his forceful elder brother, the young Jonathan turned to the Government as his father had done before him to safeguard his interests, thus becoming one of the few chiefs of Moshoeshoe's family to remain loyal. In contrast, most of Jonathan's half-brothers supported Joel once Jonathan had indicated his intention of obeying the disarmament law.[51] In this way the extremely bitter family squabble over the Leribe inheritance became inextricably bound up in that district with the challenge to the Government's right to rule, and was to complicate the pacification of the district.

The polarisation of Molapo's family was just beginning when three members of the Cape Town deputation reported their failure to a great *pitso* on 3 July, the day after Molapo's funeral, which had drawn a large part of the nation to Thaba-Bosiu.[52] They also told the Sotho that letters from Griffith and Bell expressing disapproval of disarmament had been read out during the Parliamentary debate. But although the Sotho did not question the goodwill of their magistrates, several speakers expressed indignation that the delegation had not been allowed to put its own case. 'When I appeal against any judgement I am allowed to speak myself to Griffith', pointed out one. In the speeches during the meeting the division between the two groups who were to be called rebels and loyals could be clearly seen. Lerotholi spoke out plainly against disarmament, ending with the words:

> We regret our guns we cannot part with them, if we have done anything wrong we must be told so.—We were not annexed to Natal, because we did not want our guns to be taken from us.—It is hard for me to give up my gun.

And Masopha threw down as unambiguous a challenge to Letsie as was permissible in the setting:

> Chief Letsie, I stand up when I see you move; it is the custom to follow the chief; but the common people are like crows which roost in the galleries of different precipices & we know that a chief reigns by the people. If the chief does wrong he must not be followed; the voice which must be listened to is the voice of the people. Plead, Chief, plead for Peace that the people may thrash out their grain!

Letsie reprimanded him and Lerotholi and counselled compliance with the Government's demands:

> If the people were still *mine* I would say that all the guns will be surrendered. . . . O, my people my gun is going to the Government: All those who like me will follow my example. If a house is devided [sic] that house will not stand.

But a few days later the nine guns Letsie was sending to the magistrate in fulfilment of this pledge were forcibly seized by some of his younger sons and their followers, probably acting on Lerotholi's orders.[53] An angry Griffith, after reporting this, spelt out the situation as clearly as he could to the Government in Cape Town:

> It is now my duty to bring to your notice that in consequence of the above proceedings . . . the whole Country is now in a state of chaos; I could almost say in a state of open rebellion, although no overt act of rebellion has been committed. The principal rebel leaders are the Chiefs Masupha and Lerothodi. . . . These men have declared that they will not surrender their arms; that they intend to offer only a passive resistance until such time as the Government take steps to enforce the Peace Preservation Proclamation either by sending up troops to support the Magistrate or by sending Constables or Police to search for arms; that then in such a case they will resist by force of arms and will commence by plundering the shops and murdering every European in the Country as they know it will be the only chance they will have of doing harm to the Whiteman.
>
> This being the state of affairs at present, I do not think it can be described in any other way than as simply an armed truce which at present exists in this Territory. Yesterday was the final date fixed for the surrender of arms and as far as the Mags. [sic] office at this place is concerned no arms were surrendered.[54]

The letters and telegrams sent after this event show the final collapse of the magistrates' authority. They tell of widespread victimisation of loyals whose property was 'eaten up' and who were sometimes killed fighting to protect it.[55] Davies, reporting on confiscations by Letsie's son Bereng in the Thaba-Bosiu District, gamely wrote that he would be glad to comply with Griffith's instructions in the matter 'and if in your opinion I ought to resort to the ordinary courses of the Law in this case I will do so without loss of time';[56] but when he subsequently served Bereng with a summons, the chief tore it up, burnt it, and threatened to punish the bearer: and Davies was quite unable to punish Bereng.[57] Even in districts where such dramatic events did not occur, the magistrates' power ebbed away, as Surmon clearly described in his annual report:

> Now came a time of anarchy. The natives, who had always before behaved respectfully, and implicitly obeyed the Magistrate in all things except that of disarmament, now defied his authority, first in one thing, then in another, till in a short time it was respected only by a very few.[58]

Many who would have preferred to have remained neutral joined the rebels in self-defence. Without more detailed records than exist, it is impossible to estimate the size of the potentially loyal minority. Despite the gulf between Christians and chiefs, many Christians went into rebellion too. This can probably be partly explained by the sympathetic attitude of the French Protestant and Catholic missionaries towards the Sotho dislike of being disarmed, although they never advocated revolt.[59] Those who remained loyal flooded into the magistracies as refugees, and arrangements had to be made to feed them. All orders to Masopha and the other rebel chiefs to restore captured cattle had practically no effect except where Letsie intervened.[60] The whole country was patrolled by armed bands and, though no European was molested, the traders began to leave or send their families and goods out of the country, and at least one shop was sacked.[61] Masopha fortified Thaba-Bosiu and people from the Orange Free State began to cross freely into his district and traded without obtaining licences from Maseru.[62] After several villages of loyals in the Berea District were attacked, at Griffith's orders C. G. H. Bell abandoned the Berea magistracy and fell back on Maseru with his Clerk and police, since they could not hope to withstand a similar attack from Masopha.[63] Only the Leribe District remained fairly quiet,[64] and even there, when Jonathan surrendered his guns, the Government felt obliged to return them to him for his own protection.[65] Taylor wrote of Leribe at this time that 'instead of hearty and respectful greetings as we rode about the country, people passed us without saluting and with averted faces, or would greet us contemptuously with "Dumela Lekhoa" ("Good day, white man")—the equivalent of saying to a native, "Good day, you nigger." '[66] Arthur Barkly, barricaded in his magistracy in the south, in danger of being cut off from Maseru, was ordered to report anything serious directly to the Colonial Secretary as well as to Griffith.[67] On 8 August Surmon's report to the Governor's Agent gives some idea of the complete breakdown in communication between the magistrates and the rebels in their districts: 'All the ordinary business of my office, such as hearing cases, receiving hut tax, &c., is suspended. It is very seldom that anyone living off the Reserve comes to the office.'[68]

Griffith was in the same position but was able to fall back upon the still considerable respect for the Paramount Chief, and for a few weeks it looked as if this might yet save the Administration. Letsie was persuaded to risk rebuff and exert his authority, which was still sufficient to enable him to recover captured cattle from Bereng and to fine him.[69] Lerotholi's supporters melted away[70] and at Letsie's orders both he and Nkoebi, another son of Letsie, restored most of the property taken by them.[71] Masopha refused to allow his warriors to attack Maseru, and the magistracy at Berea remained untouched.[72] Letsie, taking heart, on 11 August led a 1,000 men to Thaba-Bosiu, where he met Masopha and Lerotholi, who were waiting with about 700 or 800 men, fully armed. The two groups faced each other over a distance of about twenty yards and negotiations opened with a messenger from Letsie carrying an exchange of verbal messages between him and Masopha. But it took several days for Griffith, anxiously waiting in Maseru, to receive news of how negotiations were proceeding. Sprigg demanded that Letsie force Masopha to surrender unconditionally, with only the assurance that his life would be spared. All the people with him were to lay down their arms, and fines would be inflicted on the leading rebels. 'If Masupha does not surrender and agree to the terms,' telegraphed Sprigg, 'then Letsea is to hold possession of the mountain until a force of Cape Mounted Riflemen can arrive to support him.'[73] When these instructions were relayed to him, Letsie pointed out that they were totally unrealistic:

> Letsea . . . says that he cannot arrest Masupha, as he is too strongly supported by the tribe, [telegraphed Griffith to Sprigg] and also that as most of his (Letsea's) sons have compromised themselves one way or another, they will sympathise with and join Masupha if any attempt is made to arrest him. Mr. Cochet, who brought me a letter from Letsea this afternoon, says that he believes Masupha will consent to pay any fine that is imposed upon him, but that he will never give himself up or allow himself to be arrested, as he has so great a horror of being sent to Robben Island.[74]

Sprigg was willing to accept a fine from Masopha but demanded that the defences upon Thaba-Bosiu be destroyed as proof of good faith upon the part of Masopha—something that Masopha would never have allowed. Letsie's people began to slip away and on 15 August he informed Griffith that he was not strong enough to enforce his demands on Masopha and wished to leave the mountain to gather a stronger force together. Griffith told him to stay where he was, but by 17 August Letsie's messenger reported that the Paramount Chief feared to remain any longer at Thaba-Bosiu lest Masopha either kill him or retain him by force. On 19 August he returned to his village.[75]

The failure of this last attempt to bring Masopha to heel merely highlighted the way in which both the Government and even Letsie had lost virtually all control over the rebellious chiefs. On 18 August Griffith acknowledged this, reporting to the Secretary for Native Affairs that law and order had for some time been in abeyance. 'It is evident that the crisis through which we are passing is an endeavour on the part of some of the Chiefs to re-establish their arbitrary power and if possible regain their independence',[76] an opinion shared by Barkly, Austen, C. H. Bell, C. G. H. Bell, and at least one missionary.[77] Several of the magistrates stressed how the chiefs drummed up support from the people by spreading stories of imminent changes to be made in Sotho law, such as the suppression of polygamy. But although the magistrates retained virtually no power in their districts, they had not yet been attacked; the possibility of regaining control, though slight, remained, and Griffith again repeated past requests for a large force to be stationed in Basutoland to enforce the law.[78]

It was at this point that Sprigg arrived in Basutoland. By the beginning of August he had already begun to complain about the conflicting reports and advice he was receiving from Barkly, Surmon, Griffith and a French Protestant missionary visiting Cape Town, each of whom was reporting conditions in only a small area of Basutoland.[79] Eventually he decided to visit Basutoland to inspect conditions for himself.[80] Shortly after Letsie had left Thaba-Bosiu, the newly arrived Sprigg visited him and also had interviews with George, Tsekelo, Sofonia and Ntsana Moshoeshoe, and with Jonathan Molapo, at which the seriousness of the situation was finally impressed upon him. Letsie called a *pitso* at which to try to obtain the nation's submission to terms offered by Sprigg in a last-minute attempt to prevent full-scale rebellion and to restore the magistrates' authority. J. M. Orpen, as a champion of the Sotho in Parliament who was also acceptable to the Sotho, put forward

Sprigg's terms: if the rebel chiefs and people would comply with summonses and appear personally in court, they would only be fined; compensation for seized property would have to be given and a token number of ten guns surrendered by Lerotholi and the other rebel chiefs as earnest of future disarmament.[81] But the moment for such negotiations was already past. Masopha now knew his own strength. He did not attend the *pitso* but simultaneously held a gathering at which his young warriors were prepared for war; and Lerotholi, who at first appeared to cooperate with Letsie, refused to surrender any guns.[82] There was no apparent need for him to do so: not only had he seen the incompetence of the Cape forces against Moorosi, but had heard that the British Government had repeatedly refused to send troops to assist the Cape.[83]

With all hope of compromise gone, the inevitable outbreak came a few days later, in Lerotholi's district. On 13 September Arthur Barkly, Lerotholi's magistrate at Mafeteng, heard that a column of Cape Mounted Rifles under Colonel Carrington had crossed the border and was moving up to Mafeteng to garrison the magistracy. He placed the magistracy in readiness for an attack and 'rode out with sixteen or eighteen native police, and three or four Europeans to reconnoitre'. About two miles from the magistracy he encountered some 300 Sotho holding a line of hills to the right of the road. By placing his own men parallel to them to the left behind rising ground, he was able to keep the Sotho within range of his rifles but his own men out of range of two-thirds of their opponents' inferior weapons. His father received his first-hand account of what followed.

Presently a messenger came down and shouted that he wanted to parley, so I sent forward a native constable to him, who reported that Lerothodi was commanding the rebels in person, and wished to know if I meant to fire on him. I said I should not commence firing, but would of course return it, and added that he had better go home. The messenger returned, and I moved forward to meet some videttes of the C.M.R. who now came in sight, and sent one of them back to tell Carrington the road was commanded in his front by a strong party of rebels. Lerothodi sent to me again to say that he wanted to see me himself, to which I replied that if he would ride forward with two or three men I would do the same. The answer came that he would do so if he could, but was prevented by his people. I heard he was himself in the road with about twenty men, so I rode forward with a white volunteer and my chief constable, who is a connection of Lerothodi's. As I came up I saw a queer spectacle. Lerothodi dismounted was engaged in a violent struggle with two of his men, who were forcibly holding him back. I shouted to him, and he waved his hat to me, but as I rode on they all prepared to retreat, so I stopped and told Dechaba (the chief constable), to ask what on earth they were afraid of. 'Of Morena's (the chief's) revolver,' replied the heroes. Accordingly I divested myself of this deadly weapon, dropped my reins, and rode in among them unarmed, with my hands displayed to show that 'there was no deception.' Lerothodi then shook off his brother who was detaining him, and came up to me with proper salutations, calling me his father and his mother and so on, after Basuto fashion. I shook hands with him, and said that out of friendship for him I had come to try and save him from utter destruction if possible, and told him that nothing could delay or stop the march of the Cape Mounted Rifles, whatever he might think, and that if he attempted it he would simply be sent flying (which occurred accordingly, five minutes afterwards). I then suggested that he should withdraw his men and surrender to me *pro forma* as proposed by Mr. Sprigg. When I would inflict such fine as I thought proper, and refer the sentence for confirmation. He said he would do this if I would stop the 'polices', which of course I could not do, a fact of which he was perfectly aware. By this time Carrington had bent to his right, and moved up with his waggon, out of range to the rear of my police. Lerothodi pointed to the column, shouted and stamped with rage, seizing his gun (a very neat Snider sporting rifle). I laughed at him, upon which he put down his gun and calmed himself a little. A moment afterwards he snatched it up again, however, and pointing it at Dechaba, said he would disarm him.

I told him not to make a fool of himself, and shaking hands with him again, turned to go as the rebels were unslinging their guns and preparing for action; just as I turned, one of them fired and the ball passed over my head. To do Lerothodi justice, he 'went' for the man, who swore it was an accident. I must own, however, that I did not expect to get back alive to my men. No more shots, however, were fired till I rode down to meet Carrington, when three or four were sent after us, very wild ones. I sent my police forward in front of the column as guides, and was riding along talking to Carrington, when down came the whole body of

Basutos mounted, apparently to get possession of the rocky rising ground, where my men had been drawn up.[84]

A skirmish followed in which the Sotho suffered light casualties before they withdrew, and Carrington moved on to form camp at Mafeteng.

The attack, however, marked more than the beginning of the Gun War; it marked the end of the magistrates' carefully constructed network of trust and interests. That network had for a decade enabled the Sotho to accept them as rulers of the country, backed only by a token police force and British prestige. They had even enjoyed active cooperation from the Sotho despite widespread—and, in the case of the chiefs, strong—opposition to the regulations. The Cape was never to be able to control Basutoland again in the same way.

11 Defeating Disarmament

The war which followed was far more disastrous than Sprigg had feared. It lasted for almost exactly seven months from the attack on 12 September on the column of 212 Cape Mounted Riflemen being brought in to defend Mafeteng. They had been withdrawn from Griqualand East, which was left completely undefended as a result. This no doubt explains the timing, if not the cause of the revolt of the Sotho in the Matatiele District of Griqualand East, which erupted on 4 October. They were promptly joined by some of the Griqua, followed shortly by the Mpondomise in the Qumbu and Tsolo Districts (Hope was murdered in the former, where he had been transferred as magistrate), the Qwati and some of the Thembu in Thembuland and Emigrant Thembuland. Many whites suspected that the revolt was the result of a conspiracy, but the evidence of lack of cooperation between the rebel groups does not bear out this theory.[1] Nonetheless, there is strong evidence that Letsie was in contact with and encouraged the Sotho involved in the revolt,[2] and the Cape authorities' concern over the Basutoland Rebellion—or War of the Guns, as it is known by the Sotho—must be seen against the background of Cape forces being required to fight in this second arena as well until February 1881.

Within Lesotho the rebels made their presence felt in several areas and forced the Cape commanders to spread their forces too thinly to have any major impact. Masopha for most of the war did little fighting but blockaded and twice attacked Maseru, where an uncooperative commanding officer insisted on keeping half the available Cape Mounted Riflemen for its defence. In the north Joel's initial attack on the magistracy was beaten off, but he then besieged it and after it was relieved, continued his own war to keep Bell, with the assistance of Jonathan, fully occupied. In the south, Mohale's Hoek and Quthing were besieged and were subsequently abandoned. Most of the fighting of the Cape troops was against Lerotholi and concentrated in the area around Morija and Mafeteng, where the magistracy was initially besieged and attacked. Until it was relieved on 19 October, communication from there had to be conducted directly with Cape Town by means of African runners (on occasion carrying their messages in Greek, since some of the Sotho chiefs read both English and French), who at night would slip through the rebel posts on the border with information to be relayed to the nearest telegraph office, at Aliwal North, a day's journey away.[3] Direction of the war was made even more difficult by the commanders themselves, who were divided on what to do or how to do it, and were further hampered both by the weather and unsuitable tactics for the type of warfare in which they were engaged:

> The Basuto leader [Lerotholi] did not attempt to hold the hills and mountains in force; he maintained a fluid defence which gave way when attacked and counter-attacked wherever a weak spot offered itself. It was one of the wettest seasons on record,[4] and the white troops moved slowly and painfully over the sodden veld, dragging with them heavy guns drawn by oxen, and ox and mule wagons. They had to form laagers at every camp, circles of wagons with a sod wall and trench outside, with the interior a sea of mud. When the troops moved out to fight, at the pace of the infantry, they showed up in great splashes of contrasting colour, black, blue and yellow uniforms with many white helmets, against the brilliant green of the veld grass. Round the attacking force, moving in a rough square, the Basuto rode at will, pouring in gusts of ill-aimed rifle fire, and sometimes charging two or three times in succession against selected points. Lerotholi fought when and where he wished, and towards dusk the troops would trail back to the laager with small consciousness of having scored a success.[5]

Underestimating the effectiveness of Sotho methods of fighting cost the lives of many, especially as until late in the war the Cape troops were not issued with bayonets and, if they could not keep the enemy at a distance with rifle fire, the Sotho battle axes had a devastating effect among the Yeomanry. Taylor, the Leribe doctor, recorded that few ever recovered from the frightful headwounds caused by the axes.[6] Of the magistrates, Austen was killed, an event which occurred at the end of January 1881 in a badly planned sortie against rebel Tlokwa who had fled over the Drakensberg from the Transkeian territory. No doubt inspired by the example of the colonial troops' mutilation of Moorosi's body in 1879, the Tlokwa decapitated Austen's body and sent the head to Letsie as a peace-offering for a past attack on Thaba-Bosiu in Moshoeshoe's time.[7]

Humiliating and expensive casualties without results did not increase the popularity of the Cape Government with its electorate. Imperial troops were not used in the Gun War or the contemporary revolt in the Transkeian territories—indeed, Sotho leaders were always careful to stress to their own men that they were fighting Sprigg's troops, not the Queen's soldiers—and when imperial troops did go into action in southern Africa, after the Transvaalers rose in revolt against the British Administration there in December 1880, they merely increased the Cape Government's problems. As the Free State burghers were known to sympathise with the Transvaalers, the import of ammunition to them was restricted, whereupon the Free State refused free transit across their territory for volunteers to fight in Basutoland. Rumours began to circulate, such as were retailed in a letter home from a young Cape Mounted Rifleman:

> Colonel Colley having suffered defeat in the Transvaal,[8] the Dutch in all parts of the Colony and Free State are quite ready to join the Transvaalers and, with the natives on their side, have a war of races with the British, both Imperial and Colonial Forces, in which, I am afraid, we would come off second best for some time . . . [9]

As a result, the Cape Authorities began with some reason to fear collusion between the Free State Boers and the Sotho, and by the time the Cape expenses for the war had reached over £3,000,000, the ministry was exceedingly anxious to make peace.

The Sotho also had good reason for wanting at least a truce, for their maize was just ripe and needed to be harvested if they were not to starve through the following winter. Therefore in January they petitioned for peace, with the assistance of J. W. Sauer, the young Opposition member for Aliwal North; he had, no doubt, scented a good opportunity for embarassing the Government, and kept the newspapers informed of what followed. The peace offer was made on conditions that the Sotho be allowed to keep their arms and their country, and, not unexpectedly, was rejected as such by the Cape Government. The ministry demanded that the Sotho surrender their guns, submit to the laws of the Government, and that

Lerotholi, Masopha and Joel should stand trial, although guaranteeing that they would not be condemned to death. In addition, the future of Quthing was still to be determined by the Cape Parliament. This the Sotho could not accept, but they had had a useful seven-day armistice in which to reap their crops, and the chiefs were ready to continue fighting. It was yet another blunder by the Cape ministry, which by early April was being subjected to such fierce attacks in the 'No Confidence' debate that it was obviously about to fall.[10]

However, the new Governor, Sir Hercules Robinson,[11] had been involved in the first attempt to secure a settlement, and continued to put out peace feelers. As winter approached, the need of the Sotho to conclude an agreement increased, for once the rains stopped the Cape Forces would be able with fewer hazards to obtain supplies from the Free State and to move more freely, while Lerotholi would have greater difficulty keeping his men together in the cold weather. He was also suffering from a painful inflammation of the bladder.[12] Robinson therefore had some hope of success in his efforts to persuade the Sotho to come to terms, and through Griffith and the French missionaries established contact with Lerotholi. But when, on Robinson's orders, Griffith met Lerotholi and his missionaries near Maseru on 17 April, Lerotholi pointed out that although he would accept Robinson's arbitration and that hostilities would cease, he did not think his people would give up their arms.[13] That was, after all, what the whole war had been about, and the Sotho had not been defeated. The experienced Griffith prophetically informed Robinson:

> Knowing the Basutos as well as I do, I am bound to express my opinion that if the unconditional surrender of arms is not now enforced it would be better to withdraw from the country and let the Basutos manage their own affairs; if they are allowed to keep their arms now, after all that has been gone through, the magistrates, and the loyal people who have stuck to them, will return humiliated to their respective stations, without 'prestige', and without power to do any good, and the Government of the country will be virtually back again in the hands of the chiefs, as it was before they became British subjects.[14]

But Robinson was more preoccupied with the immediate problem of ending hostilities before the bill became even higher, and if this

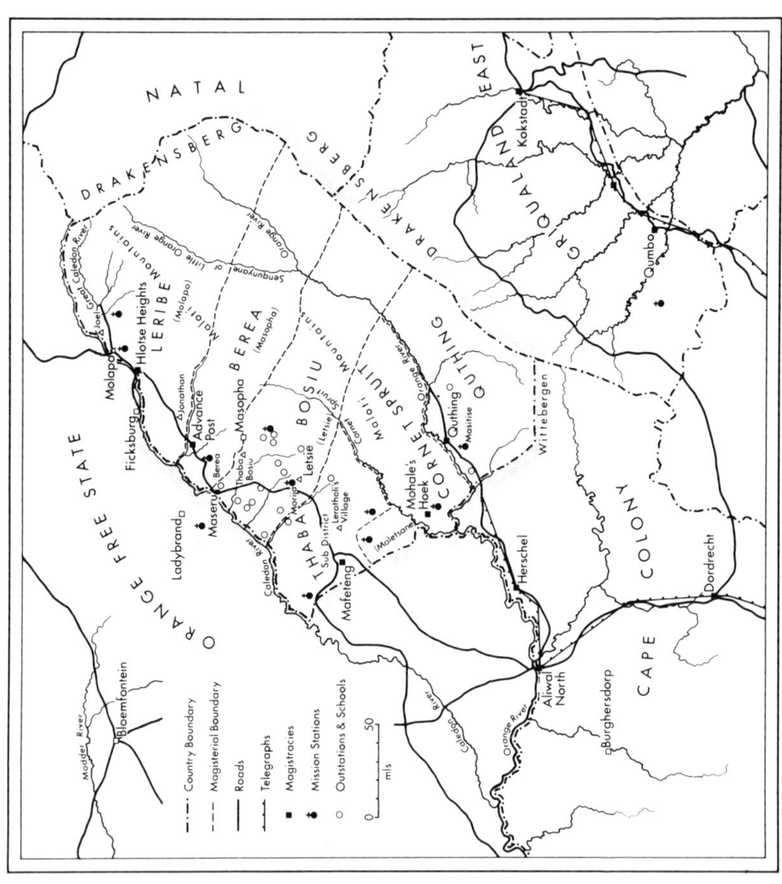

Map 6   Basutoland after the War of the Guns, showing magisterial districts

was to be achieved, the unconditional surrender of arms could obviously not be enforced. 'Have you estimated the force it would require, the time it would occupy, and the cost?' he demanded.[15] Therefore, with the Sprigg ministry's concurrence,[16] he announced his Award on 29 April 1881,[17] and with its announcement the Gun War petered out.

The Award nominally provided for disarmament, but the licensing of guns would be freely allowed, and compensation would be paid for those surrendered. There was to be a complete amnesty; Quthing was to remain part of Basutoland, and a fine of 5,000 cattle, together with compensation for loyals and traders, was to be paid. This met all the rebels' demands, for it was obvious that the Cape could no longer enforce the disarmament provision—or anything else; although all the chiefs eventually accepted the Award, they were back in the saddle and intended to stay there. Even Letsie could not be relied upon to help bolster the magistrates, for his role throughout the war had been highly questionable; apart from his intervention in the Transkei, there was evidence that his men had participated in the attack on the Mafeteng magistracy[18] and throughout the war he had remained in contact with the rebels,[19] who on some occasions at least would even surrender captured property to him if ordered to do so.[20] He was undoubtedly in a most uncomfortable position, desiring peace and protection for Basutoland, but also wishing to retain at least the nominal leadership of a nation unwilling to accept the Cape's conditions for peace. That he played a double role to some extent seems certain, since he retained his position as paramount Chief in the eyes of his Sotho and at least some of his authority, while ostensibly working for the enemy against which his heir and the majority of the nation were fighting. How far he remained loyal to the Government is extremely difficult to judge from the scanty and conflicting evidence available, especially when it is borne in mind that he had learned his skills from Moshoeshoe, who had lived by the maxim that language is not given to man to reveal his thoughts, but to conceal them.[21] In assessing how far chiefs who theoretically were enemies cooperated with each other during both the war and its aftermath, it should be remembered that the Sotho custom of marrying cousins knit all Moshoeshoe's descendants in a web of relationship which would have been difficult to ignore. Jonathan, for example, was not only the son of Masopha's favourite brother, but married to one of his best-loved daughters.[22]

That there would be difficulties in implementing the Award was therefore obvious to the new Government which replaced the Sprigg ministry on 9 May 1881 in the middle of the negotiations over the Award. The Secretary for Native Affairs in the new ministry was J. W. Sauer, who had been M. P. for Aliwal North, very near the Basutoland border, and was known as a staunch friend of the Sotho.[23] He was, however, only thirty years of age when he took up his appointment and was neither experienced nor decisive. To make matters worse, the new ministry's policy could not be implemented by Griffith—as he himself pointed out, even if he were able to set aside his strong personal sympathy for the loyals, he was too deeply identified with the previous Government and its failure to enforce disarmament to be able to re-establish the prestige of the Government[24] – and so on 25 August he was given a year's leave[25] prior to retirement. His departure meant a very real loss for Basutoland, as even the new ministry which dispensed with his services realised:[26] not only was he a most able and upright administrator, but he was liked and respected by all sections of the community, black and white.

But the 'Lion of Maseru', as the Sotho called him, was fortunate in not being responsible for the new ministry's policy; it aimed to avoid the expense of recruiting more troops or police, and to rely entirely on the chiefs to persuade their people to surrender the cattle required for compensation and the national fine. This was unrealistic. Very few chiefs, ruling ultimately by consent, could afford to antagonise their people to the extent of enforcing the restoration of all the loyals' stock: the Sotho regarded as rightful spoil anything captured in the war and would not easily surrender it.[27] Finding a suitable Acting Governor's Agent in these circumstances presented problems. Bowker, in retirement in Natal, declined the post, as did W. B. Chalmers, the Civil Commissioner at King William's Town.[28] Eventually Rolland's brother-in-law, Joseph Millard Orpen, was persuaded to take Griffith's place. He had been elected to the Cape Parliament in 1871, where he was a long-standing champion of the Sotho and regarded as an expert on them, having known them and Moshoeshoe's family personally for many years.[29] However, he began his new work at a great disadvantage, for the unfortunate policy which he had agreed to implement necessitated pandering to those chiefs lately in revolt to ensure their cooperation. Not unnaturally the much-tried loyals were extremely bitter about this, and were to become progressively more so as the policy failed to produce most of the compensation owed or to enable them to return to their villages.[30] At Orpen's installation at a *pitso* in August—attended only by loyal chiefs and their followers, apart from Sauer, the Administration and officers of the Cape Forces—he was left in no doubt of the alienation of the 'loyals'. George Moshoeshoe, the leader of the loyalists in the Maseru area, made a long speech unique in its directness and acerbity. At the call of the Queen, he pointed out,

they had given up their guns, had left all their property behind, and had come to Maseru, where they were promised the protection of Government, which had been represented to them as strong enough to afford it. But when they arrived at Maseru guns of another pattern than those given up by them were put into their hands, cartridges were given to them, and they were told that, instead of being able to protect them, the Government expected to be protected by them, and they had to fight for their lives and for the protection of the lives of the white men against their own brothers and against men of their own race and tribe. And now what could they think of a peace by which the rebels obtained all they chose to ask for, whereas the loyals lost everything they were possessed of? . . . If it were only the black loyal men who had lost lives and property in the war, the thing now agreed to might seem strange; but when he, George, considered that white men had been killed by the hundred, and white men's property destroyed to the extent of thousands of pounds in value, and that yet in the face of such losses the Government of the white man had submitted to such an award and did not even wink at the non-fulfilment of that award, could any man come to any other conclusion than this, that the Queen's Government was dead in Basutoland and that the rebels were the chiefs and not the Queen? How could the loyals live among the rebels after such events? Would they not be sneered at and ill-treated, and if they dared to ask for their rights would not the rebel chiefs tell them to go to Maseru? And if they did go to Maseru could Mr. Orpen or Mr. Davies or any other magistrate in Basutoland protect them or help them to obtain their rights? They had been told by Mr. Sauer that Colonel Griffith was about to take leave of absence on account of recruiting his health and to have a little rest. Did any Basuto here believe that this was the true reason why Colonel Griffith was leaving? No; he would tell them that the reason was this—Colonel Griffith's heart was aching on account of the miserable peace which would now bring the loyals again under the power of the chiefs, and Colonel Griffith was leaving because he could not see the loyals so utterly abandoned to the mercy of the rebels after they had defended and saved his own house in Maseru. As far as he, George, could judge, Griffith was to be congratulated upon his being able to go away, and all the people, both white and black, that were now here about him thought Colonel Griffith was the only fortunate one.[31]

Some of the magistrates who had defended their magistracies almost entirely with the aid of the loyals, felt unable to accept the new policy either. By the end of September C. G. H. Bell asked for a transfer,[32] and Davies, making a similar request in November 1881, expressed their feelings clearly:

I beg further to urge in support of my application that, having hitherto used my utmost endeavours to carry out the policy of the late Ministry; viz.—that of undermining the power of the Chiefs, & having taken part in the application to this country of the Peace Preservation Act, and persuaded as many as possible to remain loyal, I am very heavily handicapped in having now to work out the new order of things:—nor can I fail, under the circumstances of the case, to be partial to the loyals, who have fought side by side with us & risked their lives to save ours.[33]

Sauer appreciated these problems and was probably keenly aware, as the *Kaffrarian Watchman* alleged on 4 January 1882, that the pre-war magistrates were unlikely to write glowing reports on their districts for the Cape Native Blue Book in 1882.[34] By September 1882 almost all the pre-war magistrates and the more politically-minded clerks were no longer in the Basutoland civil service: in January 1882 Maitin was obliged to resign to escape an unacceptable transfer, which he believed to be deliberate victimisation for his known sympathies with the loyals;[35] in March 1882 Fitzwilliam Bell, who shared his brother's views, was transferred to Kokstad on unfavourable terms;[36] Davies did not serve as a Basutoland magistrate after December 1881;[37] C. G. H. Bell was transferred to the Transkei in 1882;[38] Arthur Barkly left Basutoland on sick leave in May 1881 and resigned without returning;[39] Major Bell, who had been in poor health for most of the war, died of double pneumonia in July 1881;[40] Rolland since mid-1877 had been in charge of the Basutoland Education Department and had held his subsequent magisterial appointments on a temporary basis.[41] Of the pre-war magistrates in the territory, only Surmon remained in a permanent magisterial post there. Of the pre-war clerks who had served in Basutoland since the Cape took charge, only William Carlisle remained, and in August 1882 he too had applied for a transfer, which he eventually received in May 1883.[42] This meant that throughout the crucial period until October 1882, in which the Cape Government was trying to re-establish magisterial rule, almost all the magistrates and clerks involved were either out of sympathy with the way in which they were expected to implement the policy, or relatively inexperienced in Basutoland politics and attitudes. To add to the problem, Orpen proved to be not only a most incompetent and spendthrift administrator,[43] but also to be so obsessed with his need for support from the rebel chiefs that he lacked understanding of both the loyals and the magistrates who sympathised with them. The Administration split into two camps— pro- and anti-Orpen—highly distrustful of each other.[44] At the same time white sympathisers with the loyals, both inside and outside Basutoland, kept up a steady—and occasionally blatantly untruthful—agitation amongst the loyals and in the Cape press against Orpen and 'his' magistrates.[45]

The task that faced the Administration would have daunted even a well-established and united magisterial team. Ultimately the re-establishment of magisterial rule depended on the magistrates' ability to secure the property and safeguard the rights of anyone who entrusted himself to Government justice, and this the magistrates would have had difficulty doing even had there been no opposition party in the country. Unfortunately, there was: Masopha at first refused to accept the Governor's Award at all and was only coerced into nominally doing so in September 1881, when Sauer began to organise an expedition by Letsie and Lerotholi against him.[46] This removed the main focus for disaffection in Basutoland and augured well for the enforcement of the Award by the chiefs; but as soon as Sauer returned to Cape Town, having already withdrawn all colonial troops except the Cape Carbineers, the problem reappeared. An extract from the minutes of the 1882 General Assembly of the Paris Evangelical Missionary Society in Paris paints a vivid picture of what followed:

This is the opportunity for which Masopha has been waiting. No sooner has Mr. Sauer left than he throws off the mask and, from his mountain-top, announces his refusal to submit. An attempt is made by Mr. Orpen with Letsie and Lerotholi's warriors, to capture him on January 24th and fails lamentably. It is henceforth obvious that the country is incapable of pacifying itself unaided. Is it in the power of the Colony to restore order by force of arms? By no means. It is not the solitary cavalry regiment left in Maseru which will achieve what the entire forces which the Cape Government could bring into line have failed to do. The situation is therefore grave, more so perhaps than ever before: in Basutoland anarchy, at the Cape impotence.[47]

Given this situation, the magistrates remained equally impotent. The picture that emerges from magisterial reports and other sources shows that the magistrates were unable to administer the law except amongst the loyals still living in the camps huddled round the magistracies; as Mabille wrote: 'the authority of the magistrates is not yet sufficiently recognised to induce people to take them their cases'.[48] A secondary reason, especially in the Leribe District, was that feeling was still so strong between the ex-rebels and the refugee loyals living at the camps that the former would not come to the magistrates' reserves.[49] At the end of November, Surmon reported from the Cornet Spruit District that all cases except one had been settled by the chiefs, and the exception had been brought to him at Letsie's specific direction.[50] Only three cases were brought to Bailie at Mafeteng during November,[51] while Hatchard reported that to his knowledge only two cases had been brought by rebels before the Magistrate at Maseru since the beginning of the peace negotiations, and both were cases against loyals residing in Maseru.[52] In the few cases where magistrates were able to secure restitution of loyals' stock, reinstatement of loyal headmen on their land, or witnesses for serious charges, it was usually only as a result of intervention by either Letsie or his sons on their behalf.[53] The practices of circumcision and of 'smelling out' witches were revived in some areas to a great extent, and drink from the Free State circulated illegally but freely, with disastrous results among both chiefs and people:[54] the strongest was known, with some reason, as 'Kill at forty yards', and all private and official accounts of the period speak of the widespread drunkenness among the Sotho, including Masopha, Letsie and Lerotholi.[55] C. G. H. Bell's report of 30

November 1881 on the Leribe District seems to have been true for the whole country:

> On the conclusion of Peace with the Rebels there was an apparent desire on their part, to a certain extent to attempt compliance with the Governor's Award, and a wish to bring about a peaceful order of things.—Since then however, the rebel chiefs have gradually recovered breath, and they are now beginning to forget the anxiety and hardships they experienced during the rebellion, with the result that their attitude towards the Government is assuming a style of independence and defiance which must eventually necessitate coercion before the authority of the Government can be upheld in the country.[56]

Even the missionaries' converts no longer automatically identified their interests closely with the Administration, as they had before the disarmament crisis. For their outspoken sympathy with Sotho objections to disarmament, the French missions themselves had become suspect in the eyes of the Administration, and the fact that many of their converts had joined the rebels[57] rather than disarm was blamed on their attitude. During the war the French Protestant and Catholic missions had not been attacked by the rebels—Lerotholi, for example, held at least two *pitsos* forbidding it—and some missionaries had remained in contact with the rebels during the hostilities. When Lerotholi became ill, for instance, he was nursed by the missionaries at Morija.[58] After the war those converts who had not been swept into the flood of reviving paganism were acrimoniously divided between 'loyals' and 'rebels', and the French mission reports speak of very little progress in gaining or regaining converts during the succeeding year. The Church of England mission stations, being identified with the Government, had been attacked during the war and only the one at Hlotse Heights was able to reopen in 1881, when it too found the Sotho unreceptive to its message. As John Widdicombe, the Director of the Leribe mission, wrote with some asperity, in his official report to the Government on the year 1881:

> . . . until a definite, just, and common-sense native policy is inaugurated and faithfully carried out by the government, the Christian Missionary will find it extremely difficult to teach his converts to be thoroughly loyal 'to the Queen and all that are put

in authority under her.' My brother priests and myself have hitherto uniformly abstained from taking any active part in native politics, and have steadily refused to become the political agents of this or that chief or faction. We have striven, according to our powers, simply to be the heralds of the Great King, and to build up His Kingdom in the midst of the empire of Satan. We teach our people to 'render unto Caesar the things that be Caesar's, and unto God the things that be God's.' We desire to teach and we do teach loyalty to 'the powers that be'; but it is very difficult to do this when the principle of authority has been seriously weakened, if not destroyed, and when 'the powers that be' seem to the native mind to be altogether an incomprehensible abstraction.[59]

Orpen was an ebullient, vain man and in his reports had a tendency to paint a rosy and over-optimistic picture of the effect of his policy, but eventually the facts were borne in on the Cape ministers, who could not let this situation continue. Some other solution of the problem had to be found. They requested Britain to take over Basutoland, but this Britain declined to do, or to sanction the abandonment of Basutoland by the Cape Government. Eventually, with the British Government's consent, they decided to use Cape troops to enforce fulfilment of the Award, offering cheap farms from confiscated land as the lure to persuade colonists to enlist. It was a desperate measure. The Sotho were given the deadline of 15 March 1882, a month away, by which to fulfil the Award; otherwise it would be cancelled, Quthing confiscated, and the Cape would enforce order in the rest of the country and confiscate the property of any who resisted their authority.

The ultimatum drew a storm of criticism from the humanitarians in England, the colonial press, and, most important, members of the Cape Parliament.[60] Orpen, moreover, telegraphed from Basutoland that the entire nation would unite to fight for Quthing. 'I do not believe a man will remain loyal at heart.'[61] The Cabinet, faced with this warning and without parliamentary support for the proposed renewal of the war, was forced to modify its ultimatum. Using as an excuse a plea from Letsie for more time, it announced that the Award would still be cancelled on 15 March but that confiscation would not automatically follow on incomplete fulfilment of its terms. With this, it admitted the final defeat of its disarmament policy. The Peace Preservation Proclamation itself, which had been the cause of all the trouble, was repealed on 6 April, and with its removal the Sotho at last once more held their guns legally. They had defeated the Government's intention to disarm them. Under the leadership of their chiefs, the struggle over the guns had been won, and in the end with only one effect on the guns of Basutoland: to the Sotho those guns were no longer 'the Queen's guns'.

12 The Triumph of the Chiefs

The Cape ministry was, however, still faced with the need to solve the problem of how to reduce Basutoland to order again and so enable the loyals to return to their villages. Its third attempt at a policy to achieve this was unveiled to the public in the Governor's Speech at the opening of Parliament, whose members were asked to endorse a policy which aimed 'at the gradual restoration of Law and Order by means of a force strong enough to support the authority of the Magistrates and to protect those who have proved themselves faithful in their allegiance to the Government'.[1] No force anywhere near sufficiently strong was ever in fact provided or likely to be, given the sorry state of the Cape's finances, but the Government did try to create a more favourable atmosphere by announcing that a commission would be set up to examine compensation claims by loyals, and that those who were unable to return to their villages were to be provided for either in Quthing or below the Drakensberg. Quthing, though not to be confiscated, was to remain under the control of the Government for purposes of settlement, as it had been since Moorosi's rebellion. This was done to provide the loyals with land away from ex-rebel chiefs, but Letsie became very bitter about it;[2] and by omitting even to consult him as the only chief still with a claim to supremacy over the district, the Government was itself violating the spirit if not the letter of the regulation providing for consultation with the relevant chiefs over land allocation.

In the first wave of relief after the new policy was announced, however, that problem was not yet in evidence. At a *pitso* held on 12 April the majority of the people welcomed the Government's move and Letsie was 'repeatedly cheered when urging on people to pay tax and return to order'.[3] For a tense few days it looked as if even Masopha would come to heel. Rolland, who was at that time acting as deputy for Orpen, sent Nehemiah to him secretly before the *pitso* and telegraphed his report to Sauer:

Masupha said he had full confidence in the present Government and Orpen, but disliked the idea of coming under Letsea; that he was almost persuaded, but would wait till he had spoken to Letsea's sons, and would then send direct answer to me, confidentially. . . . After Masupha retired, his sons remained to say they were in favour of peace, and had never heard their father speak so reasonably.[4]

But Masopha did not appear at the *pitso*, and even the deputation sent to him from the *pitso*, composed of all Letsie's sons, two sons of Molapo, and all the Morija and Thaba-Bosiu French Protestant missionaries, could not persuade him to submit. He refused to pay tax or have anything to do with the Cape Government.[5] 'They all seem to think that Masupha is not sane', Rolland reported. 'He is much altered and would not look anyone in the face.'[6] However, Rolland was optimistic. Letsie's sons, he subsequently telegraphed, had officially reported to him on the deputation.

> They beg Government not be anxious, and believe that, with the aid of the Magistrates, they will be able to overcome his [Masopha's] resistance, without necessitating warlike interference by Government. It is now a family quarrel. . . . All the sons went, by order of Letsea, to their districts, and will press the payment of tax peremptorily. They are extremely angry with Masupha, and refused to shake hands or return his greeting, when they left him. He followed, begging they would not cast him off, but received no answer. . . . Letsea's sons seem in earnest, and very friendly to each other. A good sign.[7]

And for a while the telegrams showed hut tax coming in steadily, even though money was scarce as a result of a slump in demand for grain at the diamond fields. Then the flow of tax money slowed to an irregular trickle. Rumours had found their way up to Basutoland and began to circulate that the Cape Government was about to fall, that the current policy was about to change, that the Cape would abandon Basutoland . . .

This last rumour had strong foundations. In Cape Town the latest policy had not received the support of the Opposition, which regarded it as extremely humiliating. In the Assembly a bill to repeal the Annexation Act of 1871 was defeated by only twelve votes, and the Legislative Council actually passed a resolution favouring its repeal, although Britain again refused to allow this.[8]

As an irate Orpen subsequently pointed out,[9] it was all very well for the Government to instruct him to use the 'old tribal legitimate authority which was in professed unity with Government' to support the authority of the magistrates, but for this to succeed the policy of the Government had to be clear and stable. Letsie, who in Orpen's eyes was 'very old, gouty, sick, weak, double-minded, undecided, failing in intellect, and full of procrastinations', was most unlikely to antagonise his powerful, anti-Government brother and sons if at any moment he might be left at their mercy.

Faced with this increasing non-cooperation in Basutoland, the Cape Government cast about in desperation for some solution to the problem—and came up with 'Chinese' Gordon. Major-General Charles Gordon was to win immortality for himself when he was killed by the forces of the Mahdi in Khartoum three years later.[10] In 1882 he already had a reputation for being able to 'manage native peoples', and had an intense, mesmeric personality. Unfortunately, he was also given to impulsive judgements, excessive enthusiasms, and bewildering changes of opinion that could make cooperation with him over Government plans or policies extremely difficult. He had originally been invited to the Cape in March 1882 at the height of the crisis over the Governor's Award, 'to assist in terminating the war and in administering Basutoland'. He arrived in May with a fixed belief, although he had never been to Basutoland, that the chiefs were being unnecessarily antagonised by their magistrates.[11] However, by that time the crisis of February which had prompted the Government's invitation had been temporarily solved by instituting the policy outlined in the Governor's Speech. It was thought inadvisable to replace Orpen at that stage, and so Gordon was appointed Commandant-General of the Cape Forces and spent his first months in South Africa inspecting the Cape Forces in the Transkeian territories. By July, however, the new policy in Basutoland was obviously not producing the desired results, and, as the influential Cabinet Minister, J. X. Merriman, wrote to Prime Minister Scanlen: 'We cannot go dangling on forever, fed up by telegrams and spending Colonial money. We have only nine months [until Parliament meets] to put our house in order and make up our minds what the next step is to be.'[12] Gordon, who had continued to take an interest in Basutoland, had recently drawn up a Convention outlining his solution to the problem, and submitted it to Merriman. It incorporated elements of earlier, tentative schemes he had developed and was also partly based on discussions with

Orpen (who, when Gordon first arrived in South Africa, had been in Cape Town to give evidence before a Parliamentary select committee).[13] Gordon favoured a plan of indirect rule through the chiefs and two consultative councils, with no magistrates in the country except a Resident and two Sub-Residents, whose main task would be to control the Sotho's relations with adjacent territories. His plans were derived from analogies with India, and Merriman dismissed them as inappropriate. He told Gordon that there was no recognised chief of all the nation with whom they could place a Resident and that the Sotho were 'simply a collection of jarring clans held together for the time by animosity against us'.[14] As time was to prove, Merriman was mistaken; Sotho unity was greater than he realised and Gordon's plan was the only type of arrangement that might have induced Masopha to cooperate.[15] But Merriman followed up this mistake with a far greater: he persuaded the Prime Minister to send Gordon, still convinced that his plan was the correct one, to Basutoland. At his instigation, it was agreed that Gordon should accompany Scanlen to Basutoland, ostensibly to inspect the Cape Mounted Rifles detachments, but actually in the hope that, having seen the situation for himself, he could come up with some solution.

Unfortunately the problem was complicated from the start by Gordon, who had taken one of his strong dislikes to Orpen and was not discreet in his views.[16] The local press carried comments on them even before Gordon reached Basutoland, and Orpen returned the dislike with interest. He complained bitterly that Gordon's public pronouncements on what he thought should be done in Basutoland, as well as completely unauthorised contact with Masopha *via* his missionary, had given rise to an increase in the rumours of abandonment or war, and caused considerable unrest. Letsie called all the chiefs to a *pitso* at his village, 'it is surmised', reported Orpen, 'to decide what will be done on the arrival of the General. They are told he will give them abrupt alternatives, such as abandonment, and, possibly war.'[17] The atmosphere was therefore bristling with mistrust by the time Sauer and Gordon held their first meeting with the Sotho on their arrival at Morija, and was not improved by Sauer accusing Letsie of prevaricating whenever called on to support the Government. This drew forth an unusually direct and angry protest from Lerotholi, and his temper cannot have been improved by being publicly lectured by Gordon: 'I must tell Lerothodi that his chance of being paramount chief is not worth one shilling unless Masupha's power is put down, and if this is not done quickly, it will lead in the future to fights between chiefs, and then other enemies of the Basutos will step in . . . '[18] But Sauer did categorically deny that Basutoland was to be abandoned, and after the meeting Letsie and Lerotholi saw him privately in Mabille's study to ask permission to collect an armed force for compelling Masopha to submit, to which Sauer agreed.[19]

It is difficult to judge how sincere Letsie was in making this proposal. As he had already shown in his earlier attempt to subdue Masopha in January that year, he was unwilling actually to fight his brother. Moreover, he feared—rightly, in the light of subsequent events—that the mistrust between members of the Administration might result in his betrayal. The next day he sent a messenger to Rolland specifically to point out that 'the disagreements of the officers of the Government, which are harmless and bloodless as regards these officials, are in their effects upon natives productive of death, destruction and bloodshed.'[20] Lerotholi was probably rather less hesitant. He and Masopha disliked each other, and there is a ring of authenticity about Lerotholi's declaration to Sauer: 'Anything that Government tells me to do for my father I will do, for I am the chief son of Letsie. . . . I am responsible for my father, and I don't wish the country to be destroyed by my inferior, Masupha.'[21] But as Gordon pointed out in a perceptive memorandum to Sauer three days later, Lerotholi would never act against Masopha and incur odium among his people unless he was certain not only of success, but also of involving Maama, his brother next in the succession; if he did not have this, Maama was quite likely simply to replace Masopha as the leader of the disaffected elements in the nation. 'It would never do,' added Gordon prophetically, 'to have a repetition of Thaba Bosigo, for the ridicule attached to a second failure would be fatal in its results both in the Colony and throughout Basutoland . . . '[22]

Sauer took the point, and on the visit that he and Gordon then made to Leribe allegedly went so far as to offer Jonathan's lands as a bribe to the much stronger Joel if the latter would join Lerotholi in coercing Masopha. As, on the same visit, he also apparently promised a deputation from Jonathan that he would settle the dispute between the brothers fully and fairly,[23] the Government can hardly be said to have contributed towards peace in the troubled northern district. With equal duplicity, Sauer decided at about this time to allow Gordon to visit Masopha, in the hope that Gordon's magnetism might somehow induce the chief to submit; yet Sauer was simultaneously encouraging and assisting Lerotholi's coercive expedition, two inconsistent tactics that could succeed together only if Masopha remained in total ignorance of the proposed use of force, or was completely intimidated by it. Neither alternative was likely: Sotho cohesion was such that anything happening at Morija was known within hours at Thaba-Bosiu, and vice versa; while it was most improbable that the highly intelligent old warrior at Thaba-Bosiu would not realise the uses of Gordon as either hostage or shield against the coercive expedition.

Subsequent recriminations centred on the question of whether Sauer acted with deliberate duplicity or merely muddle-headedness, but in any event, once back in Maseru from the Leribe visit, on 24 September he agreed to Gordon visiting Masopha.[24] However, well aware of Gordon's unpredictable temperament and his admiration for the rebel leader, he insisted that Gordon first commit to writing the limitations of his brief:

> I understand what you wish me to ascertain in the visit I propose making to the Chief Masupha (in a completely private capacity) is what he has to say in *re* the acceptance of a magistrate and consequent acknowledgement of the Government and the payment of hut-tax; that I am to represent to him the impossibility the Government is under *in re* the abandonment of Basutoland, and to endeavour to obtain from him an announcement of what he would be content to agree to in order that you may be able to consider whether his wishes are acceptable to the Government. I understand I have no power to make any promises whatever to him.[25]

(As a further precaution, Sauer arranged for Arthur Garcia, Inspector-General of the Colonial Forces, to report to him on Gordon's activities.) Gordon was subsequently to claim that the document was not intended to bind him if he found Masopha amenable to alternative arrangements,[26] and he certainly did not allow himself to be bound by it.

By the time he and his party set out to visit Masopha on 25 September, Lerotholi had already gathered a large force for his expedition against Masopha. This Gordon knew,[27] but later declared that he did not think Sauer intended actually to use it. Masopha had no doubt heard what was in the wind too, and had probably had reports by then of the obvious friction between Gordon, Orpen and Sauer, which he was too shrewd a politician not to exploit. Gordon and his party arrived at the Reverend Keck's mission station, which served Masopha's people, at 11 a.m., and two hours later a reception party of Masopha's sons and counsellors called on him to discover the purpose of his visit. Mr Keck read them the letter Gordon had written to Masopha for this purpose, in which in one sentence he explained that 'Government wants you to take a magistrate, and to persuade you to order your people to pay a hut-tax', and then went on to suggest that Masopha ensure that he chose his own magistrate, decided with him how the hut-tax should be spent, and that the Government 'order this magistrate to consult with you on all large matters, to treat you with all proper respect as a great chief'.[28] This certainly went beyond current Government policy—in fact, it sounded remarkably like Gordon's original plan of a Resident and two Sub-Residents based with the three major chiefs, with the latter virtually controlling internal policy—but Gordon explained to Garcia that he did not think Masopha would meet them if he appeared merely to be putting forward the old demands of hut tax and the acceptance of a magistrate.[29] When Masopha did finally meet them next day, the chief merely continued his delaying tactics by replying to Gordon's offer that he would consult his chiefs and people and send an answer. In playing for time, he was aware that Lerotholi's men, on the move towards Thaba-Bosiu, were not supplied by a commissariat and were already complaining of hunger; in addition, 'a good downpour' was threatening.[30] The longer he delayed, the lower would morale drop, and the more likely were Lerotholi's men to disperse.

Shortly after the meeting, Gordon received a letter from Sauer telling him that Lerotholi was ready to attack, and that he could be delayed only until the next day.[31] Gordon was furious. The effect on Lerotholi of an order to delay his attack was no doubt much the same, especially as the rain had by then set in and Letsie had informed him of Gordon's presence with Masopha, thereby aggravating his mistrust of the Government.

Gordon was to remain convinced that Masopha would have accepted his terms had the expedition not been threatening. Garcia was frankly sceptical, and it is uncertain whether the Government would have agreed to them anyway.[32] As it was, Gordon decided to leave for Maseru immediately since no purpose could be served by his continued presence, but modified his plan when it was pointed out to him that this sudden departure might make Masopha think that he was frightened. Masopha was therefore informed that he was leaving at 9 a.m. the next morning, as Sauer had requested his presence in Maseru. Arthur Garcia maintained a stiff upper lip in reporting on what must have been a highly alarming eighteen hours thereafter:

The man who took this letter to Masupha sent back word he wished to know why the Secretary for Native Affairs ordered General back after the morning's conversation. General sent message to say that he (Masupha) had better ask the Secretary for Native Affairs. Then up to midnight came messages and reports saying Lerothodi meant to attack at daybreak. Masupha sent to say he was astonished; that he had determined to agree to the proposals of General. General replied he was going at 9 a.m., and that he had nothing to do with Lerothodi's actions, about which Masupha had better ask the Secretary for Native Affairs.[33]

Masopha made no attempt to detain him and the next day Gordon took the shortest road out of the country, 'expressing his fury in intermittent expressions of violent rage and fist-shaking at the astonished warriors of Lerothodi's coercive force whom he passed along the way'.[34]

Inevitably in the circumstances, Lerotholi's force disintegrated and Sauer found himself exactly where he had feared: 'come to ground between two stools'.[35] As Letsie pointed out to Sauer in a letter some weeks later: 'the visit of General Gordon in coming here has been far from producing the smallest good—it has only come to greatly increase perversity on the part of Masupha and others'.[36] This Sauer found for himself when on 18 October he had an interview with Masopha and about 1,000 of his people at Thaba-Bosiu. Masopha was adamant that they did not wish to have a magistrate or to pay taxes. The arrangement which had existed in Basutoland between 1868–70 suited them far better. 'We wish to be ruled' he declared, 'in the same way as in the time of Moshesh.'[37] In November, his ally, Joel again mounted an expedition against the loyals at the Leribe District magistracy, although Jonathan managed to drive him off in a battle that greatly enhanced his prestige.[38] Orpen, as Chief Magistrate, held a farcical trial of Jonathan and Joel in the presence of Lerotholi and other chiefs, but the fine imposed on both was too light to act as an effective deterrent for long. And at the close of 1882 the situation throughout the rest of the country was if anything worse than it had been at the end of hostilities.[39]

Faced with this situation, the first major economic recession since the boom begun by the discovery of the diamond fields, and with frontier problems in the Transkei and Bechuanaland as well as Basutoland, public opinion in the Cape veered increasingly in favour of abandoning Basutoland.[40] To make matters worse, the Orange Free State objected to the fighting that had developed along the border as a result of refugees fleeing from the Leribe District.[41] The Scanlen Government made one last desperate effort to produce a solution, which it put to a Special Session of the Cape Parliament in January 1883. It was the only policy that under the circumstances had any chance of succeeding, but how great a concession the Government was making is indicated by the fact that the policy was completely contrary to all Cape principles of control in African areas, being far more akin to the plan suggested by Gordon. For the first time since 1868 a government proposed to leave the management of Basutoland's internal affairs to the chiefs, and to control only external relations. In terms of past Cape policy, it was a retrograde step.

However, the scheme never really got off the ground, for it failed to gain adequate support from the Sotho chiefs and had only half-hearted support in Parliament: although the Assembly agreed to it, the Legislative Council voted for outright abandonment.[42] At first sight the lack of Sotho enthusiasm seems surprising, since the repeated demand of Masopha and his many sympathisers was for external protection from the Orange Free State but internal self-government, free from magisterial control and interference in Sotho law—the policy the Cape was proposing. The reason however became clear when in mid-March Scanlen and Sauer went to Basutoland to sound out Sotho reactions to the proposed policy, and indicated at the numerous meetings they held[43] that the alternatives to it were either complete withdrawal or, possibly, handing Basutoland back to imperial rule. It seems that the Sotho chiefs were so disenchanted with the Cape Government that almost all would have preferred to be under imperial rule again, and to some chiefs even complete abandonment seemed preferable.[44] At the meetings many old grievances against the regulations were aired once more, most of them resulting from the Administration's policy of undermining the power of the chiefs.

There were more recent grievances too. In December the Government had succeeded in antagonising both Letsie and the loyals by its indecision on whether to allow Nkoebi, an ex-rebel son of Letsie, to settle in Quthing or not, Letsie being angered that his nominee was not installed immediately, the loyals because they had moved to Quthing specifically to escape the control of the ex-rebel chiefs.[45] The loyals were further disappointed by the failure to compensate them for their losses, despite the Government's promises the preceding April. Admittedly the commission to enquire into losses sustained had eventually appeared in August 1882, composed of Griffith as Chairman, Cecil Rhodes and two other members of the Cape Parliament, and had proceeded to take evidence at the various magistracies. With Griffith in the Chair, hopes had risen that full compensation would soon be forthcoming, but the Cape Parliament voted only £75,000 of the £100,000 compensation recommended, and payment was very slow. Moreover, as a result of Rhodes' minority report against compensating traders, this group received nothing, which had left them as a powerful propaganda group among the Sotho very disenchanted with Cape rule.[46]

The most recent grievance, however, concerned the new Acting Governor's Agent. Captain Matthew Blyth had been appointed to replace Orpen, who was felt to be too closely identified with past policies.[47] Blyth was the first Chief Magistrate of the Transkei and one of his Assistant Magistrates has left a description of him which does much to explain his subsequent problems with the Sotho:

> My chief, Captain Blyth, was a dear old thing, as good as gold, but an old woman from the sole of his shoe to the top of his hat, an awful old woman, but with a good heart and a most awful temper. When he lost the latter no punishment was sufficient even for a trivial offence. But when some infernal scoundrel, who had committed an atrocity for which he ought to have been most severely punished, shed crocodile's tears and prated a heap of nonsense about his wife and children, the heart of the Chief Magistrate became as water, and his tears not infrequently flowed down onto the chief magisterial bench while those of the culprit watered the dock.[48]

He was hardly a tactful choice as Acting Governor's Agent: the Sotho suspected him of being mainly responsible for Nehemiah's wrongful imprisonment and his temper had earned him a reputation for severity which, after the easy-going Orpen, was not welcomed.[49] No doubt to many imperial rule was preferable to a future spent collaborating with Blyth.

While the Government was unwilling or unable to remedy some of these grievances, Scanlen and Sauer did attempt to counter many of the Sotho objections to the proposed scheme. Various modifications were made before the final draft was sent to Letsie on 31 March and presented to the chiefs and headmen at a meeting at Hlotse Heights on 2 April 1883.[50] Although born of necessity, these were by far the most liberal regulations the Cape had ever offered an African people. They removed the magistrates (and, in practice, Cape law) from the average African's life unless he chose to appeal from his chief's decision. Only in a few, specific instances were cases reserved for magisterial attention. Although the Governor was still to make the laws, the provision that the chiefs and headmen were to administer them was a farce; as shown above, many chiefs and headmen disapproved of the existing laws where they were contrary to Sotho law, or did not understand the principles on which they were based. With magisterial authority under the proposed constitution far less in evidence than before the war, the only incentive to such chiefs to administer the modified law was fear of having their decisions set aside on appeal to the magistrates; and appeals were likely to remain rare while the chiefs retained their greatly strengthened position. It seems unlikely that the missionaries, who often acted as interpreters at the meetings held by Scanlen, Sauer and Blyth would have allowed the Government to remain in ignorance of this fact, but they were also keenly aware of the evils abandonment would bring, and would have preferred even the proposed system to that alternative.[51]

The chiefs were not required to make an immediate response to the proposals of 2 April, and only after three weeks had elapsed was a national *pitso* held to receive their answer. It lasted for two days and the Reverend Alfred Boegner, the Director of the French Protestant Mission, wrote a vivid description of the first day.

> The plateau on which the Pitso is held under a grey sky is vast in extent and set in a frame of mountains. On one side stands the camp of Captain Blyth and other officials; on the other side the native horses in their hundreds are grazing. The ground is strewn with red saddles. Here and there a European appears; the surcoat

of a Roman priest, the white helmets of other visitors, the broad black hat of Mr. Dyke, père.[52] All the crowd talks, shouts, discusses, laughs. They are awaiting Masupha. Horsemen by the score continue to arrive—but Masupha comes not. The Pitso begins without him. The men arrange themselves in a huge hollow square, those in front sitting on the ground, those behind standing. The chiefs and missionaries take their places within the square: Letsie, Captain Blyth and the six magistrates seat themselves there apart. The Captain has a soldierly bearing and inspires confidence. Mabille opens with a prayer. Then Letsie rises, '*Lumelang!* Hail!' he cries, and the thousands of voices respond with a long-drawn-out '*Eh!*' Letsie addresses his people by their honorific title: 'Bakuena! Crocodiles!' and the response comes thunderously back: 'Thou art the Crocodile!'. 'I have nothing to say . . . ' so he begins with the customary exordium, telling his father's and mother's names. 'As Moshesh was a servant of the Queen, so am I. . . . Now listen to what will be said on the part of the government. As for me, I sit down, having nothing more to say'. Captain Blyth speaks clearly, explaining the purpose of the assembly. The question to be answered is: Do the Basuto wish to remain under the government, and will they accept the new arrangements? The future is in their own hands. The answer must be a plain Yes, or No. Mabille is called upon to read the government's proposals; and Captain Blyth goes on to insist that the answer must be unanimous; the new law must apply to all, or to none.

Now the discussion opens. Letsie declares that for himself he accepts; and he deplores Masupha's absence.

Having listened to the Paramount Chief the officials retire to allow the Basuto to talk it out among themselves. The chiefs present are unanimously favourable; but messages from Masupha and Ramanella declare their hostility to anything and everything proposed by the government.

Now Mabille rises to his feet and all eyes are fixed upon him. This is more or less what he says: 'Letsie, chiefs and all you Basuto, allow me to say a word. Though I am a missionary I am also a Mosuto, having lived over twenty years among you. If I speak it is to warn you that the hour is serious, solemn, and to ask you to show yourselves men. You have heard what was said: the new laws must be accepted in their entirety and by the entire nation. Will you remain divided? Cannot you act? Cannot you unite? Or are you still counting upon something to happen in the future? Do you not see that you must give a clear and decisive answer, here and now? Weigh well the consequences of the resolution you take. If you do not accept these proposals the consequences will be that sooner or later your country will be abandoned. And do not imagine that things will be then as they were before you came under the shadow of the Queen. Once the British have gone the Boers will come and claim the country which once they nearly conquered. They will say: "Moyela, clear out! Lerothodi, clear out! Letsie, clear out! All this land is ours." And you will be servants where now you are masters. One man troubles you—Masupha. He thinks that he has nothing to fear; he will keep his country. So thinking, he shows himself selfish. He kills us all by his selfishness. Son of Masupha, are you here? [Response: Yes!] Well, tell your father: You kill us, you kill the churches, you kill the nation. And all of you, when some day you are scattered abroad or serving the Boers in the land that was yours, herding the cattle of others, ploughing the land of others— then your children will say, and you will say to yourselves: "A curse upon Masupha! It is he who brought us to destruction". To-day it is not too late. Reflect—act—be men!'[53]

The speeches continued all day, but at sunset a second day was needed to obtain a definite answer from Letsie. In the end, his consent to the new constitution was wrung from him only by the concerted efforts of Blyth, Lerotholi, and some of the other chiefs:

Captain Blyth.   Your own chiefs have asked you, and I ask you for a direct answer, do you, or do you not accept the regulations?
Letsea.   I don't want the Government to leave. I don't want Europeans in the country to eat up our country.
Captain Blyth.   That is beside the question. I must have a clear and decided answer.
Mathlehbe.   The laws are good, answer chief.
Captain Blyth.   Lerothodi, all I want from your father is, does he as Paramount Chief accept these regulations on behalf of the Basuto nation? That is all I want. We are not here to be put off like children. I am not here for that purpose on behalf of Government.
Letsea.   I have not had time yet.
Captain Blyth.   We all knew this Pitso was only called for the

purpose of giving a direct answer to this. All knew this. Letsea knew it more than a month ago.

Letsea. I accept the laws but—

Captain Blyth. There must be no buts; 'either I Letsea, accept these regulations on behalf of the Basuto nation,' or 'I Letsea do *not* accept.' It must be clear and decided. If you Paramount Chief wish to say 'no' say 'no,' or 'yes' say 'yes,' but no 'buts' and 'ifs.'

Molomo. When you began by saying 'yes,' did you not mean you accepted, but would he read the regulations.

Letsea. Yes, I meant that.

Captain Blyth. I only want to know your minds but no uncertainty.

Lerothodi. My chiefs, I don't see why all this talking should go on. I accept these regulations. We live by the Government. We cannot let the Government go.

Nehemiah. I wish to explain a few things which have happened with reference to regulations. When Basutos handed themselves over to Government, Mr. Bowker distributed regulations over Basutoland, and told people to come to him if they did not understand them. I don't remember that any one did go back to Mr. Bowker.

Letsea. I have already said, I have accepted these laws, but I want to read them, and reconsider them.

Captain Blyth. That is no answer. I must only say to Government I have got no answer. There has been eighteen months of shuffling. There must be no more.

Seta says, Tell the Governor's Agent we accept. (The people acclaim.)

Captain Blyth. Let Letsea say himself what has to be said.

Letsea. According to Sesuto custom that was just as good.

Captain Blyth. I have come as an Englishman, and an officer of the Government, and want a straightforward answer.

Letsea. Do you hear there are laws proposed for us, they were read to us. Some of these which were read to us at Morija I have not heard read here. I say to you, Maama and others as Moshesh gave us over to the Queen. I have accepted these laws with my whole heart.

Captain Blyth. I now wish to ask Letsea and others do you all accept.

We all accept.

Captain Blyth.   Is that the answer I am to send?
The people acclaim 'let the Government remain.'
Captain Blyth.   I shall let Government know at once that the
Pitso was held two days, and that on the afternoon of the second
day, &c., &c. Do I understand right?
'The people acclaim'.

I shall also tell the Government, Masupha was sent for, but
sent a message that he had not killed the taxes, let the man who
killed them come. Ramanella was also not present. I am
confident the Paramount Chief has sufficient authority to carry
out this if he wishes, when the answer of Government comes, I
shall communicate to you. We will carry out our part of the
agreement faithfully and well.[54]

But such a consent to the constitution was virtually worthless, as
Blyth pointed out: Letsie could not be counted on to lend his weight
to the new laws. His reluctance seems strange, given his people's
willingness to accept the constitution, but Blyth explained: 'he is
entirely in the hands of his sons, two of them, "Bereng" and
"Mama" secretly side with Masupha, and the arrogance and
general bearing of these two Chieflets bode but little good to the
general peace of this country.'[55] Masopha's reasons for refusing to
cooperate were no doubt similar to those of his nephews, jealous of
their brother Lerotholi. In Masopha's case the Government's
agreement that Letsie's position as Paramount Chief should be
enhanced in order to restore his old powers would effectively have
ensured Masopha's opposition.

The failure of Letsie to accept the new constitution wholehear-
tedly at the *pitso* sealed Basutoland's fate. Although the new
regulations were promulgated, it was obvious that there was no
hope of their being accepted by a united country, the Cape
Government's precondition for remaining in Basutoland. Letsie
would never take the necessary steps to ensure Masopha's compliance. As if to emphasise the divisions in the country, only five
days later news was received from Leribe that Joel had attacked
Jonathan with the support of Masopha.[56] Widdicombe later
recounted how Joel, on capturing Jonathan's village at Leribe,
burnt every hut in the place and then proceeded to 'a deed which
struck awe into the hearts of the whole people'.

He burnt down his father's house with his own hands! This act, so
unparalleled in native warfare, displayed the depths of his

jealousy and hatred of his half-brother; for the house, a large and, in its way, not unhandsome structure of stone, went with the chieftainship, and was, of course, claimed by Jonathan, though he had been as yet unable to occupy it. There is, as we know, among the Basutos a great reverence for their ancestors, and a father, whether living or departed, is always held in honour by his sons; and thus the burning not only of his father's village, but even of his very house, the house which was Molapo's special pride and boast, was an act which drew down upon Joel the execrations of the whole tribe. There can be no doubt that old Letsie marked it and remembered it; for from that time forth the Paramount Chief showed Jonathan more favour, though he was not yet prepared to side with him openly.[57]

After taking Jonathan's village, only Joel's failure to carry through the attack saved the undefended magistracy and loyals' village from being taken (Jonathan and his men were in pursuit of another part of the attacking force). Serious fighting continued until Letsie was persuaded to pass judgement on the Molapo inheritance at a national gathering held from 22–6 May to hear the case. Possibly with Joel's recent action in mind, he recognised Jonathan as the rightful chief.[58]

But by that time the Cape Government had lost confidence in its ability to cope with the situation. At the beginning of May it opened negotiations with the British Government to hand over Basutoland to its care,[59] and the news quickly spread. The resulting uncertainty as to the future placed Blyth and the magistrates in an increasingly uncomfortable position, and Blyth appears to have been hampered by the magistrates of the pro-Orpen faction among the officials, who resented his criticisms of Orpen's and their administration.[60] But as the evidence (such as Blyth's report on 22 June 1883) showed, the Government's new policy which he was attempting to implement did not appear to be very effective anyway.

After three months careful and cautious working of this new system, I cannot say that it has met with that measure of success its liberal spirit deserved. The Chief Letsea is willing enough to take all the power to himself in dealing with cases,[61] and the general management of the tribe, except when grave difficulties arise as in the case of Masopha, when Letsea says he is powerless, 'the Government must deal with that,' but he is not so willing to recognise his obligations to the Government. The above remarks apply also to nearly every Chief in the country who now exercises his authority, and seeks his own aggrandisement without let or hindrance, and already the common people are sorely feeling the burden of their position, and would gladly welcome the just and humane rule of British Magistrates, but are afraid to make any move in this direction as they would incur the displeasure of their chiefs; and the power of the Government in Basutoland is not strong enough to protect them.[62]

Blyth's increasing and extreme distrust of Letsie[63] was probably aggravated by Blyth's own ill health,[64] but was also partially justified by Letsie's behaviour. However loyal the Paramount Chief might have desired to be, he had very little power with which to assist the Government: his heir, Lerotholi, was loyal to the Government, but he too was in poor health;[65] and Letsie's son next in the succession, Maama, and several of Maama's more influential brothers supported Joel and Masopha[66] and would have refused to help to subdue them. For the same reason, Letsie could not always ensure that the regulations were observed.[67] Besides, it is very possible that both Letsie and Lerotholi were happy to see magisterial control kept to a minimum, and found the rebel chiefs provided a useful excuse for inaction when required to bolster magisterial authority. Unfortunately the lack of force at Blyth's disposal obliged him to rely entirely on Letsie to bring him those cases which according to the new regulations were to be tried by a Government officer, such as cases of murder. Hence his frustration in October, for example, when Joel refused to surrender an accused man to him, saying Letsie had told him to deal with the case himself. Blyth angrily reported: 'This is Letsea's way of working, sending one message to Joel as in this case and he will tell me he will see to it at once.'[68] But as he must have realised, such behaviour on Letsie's part was inevitable, given Letsie's political circumstances and character: the Paramount Chief was unlikely to retain his position if he was blatantly and regularly disobeyed by rebellious chiefs, but was on the other hand too shrewd a character to defy the choleric old administrator openly. Prevarication was the only solution.

How close the new system of self-government came to total breakdown as a result of Blyth's frustration with Letsie's alleged impotence and manoeuvres is perhaps best indicated by the exchange of letters between them on the subject of Letsie's abdication. Whether Letsie was in earnest or not is unclear, since events intervened before he could act. Possibly he was merely trying to enrol Blyth's sympathy, and perhaps to frighten the Government into demanding less of him; but on 20 October he wrote to Blyth that his loss of influence had made him decide to announce his abdication at a *pitso*, provided Blyth thought it advisable and that the Government would appoint a more readily obeyed Paramount in his place.[69] Blyth's exasperated reply reduced Letsie to angry sulks[70] and might have had far worse results had the British Government not intervened.

> I am quite aware that for some time past you have not carried out anything that I wished you [sic] although it was for the good of your country.
>
> I cannot and do not think that your influence is so little as you say, and I am sure that if you really desired it, and gave positive orders that they would be obeyed, and any instructions I have given you would have been carried out at once.
>
> You can do as you like about calling a Pitso and perhaps it would be a good thing, as anything is better than this present way of going on. The presence of the Government in your country is a farce. I have honestly tried my best for your good, and that of your people and I have worked only through you as Paramount Chief, but I can do nothing more.
>
> I hear what you say about resigning your position as Paramount Chief. The Government will be sorry to learn that you have no power and influence. They will not mind who is Paramount Chief so long as their orders are obeyed—and the Basutos ruled justly and properly, so that there may be peace in the land and the present evil state of things come to an end.[71]

Fortunately at this stage the Cape's negotiations with Britain—prolonged by a dispute over financial contributions—were completed, and the British Government very reluctantly agreed to take over Basutoland on certain conditions, mainly for fear of the repercussions in southern Africa if it did not.[72] A *pitso* was called for 29 November to ask the nation if it was willing to be ruled by Britain or if it would prefer abandonment. The Bloemfontein newspaper, the *Friend of the Free State*, carried a detailed report of what everyone realised was an historic occasion.[73] Some 3,000 Sotho assembled, together with most of the leading chiefs, and Letsie arrived in impressive style in a carriage drawn by four greys. Virtually all the white population of the country was reported to be present, headed by 'Capt. Blyth, C.M.G. (who wore the insignia of the Order upon his left Breast)'; but three leading chiefs were conspicuously absent: Masopha, Joel and RaManella.[74] Proceedings opened with a prayer from a French missionary and then the Queen's proposals were read to the people. They outlined the existing situation and ended with the crucial questions:

> Do you desire to remain British subjects under the direct Government of the Queen? and if so, do you undertake to be obedient to the laws and orders of Her Majesty's High Commissioner under whose authority you will be placed, and to pay a hut tax of ten shillings in aid of the administrative expenses of your country? Her Majesty's Government ask for plain straight-forward answers, yes or no, to these simple questions. — If you say yes, the Government ask further, are you united? the Queen does not want unwilling subjects. Her Majesty's Government cannot take over a divided people.

Letsie then addressed the people 'at some length, and finished by saying, "I am for Peace. What say ye?" There were loud cries from all, "We are, Chief!" Letsea: "I am for the Queen's Government. What say ye?" There were loud cries which shook the air, "So are we, Chief! Mother, do not leave your children to be killed!"' And so, after various chiefs had spoken, Letsie and the other chiefs and headmen present signed a document expressing their willingness to accept the Queen's proposals. They represented over 110,000 people; the absent chiefs represented about 20,000.

Masopha, to emphasise his rejection of the proposals, held a *pitso* of his own at which he demanded complete self-government;[75] The *Friend of the Free State* speculated that his defiance might be part of a national plot 'in order that the Basutos, when the time comes for them to kick up their heels again, may say, "We never agreed as a united people to the Imperial Government resuming rule over us." '[76] There followed an anxious period for the Cape ministers before the British Government in mid-December decided that the Sotho majority in favour of British rule was large enough to warrant it accepting Basutoland.[77] Further attempts by Letsie to induce Masopha and RaManella to agree to pay hut tax and accept a magistrate merely provoked them into doctoring their warriors for war and taxing Masopha's people to raise money for more arms and ammunition;[78] 'they say,' reported Letsie, 'that the Queen's Government is a cave which has fallen upon those who took refuge in it and is full of graves'.[79] But by then the British Government was committed to accepting Basutoland. Letsie's lengthy farewell letters of thanks to Blyth and the Cape Government were models of diplomacy for soothing ruffled plumage.

> . . . My prayer to you, Sirs, who are now at the head of the Government of the Cape Colony, is that you would always look upon us with a friendly eye, and not consider us as your enemies. I beg that you will continue to me and the Basutos your friendship and your favour and your help. We are perfectly aware that the Cape Colony occupies a large part of South Africa and possesses a great influence for good upon its neighbours. And therefore, if you consent to remain with us in close ties of friendship, we shall in the future receive much good from you. I trust that you will grant this my prayer.[80]

On 18 March 1884 an order in council was promulgated notifying the Queen's assent to the Cape disannexation of Basutoland, assuming direct Imperial control and vesting in the High Commissioner all legislative and executive power.[81] On the same day Blyth handed over his duties to Colonel Marshall James Clarke, the new Resident Commissioner who was to replace the Governor's Agent, and the following day left Basutoland.[82] With his departure ended the Cape's responsibility for Basutoland, and on 29 May 1884 the Cape code of regulations, legally kept in force by a British order in council, was replaced by a new code of regulations promulgated by the High Commissioner.[83] The chiefs had won.

But exactly which chiefs? Letsie and Lerotholi certainly, for they retained Britain's protection against the Free State and regained not only their original freedom from strict magisterial control, but far more power as Paramount Chiefs under the British form of government than would have been the case had they reverted to the loose pre-British confederation of Moshoeshoe's day. Whether Masopha emerged a winner or a loser is less clear. He certainly won his original battle to reduce the power of the magistrates and interference in Sotho law, for the British Government was in future to rule with a very light hand. But did his continued rejection of

British rule stem from a national 'contingency plan' of the kind suggested by the *Friend*? If this were so, the lack of interference by the British Resident Commissioner made it unnecessary ever to resort to the plan. Or did Masopha fear encroachment on the chiefs' powers by British officials once they were installed? Or did his resistance indicate, as some suspected, that by the time the Cape Government left Basutoland he was set on gaining full independence from Letsie, if not the Paramount Chieftainship for himself? He must have realised that while the British remained able to control the country through the legitimate Paramount and his heir, neither independence nor a seizure of power would be possible.

If independence was his aim, he never achieved it. He continued to foment trouble between his nephews who lived near him, in each case assisting one side in order to obtain its support. These quarrels frequently led to fighting, the victors invariably confiscating as much of the property of those defeated as they could find. The British magistrates were not strong enough to intervene in such skirmishes, or even to punish Masopha when he had three men put to death for witchcraft. Eventually, however, he and RaManella, his cousin, had a serious fight in which about fifty men were killed. Each chief, anxious for Government support, appealed for arbitration, and their acceptance of the resulting decision on their dispute greatly strengthened the Government's position in the eyes of the Sotho. Masopha, finding himself increasingly isolated and out of touch with the nation, asked the Resident Commissioner in February 1886 to place a magistrate in his district. The man who was sent for the first four months, Godfrey Lagden, was able to collect taxes and, for the first time in six years, re-establish a magistracy in the district. In later years, even after he had become Resident Commissioner and clashed repeatedly with Masopha, Lagden recorded that he always admired Masopha's 'attractive personality and manliness'.[84]

With the return of Masopha and his supporters to the Government fold, the country was at last united, and when the Resident Commissioner held the country's first regular annual national meeting since the British Administration had taken over, Masopha and every other leading chief were among those who attended. However, although Masopha was in his late sixties, he showed little sign of mellowing. Over the next twelve years a series of crises testified to his refusal to submit passively to Letsie or, after his death, Lerotholi.[85] The story of his final confrontation with the country's rulers reads like a sombre echo of Moorosi's fate.

In November 1897 a junior son of Masopha raided the Orange Free State to seize a young woman of his district who had run away from her elderly husband in Lesotho with a young man from her village. The raider was arrested in the Free State and sentenced to imprisonment with lashes, but managed to break jail in Ladybrand in broad daylight and rejoin his father. (Rumour had it that the people of Ladybrand, either bribed by Masopha or fearing an attack by him, assisted in the escape.)[86] Masopha, when ordered to surrender his son to justice, not only refused to do so, but declared he would resist any attempt at arrest. Lagden called upon Lerotholi to enforce the law and effect the arrest, but only when all attempts at persuasion had failed did the Paramount march on Masopha with every man he could muster. Masopha, true to the last to his Sotho name of 'the Wildebeest', decided to fight. He evacuated Thaba-Bosiu to take up a strong position on the plateau overlooking the Phutiatsana, and the two armies, each of some 10,000 men, faced each other across the river. The question was no longer merely the surrender of a criminal: it was a battle for supremacy between rival sections of the tribe.

On 5th January 1898 Lerotholi attacked and the stronghold fell next day.[87] The losses were small, but not the penalties which followed. Masopha formally surrendered his son, who was tried and sentenced to prison. Masopha himself was heavily fined, deprived of his district chieftainship, and forbidden to reoccupy his village at Thaba-Bosiu, the historic fortifications of which were dismantled. The following year he died, aged seventy-eight, a broken old man.

And yet, although he never became Paramount, he had, despite himself, set his country on the road to the independence which he sought. Had he not determinedly headed opposition to magisterial rule, through all attempts after the Gun War to reimpose it, the Cape would have remained in Basutoland, which would have suffered the fate of the other Cape-ruled African areas that eventually came under the laws of the Union of South Africa. Masopha's continued opposition sapped the Cape Government's confidence in its ability to rule Basutoland, and led eventually to its handing the country back to an imperial power which in time gave its African territories independence. Masopha could not have foreseen the eventual result of his resistance to Cape rule; and had he won his final battle, his victory would probably have spelt disaster for his country. The British would almost certainly have felt obliged to abandon Basutoland to the mercy of its neighbours, since the defeat for the Paramount's forces would have left them with no means of enforcing their decisions unless they had imported expensive imperial troops. Had Basutoland been abandoned, its own past history and that of other chiefdoms in similar positions indicate that it would very probably have been absorbed piecemeal into the Orange Free State, leaving the Sotho living as squatters on white-owned farms. Ironically, Masopha's final defeat ensured that his people survived as an independent nation; but, equally, without his victory against the Cape it is very unlikely that today his country would be recognised as the independent Kingdom of Lesotho.

Epilogue

Until the War of the Guns, Basutoland was thought of as the outstanding success of the Cape Government's 'civilising' policy as embodied in the regulations. Their apparent effectiveness in undermining allegiance to the chiefs led to glowing reports to the Cape Parliament on their use in converting a self-sufficient, subsistence society led by chiefs and based on the extended family into an individualistic consumer-producer economy. They were even adopted as the model for the subsequent Transkeian regulations.[1] And yet, alone among the tribes ruled by the South African colonies, the Sotho chiefs were able to unite their people so effectively that they achieved the only successful revolt against the colonists. At first sight this revolt would appear to negate the Cape officials' claim to have already made important modifications in the social structure of Basutoland. With rebel forces seen to include groups on whom the Cape officials had counted as certain allies against disloyal chiefs, their analysis of the degree of social change effected appears questionable. But to take the revolt as proof of the failure of the Cape's chosen means of changing Sotho society is to misunderstand the nature of both the process taking place until the Gun War and the social adjustments that were made.

Such misunderstanding stems partly from the simple equation frequently drawn by the Administration and its observers between the magistrates' success in implementing official policy and the loss of power by the chiefs. This idea arose from observing only one of the ways in which official policy was imposed—that of enforcing the regulations in court against the wishes of the chiefs—and assuming it indicated an irreparable loss of power by all the chiefs vis-à-vis both their followers and the Administration. In fact the process of imposing the law was far wider, more complex and more fluid than such observations indicated, and provided the chiefs with various openings that differed according to rank and circumstances.

For any government to introduce effective laws making radical changes in the daily practices of a population, it must either have the use of overwhelming force and be prepared to use it ruthlessly, or it must obtain the cooperation of the population. Where the size of administration is as small as that in Basutoland, virtually nothing can be done without popular support. To obtain this, the Basutoland Administration inevitably had to make concessions.[2] Its implementation of the regulations was not, therefore, a one-way process of law being imposed from above. Both the formulation and, to a greater extent, the degree of implementation of the law were the result of constant interaction between ruler and ruled, with the ruled having considerable *de facto* control over both processes. Furthermore, within the many levels of both Sotho and Cape societies, attitudes and processes were constantly affecting and being affected by the information each society received on the reactions of the other to the preceding move. As a result, a policy or the subsequent reactions to it could undergo many unexpected changes, even while often remaining unchanged on paper. To take a simple example, Griffith's attack on the custom of *letsema*[3] provoked an unexpectedly strong reaction from the chiefs, which in turn caused Griffith to write to Cape Town for instructions. The governmental level of the Cape hierarchy, being subject to different political pressures from those that Griffith experienced, was sensitive to the colonial problems involved in sending expensive troops to enforce obedience on obstreperous chiefs. It therefore recommended a more circuitous approach to altering established customs, including regular consultation with the chiefs on any such alteration before it was implemented. This in practice gave rise to a new process in later attacks on important customs, although it was not reflected in the regulations on paper. It was also one of the incidents that made Griffith propose, and the Government accept, his creation of an extra arm to the administrative structure in the country later that year, in the form of the Basutoland Mounted Police[4]—which would subsequently affect the enforcement of the regulations. Meanwhile, the chiefs, who were equally carefully monitoring the Administration's reactions, would rapidly have become aware that the Administration was taking greater pains to consult them, and so no doubt would their subjects. This would have affected the extent of the latter's support for the chiefs, which in turn would have affected their chiefs' future actions.

Given this continuing interaction, the implementation of the regulations depended on a fine balance being maintained by the officials on the spot, who therefore required great latitude in the rules to enable them to adapt their responses to every Sotho move. The ideal aimed for was the full implementation of the regulations in every case and, where possible, in such a way as to nudge the people affected ever further along the chosen path towards the Cape's definition of a civilised society. Where, however, implementation of the regulations would lead to a confrontation that the Administration could not hope to win or only at too great a cost, there had to be sufficient flexibility in the rules laid down by Cape Town for their administration to allow the officials to give ground without too obvious a loss of face. While on paper many of the regulations might not offer any room for manoeuvre, in practice, as has been shown, they could be and were manipulated by being defined by the Administration as inapplicable. Thus, for example, the regulations laid down in uncompromising language that 'the taking of the life of any person wilfully and maliciously will be held to be murder, and will be punishable by the death of the offender'. Yet, to avoid the possibility of sparking off a riot in Molapo's district in 1872 by executing some Nguni murderers, the Administration found an excuse not to apply the regulations.[5] On other occasions the regulations were enforced, but only after much political negotiation, such as where pressure from Letsie had to be used to obtain the payment of a fine under the regulations in the case of Raisa in July 1877.[6] Given this situation, the regulations should be viewed as a statement of how the Cape would have liked to rule, rather than of what law was regularly enforceable or enforced in practice. That the practice did increasingly approximate to the ideal is indicated both by the available evidence[7] and by the fact that the Government felt able to redefine the 1877 regulations more stringently. But the regulations alone cannot be taken as indicating what legal and social changes were actually enforced by the Administration, nor what the extent of its power actually was.

Nor on the other hand can the extent to which the Sotho appeared to adapt socially, economically and legally to the Cape's ideal model be taken as a guide to what the Cape policy was capable of achieving. Its apparent success during the first eight years of the Cape's administration was not all of its own making. Much was attributable to the missionaries, who had already had a marked impact on the habits of the society, and even more, there were the diamond fields. The growth in the economy of the diamond fields almost exactly coincided with the Cape's annexation of Basutoland and contributed greatly to social change there. The Sotho were the best situated of all the societies ruled by the Cape to benefit from the increasing prosperity, since their proximity and rich farm land enabled them to provide grain, firewood, wool and meat when all were much in demand. They were also able to go to the diamond fields cheaply and for relatively short periods, during which they could earn money in employment. They acquired wealth on a scale unthought of before, and the large-scale introduction of hoes, wagons and money changed their whole way of life. Ironically, the prosperity generated by the diamond fields was not only a major factor in promoting the Cape's policy, but also a major cause of its end: the guns that the Sotho were able to buy with their new-found wealth were at the heart of both the crisis that ruptured the Cape's 'civilising' policy in Basutoland and its failure to save its Administration by decisively winning the resulting confrontation. But even had the disarmament crisis not occurred, the rate of progress of the Basutoland Administration's policy would almost certainly have slowed down, though not nearly as disastrously, as the deepening recession in the Cape economy and on the diamond fields in the early 1880s reduced the flow of wealth to Basutoland and the flow of labourers from it.

As has been shown, however, the Administration also had its own tools and methods for encouraging social change. The strategy for which these were employed was to create a situation in which 'civilising forces' could have full play, and so to shepherd at least most of the people into a way of life where their interests diverged from the conservative chiefs' so radically on all important matters that there would eventually be no common ground on which the chiefs could rally them against the Administration. So long, however, as common interests existed, any blunder by the Administration that impinged on them automatically helped to unite chiefs and people, even where the people's interests diverged in many other ways from those of the chiefs. Although a general unease with the pace of change was widespread in the period under consideration, it was not enough alone to unite the people behind the conservative chiefs while the advantages of change were also in evidence. Perhaps it would have become an explosive force in its own right had the speed of change quickened even more, or recession made the benefits less accessible—though insofar as the subsequent development of the Cape policy in the Transkei can serve as a guide, it does appear that a detonating issue was required. However, general disquiet left the Administration exceedingly vulnerable to any event or policy, whether of its own or another's making, that could be seized upon by the chiefs.

It was for this reason that the Administration found it imperative not only to retain the support of the Paramount Chief and his heir, but to bolster their power. These chiefs could both assist with enforcement in small-scale confrontations and also in many cases rally the main body of the people behind the Administration so as to isolate a dissident chief and his supporters. The case of Moorosi was a prime example. But this use of the Paramount Chief put the Administration in the anomalous position of doing its best to buttress his traditional power while simultaneously attacking the power of the chiefs—which involved attacking the mainstays of the Paramount's power too. Similarly, the attempt to convert the younger sons of Moshoeshoe into Government officials was rather ambiguous, since it involved to some extent relying on their influence as chiefs. The contradictions embedded in the policy inevitably left the magistrates and collaborating chiefs rather mistrustful of one another, each painfully aware of having rendered himself more vulnerable should the other side fail him.

Given the tension inherent in the Cape's methods of changing Sotho society, was its breakdown inevitable, and at that point in time? Had Masopha not existed, would there not have been another chief to lead a revolt at such a heaven-sent opportunity as the disarmament crisis? Certainly Lerotholi's junior brothers such as Maama would have been likely candidates, but it must be borne in mind that to the Sotho the opponent appeared intimidatingly powerful. The Cape forces had put down the recent frontier revolt on the other side of the Drakensberg and had subsequently defeated Moorosi—admittedly after a delay, but with devastating effect. Moreover, the Cape was still at that point bound up in the Sotho mind with a Britain that in July 1879 had restored its reputation as a mighty fighting force by defeating the Zulu at Ulundi. To carry through a challenge to such a foe as the Cape appeared to be may well have required a warrior of the experience and character of 'the Wildebeest'. Any lesser man who faltered or came to heel at the order of the Paramount Chief would not have obtained the same national following that obliged Lerotholi to join him in revolt. And had the Gun War not occurred, then the longer the Cape's policy continued in operation, breaking down the links of common interests between chiefs and people, the more difficult it would have become for a chief to rally enough of the people for an effective uprising. The importance of a coincidence of a suitable leader and a uniting issue at a sufficiently early moment in the Cape's administration is borne out by the fact that the same policy, when applied in the Transkei in the succeeding decades, never provoked a large-scale revolt.

However, Masopha did exist and in 1880 the Cape Government was in the circumstances extremely rash to challenge the Sotho—not because the Administration had failed in its avowed aim of loosening the allegiance of the people to the chiefs, but because it had not had enough time to consolidate its gains. It had got off to a flying start as a result of missionary efforts and the flourishing diamond fields economy and, compared with administrations in the other Cape-ruled African territories in that period, it had in general been exceptionally able and judicious, especially in view of the tensions inherent in the system and the demands on the judgement of the administrators. But the loosening of allegiance to long-established chiefs was not a simple, irreversible, one-time operation analogous to the cutting of a single thread, and would have had to be far advanced to have been effective against the call of so unifying an issue as disarmament, led by a man like Masopha.

Once the eruption had occurred, the one hope left for continuing a manipulative policy like that of the Cape was for colonial or British forces to gain a decisive victory. In retrospect it can be seen that the failure to do so spelt the certain death of the Cape Administration. Since its policy depended on separating the people from most of the chiefs and retaining the loyalty of the remaining ones, it had to be able to protect its supporters from the consequences of their collaboration. For much of the time it could rely on the nebulous prestige of the mighty British Empire, but if it ultimately had its bluff called and failed to meet the challenge, there remained no credible threat to use against those who failed to obey its unpopular orders in the future. Nor could they be restrained from wreaking vengeance on those who had trusted in the Government for their protection. After the first mistake, therefore, nobody would ever risk collaboration with the Administration again in the teeth of majority opposition, and it would lose all ability to enforce its orders through the influence of collaborating chiefs. At the *pitso* to install Orpen as Acting Governor's Agent, the embittered George Moshoeshoe in fact spoke the epitaph of the Cape Administration:

They had a cry in Basutoland that once upon a time a lion died and then the carcase all rotted away except the lion's skin, and then a hare came and made his nest under the dead lion's skin, and all the people, not knowing the lion was dead, were very much frightened and would not go near the place, so that the hare had a good and quiet time of it under cover of the lion's skin; but one day a little boy came and threw a stone at the lion and then the skin gave a hollow sound and the hare jumped out and ran away. So the people all laughed heartily at the dead lion's skin and were no longer frightened.

Just so was it now with the Queen's protection in Basutoland. It was a dead lion's skin which could not even protect a hare.[8]

Notes

INTRODUCTION

1. J. A. Benyon, 'Basutoland and the High Commission with particular reference to the years 1868–1884: The Changing Nature of the Imperial Government's "Special Responsibility" for the Territory' (Oxford Univ. D.Phil., 1968).
2. A. Atmore and S. Marks, 'The Imperial Factor in South Africa in the Nineteenth Century: Towards a Reassessment', *Journal of Imperial and Commonwealth History*, iii, 1 (1974).
3. P. B. Sanders, *Moshoeshoe: Chief of the Sotho* (London, 1975) appendix.

CHAPTER I   CREATING A NATION

1. E. H. Brookes and C. de B. Webb, *A History of Natal* (Pietermaritzburg, 1965) pp. 14–15.
2. For the etymology of the word, see Sanders, *Moshoeshoe*, p. 27, n. 1.
3. The exact date of his birth is unknown: see Sanders, ibid., p. 5.
4. For other names, see D. F. Ellenberger, *History of the Basuto, Ancient and Modern* (rewritten in English by J. C. MacGregor, London, 1912) pp. 106–7. Amongst the English and settlers he became known as Moshesh.
5. Probably so-named because of the illusion created by the setting sun, and subsequent legend which arose, that the mountain grows larger at night. See Sanders, *Moshoeshoe*, p. 35, n. 21. Often called 'Thaba Bosigo' by nineteenth-century writers.
6. Though his son, Thlali, and Dr John Philip, the L.M.S. missionary, described him as short.
7. G. Tylden, *The Rise of the Basuto* (Cape Town, 1950) pp. 14–16.
8. Sanders, *Moshoeshoe*, p. 138, quoting Arbousset to P.E.M.S. Committee, 2 Mar. 1852, *J.M.E.* (1852) p. 208. Sanders does also point out that Moshoeshoe's temper was much feared, and that when enraged he had been known to attack and even to attempt to kill offenders: see Sanders, ibid., p. 139.
9. Special Commissioner of the Cape Argus (J. M. Orpen), *History of the Basutus in South Africa* (Cape Town, 1857) pp. 4–5.
10. Ellenberger, *History of the Basuto*, p. 229.
11. E. Casalis, *The Basutos* (London, 1861) pp. 22–4.
12. Many of the following methods he learnt from Mohlomi, a distant relative who was an exceptionally successful chief among the small Sotho chiefdoms and, when an old man, gave advice to the young Moshoeshoe.

13. N. Moshoeshoe, 'A Little Light from Basutoland', *Cape Monthly Magazine*, (1880) p. 16. No doubt they too were returned under the *mafisa* system, outlined on p. 26.
14. A group ruled by a senior kinsman of Moshoeshoe's father.
15. Ellenberger, *History of the Basuto*, p. 230.
16. Sanders, *Moshoeshoe*, p. 55.
17. The daughters of these men were regarded as daughters of the chief and the number of marriage-cattle paid for them was as much as ten times higher than Moshoeshoe would be obliged to give for the men's wives. Cape, G. M. Theal (ed.), (Unpublished) Basutoland Records—contracted to U.B.R. below—iv. 128: 'Notes on the Political and Social Position of the Basuto Tribe' by Rolland, 30 Mar. 1868. For an interesting legal result of this system of clientage that was later to lead to a clash with Christian missionaries, see L. Thompson, *Survival in Two Worlds: Moshoeshoe of Lesotho 1786–1870* (Oxford, 1975) pp. 95–8.
18. Ellenberger, *History of the Basuto*, p. 233.
19. Casalis, *The Basutos*, pp. 71–2.
20. See e.g. Sanders, *Moshoeshoe*, pp. 14–15, 23, 32.
21. i.e. confiscate all a man's property (and sometimes banish him), a common punishment by a chief's court for serious offences.
22. Less far-sighted chiefs were frequently known to seize their wealthier subjects' property on a trumped-up charge of witchcraft.
23. Orpen, *History of the Basutus*, p. 4. See also Cape G. H. 14/7: Statement by Moshoeshoe to Wodehouse, 27 June 1864.
24. Casalis, *The Basutos*, p. 220.
25. Cape, N.A. 272: minutes of meeting, 20 Aug. 1873, encl. in Griffith to Molteno, no. 84, 27 Aug. 1873.
26. Sanders, *Moshoeshoe*, p. xv.
27. For the way in which the placing system enabled Moshoeshoe's descendants to gain increasingly greater control of the positions of authority in the country, see G. I. Jones, 'Chiefly Succession in Basutoland', in J. Goody (ed.), *Succession to High Office* (Cambridge, 1966) pp. 61–3, 68–9.
28. Orpen, *History of the Basutus*, p. 4.
29. The efforts of his many wives also enabled him to provide the food, beer and entertainment for retainers and visitors that were expected of a chief.
30. For a discussion of some factors making for tension in the Sotho nation, see A. Atmore, 'The passing of Sotho Independence 1865–70', in L. Thompson (ed.), *African Societies in southern Africa* (London, 1969) pp. 290–3.
31. A branch of the Khoikhoi, called 'Hottentots' by the colonists, who had been living in the Cape when the Dutch arrived but had been pushed inland as European settlement advanced. Another result of Kora raids was that the Sotho acquired horses and guns for the first time, both by capture and by trade.
32. Ellenberger, *History of the Basuto*, p. 236.
33. *Little Light of Basutoland*, no. 5 (May 1877) p. 4. However, the French Protestant mission remained by far the largest and most influential mission in the country for several decades. The Catholics were of the order of the Oblates of Mary Immaculate.
34. The recent complete disruption of Sotho society may at least partly explain the receptiveness of the Sotho to the new ideas of Christianity. The first convert

was baptised in August 1839 and by 1848 the number of full Church Members was 1,003 and included several members of Moshoeshoe's immediate family as well as some of his close advisers. Well over 2,000 attended church every Sunday. Sanders, *Moshoeshoe*, p. 124.

35. In the 1860s he did have a brief period of reaction against the missionaries.

36. Casalis, *The Basutos*, p. 228. Modern spelling of 'mekoa' is 'mokhoa' (plural: 'mekhoa'). Assisted by the missionaries, Moshoeshoe reduced three laws to writing after 1854: an ordinance prohibiting the liquor trade in Lesotho, a proclamation prohibiting the killing of people imputed to be witches, and a 'Law for Trade' decreeing that traders could not own land but merely hold it at the chief's pleasure and that in matters of debt they fell under his jurisdiction. See Sanders, *Moshoeshoe*, pp. 279, 281. George and Sofonia Moshoeshoe also claimed that their father had written laws on circumcision, theft, and the drinking of the local beer called *joala*. See *Cape Parl. Papers*, 1873, evidence, Appendix III, Special Commission on the Laws and Customs of the Basutos, pp. 43 and 46.

37. Cape, U.B.R., iv. 141–2: 'Notes on the Political and Social Position of the Basuto Tribe' by Rolland, 30 Mar. 1868.

38. Ellenberger, *History of the Basuto*, p. 280.

39. *Little Light of Basutoland*, no. 6 (June 1876) p. 23. However, he was unable to enforce this order outside his family, and the people under his immediate control, and in 1865, in a period of reaction against the missionaries, he insisted on boys from Christian homes being initiated. See Sanders, *Moshoeshoe*, pp. 127, 276.

40. Where the husband of a converted woman refused to allow her a divorce, or even a separation from him, the church would not condone her leaving her husband and living apart from him, since according to Sotho law this would also have resulted in her leaving her children. A polygamist's wife still living with her husband was not, however, admitted to church membership, although she could be admitted as a catechumen. S. Poulter, *Family Law and Litigation in Basotho Society* (Oxford, 1976) p. 67.

41. *Cape Parl. Papers*, 1873, Appendix III, Special Commission on the Laws and Customs of the Basutos, p. 27: Casalis to Griffith, 1 Oct. 1872. Part of the opposition was due to Moshoeshoe insisting that the women should still be treated as his wives in receiving tributary assistance in cultivating their lands.

42. For an account of Moshoeshoe's attitude towards Christianity, see Sanders, *Moshoeshoe*, pp. 126–32; Thompson, *Survival in Two Worlds*, pp. 70–105.

43. G. M. Theal (ed.), *Basutoland Records*, vol. i (Cape Town, 1883) 85–6: Moshoeshoe to Secretary to Government, 15 May 1845.

44. Molapo subsequently mendaciously claimed Moshoeshoe had ordered him not to fight the Boers so that his country could be used as a cattle refuge, place to grow corn, and rallying point when the Boers tired. See Cape, G. H. 14/7: Molapo's message to Currie, 29 Mar. 1868. Molapo was absolved from his allegiance to the Free State in April 1870 and only then formally rejoined the nation under the British.

45. Theal, *Basutoland Records*, iii. 813–14: Wodehouse to Buckingham, 17 Sept. 1867.

46. The missionaries at once complained to both the British and French authorities, who were sympathetic. See Theal, ibid. iii. 656: Rolland, Mabille

and Cochet to Wodehouse, 6 Apr. 1868; iii. 662–3: French consul at Cape Town to Wodehouse, 21 Apr. 1866; P.R.O., C.O. 48/432: Wodehouse to Cardwell, no. 44, 12 May 1866, minute by Cardwell, 21 June 1866.

47. P.R.O., C.O. 48/438: confidential memorandum for the British cabinet, Nov. 1867, following Wodehouse to Buckingham, no. 88, 17 Sept. 1867.
48. P.R.O., C.O. 48/432: Wodehouse to Cardwell, no. 43, 12 May 1866.
49. Cape, N.A. 272: minutes of meeting held 20 Aug. 1873, encl. in Griffith to Molteno, no. 85, 27 Aug. 1873; *Cape Parl. Papers*, G. 33–79, p. 34.

CHAPTER 2   CONFLICTING VALUES

This chapter is based on the following sources as well as those specifically cited in the footnotes: E. H. Ashton, *The Basuto* (London, 1952); E. H. Brookes, *The History of Native Policy in South Africa*, 2nd edn (Pretoria, 1927); P. Duncan, *Sotho Laws and Customs* (Cape Town, 1960); T. O. Elias, *The Nature of African Customary Law* (Manchester, 1956); M. Gluckman (ed.), *Ideas and Procedures in African Customary Law* (London, 1969); H. Kuper and L. Kuper (eds), *African Law: Adaptation and Development* (Berkeley, 1965); R. W. Lee, *Introduction to Roman-Dutch Law* (Oxford, 1915); J. Lewin, *An Outline of Native Law*, 4th edn (Cape Town, 1966); A. Ramolefe, 'Customary Law Inheritance and Succession', *Basutoland Notes and Records*, 5 (1966); I. Schapera (ed.), *The Bantu-speaking Tribes of South Africa* (London, 1937); V. G. J. Sheddick, *The Southern Sotho* (London, 1953); J. H. Simons, *African Women: Their Legal Status in South Africa* (London, 1968); G. Wille, *Principles of South African Law* (Cape Town, 1937); M. Wilson and L. Thompson (eds), *Oxford History of South Africa* (London, 1969); and many of the documents cited in other chapters.

1. There is evidence that in practice many commoners had only one wife, but chiefs, particularly the higher chiefs, had several. See C. W. de Kiewiet, 'Social and Economic Development in Native Tribal Life' in E. Walker (ed.), *The Cambridge History of the British Empire*, 2nd edn, vol. viii (Cambridge, 1963) pp. 839–40.
2. Except such personal property as weapons and clothing, which were owned individually.
3. Although at least two of the missionaries in Lesotho understood its social function. See L. Thompson, *Survival in Two Worlds*, p. 5. where he cites Casalis and Lemue.
4. [Original footnote to excerpt] It was only when wars ceased and the bodies of enemy warriors were no longer available for this purpose that the notorious medicine murders began. The victims of such murders were overpowered and rendered unconscious, and various parts of their bodies were removed before they were finally killed. See G. I. Jones, *Basutoland Medicine Murder* (HMSO, London, 1951).
5. Public meeting place of the chiefdom.
6. Sanders, *Moshoeshoe*, pp. 10–11.
7. E. Casalis, *My Life in Basutoland* (London, 1889) pp. 179–80.
8. There is some dispute as to whether *bohali* was always an essential element for a valid marriage. See Poulter, *Family Law*, pp. 150–2.

9. *Cape Parl. Papers*, 1873, Appendix III, Special Commission on the Laws and Customs of the Basutos, pp. 48–9: Sofonia Moshoeshoe's evidence, 4 Dec. 1872. But see S. A. Roberts, 'Introduction' in S. A. Roberts (ed.), *Law and the Family in Africa* (The Hague, 1977) pp. 7–8 on the dangers of using western categories to analyse African marriage law.

10. Poulter, *Family Law*, pp. 149–53, 153–4.

11. A 'house' was the unit of a wife and her children, to which attached certain property, rights and status. A junior wife was not given her own hut until after she had borne a child, and certain wives who were married as 'seed-raisers', servant wives or (for a man with a large number of wives), junior wives, did not found separate houses.

12. For every wife a man married he received additional fields from the communally-owned chiefdom lands.

13. [From original footnote to excerpt] Ellenberger, *History of the Basuto*, p. 279.

14. Sanders, *Moshoeshoe*, pp. 140–1.

15. The Cape Colony, which was soon to become the ruler of the Sotho, was governed in the nineteenth century by Roman-Dutch law, modified by English law after the Cape became an English colony.

16. Z. K. Matthews, 'Bantu Law and Western Civilization in South Africa: A Study in the Clash of Cultures', (Yale Univ. M. A. thesis, 1934) p. 163.

17. *Cape Parl. Papers*, 1873, Appendix III, Special Commission on the Laws and Customs of the Basutos, p. 45: George Moshoeshoe's evidence; p. 55: Chief Jobo's evidence.

18. M. Wilson, 'Co-operation and Conflict: The Eastern Cape Frontier' in Wilson and Thompson (eds), op. cit., i, 268–9.

19. See pp. 9, 10, 11.

20. The ward was an administrative territorial division invented by subsequent administrations, but the same remarks would have applied to every chiefdom.

21. Public meetings of all adult men in the chiefdom were called to publicise announcements and discuss major issues. At these meetings great freedom of speech was allowed.

22. I. Hamnett, *Chieftainship and Legitimacy* (London, 1975) p. 90.

23. Law is here used to cover both customs and commandments, breach of which rendered the offender liable to a specific penalty at the discretion of a judicial functionary, while breach of what is termed a custom would render an offender liable to abuse, ridicule or ostracism at the worst.

24. Usually at a special meeting attended by their close relatives and presided over by the head of the offender's family.

25. This remedy was not open to him where he was wronged by the senior chiefs of the chiefdom, since it was virtually unknown for a chief to be sued in his own court. If, when approached privately, a chief refused to make reparation, the man had no remedy except to transfer his allegiance to another chief, if he could.

26. Matthews, 'Bantu Law', p. 197. See also the description of Sotho chiefs' courts in J. C. MacGregor, 'Some Notes on the Basuto Tribal System, Political and Social', *The South African Journal of Science*, vi, 7(1910) 277.

27. Even if it was an appeal from a lower court, the whole case would have been heard again in full, with the original judge in addition explaining how he had reached his decision.

28. The Sotho distinguished between sorcery and witchcraft, but as both were held

to involve evil magic, as opposed to that used by doctors and diviners, the terms 'witchcraft', 'witches' and 'wizards' are used here, as they were by contemporary writers and legislators, to include sorcery.

29. I. Schapera, *Government and Politics in Tribal Society* (London, 1956) p. 79.
30. Money was foreign to southern African indigenous societies.
31. Certain individuals were believed to possess the power to cause harm to others by use of supernatural powers.
32. See, e.g., Casalis, *The Basutos*, pp. 282–3. Where the death sentence was passed for offences other than witchcraft, the offender was usually hurled over a sheer precipice.
33. An offshoot of this was the attack by missionaries on Sotho burial rites, which the Sotho considered essential to prevent the spirit of the deceased from bringing disaster on his descendants. See Thompson, *Survival in Two Worlds*, pp. 91–2.
34. Sanders, *Moshoeshoe*, p. 71.
35. *Cape Parl. Papers*, G. 16–76, p. 15: RaMatšeatsana's speech at the annual *pitso*, 4 Nov. 1875.
36. It should also be borne in mind that the wider context of southern African economic developments, outlined on pp. 2–3, lies behind this micro-study of interaction in Basutoland.

CHAPTER 3   INTERREGNUM

1. Sanders, *Moshoeshoe*, p. 305.
2. For a detailed discussion of Wodehouse's manoeuvre, see Benyon, 'Basutoland and the High Commission', pp. 178 *et seq.*
3. See e.g. Theal, *Basutoland Records*, iii. 143, 144: Minutes of Conferences, 11–12 Feb. 1862; Cape, U.B.R., v. 331: Bowker to Wodehouse, 23 Sep. 1869.
4. P.R.O., C.O. 48/441: Wodehouse to Buckingham, no. 31, 2 May 1868.
5. Cape, U.B.R., iv. 125–51: 'Notes on the Political and Social Position of the Basuto Tribe', 30 Mar. 1868.
6. This was a more radical suggestion than it sounds. As E. H. Ashton says: 'In the old days, recognized doctors, officially attached to the chief as rainmakers, diviners, or keepers of war medicine, ranked next to the chief himself in importance'. See 'Medicine, Magic, and Sorcery among the Southern Sotho', *Communications of the School of African Studies, University of Cape Town*, new series, 10 (Dec. 1943) 3.
7. Cape, P.M. 259: copy of the original notes of the Rev. J. T. Daniel, who acted as interpreter to Wodehouse at the meeting; P.R.O., C.O. 48/441: regulations enclosed in Wodehouse to Buckingham, no. 31, 2 May 1868. For a discussion of the shaky legality of the High Commissioner's rule in Basutoland from 1868 to 1871, see Benyon, 'Basutoland and the High Commission', pp. 266–7.
8. P.R.O., C.O. 48/441: Wodehouse to Buckingham, no. 31, 2 May 1868.
9. According to s. 20, hut tax could be paid in money, stock or grain. A certain percentage, it had been agreed earlier, was to go to Moshoeshoe. See Cape, N.A. 275: Petitition enclosed in Rolland to Ayliff, no. 37, 20 July 1878.
10. e.g. Cape, G.H. 14/7: Moshoeshoe to Bowker, 24 June 1868, informing Bowker that he had ordered his people, when they found a murderer, to take him to Bowker 'that you may judge him by the law laid down for murderers'.

On the impossibility of implementing the regulations, see *Cape Parl. Papers*, A. 18–72, Report of the Select Committee on Basuto Regulations, evidence by Bowker.

11. P.R.O., C.O. 48/441: Wodehouse to Buckingham, no. 31, 2 May 1868.
12. e.g. Cape, G.H. 14/7: Bowker to Wodehouse, 23 Oct. 1868; 16 Nov. 1868; 3 Dec. 1868.
13. The convention of 1854 by which the British had recognised the independence of the Orange Free State.
14. *Brit. Parl. Papers*, 1870 xlix [C. 18] pp. 18–19: minutes of the Aliwal North conference.
15. Sometimes spelt 'Letsea' in contemporary documents.
16. Cape, U.B.R., v. 96–110: account of Korokoro *Pitso*, 22 Feb. 1869, in the *Friend of the Free State*, 25 Feb. 1869.
17. *Brit. Parl. Papers*, 1870, xlix [C. 18] pp. 69–70: Daumas to Chesson, 2 Nov. 1869.
18. For an account of the background of this move, see Atmore, 'The Passing of Sotho Independence 1865–1870', op. cit., pp. 297–8.
19. *Brit. Parl. Papers*, 1870 xlix [C. 99] p. 3: Wodehouse to Granville, 19 Mar. 1870.
20. See e.g. Cape, G. H. 14/7: Bowker to Wodehouse, 3 Dec. 1868; 20 Mar. 1869.
21. Sanders, *Moshoeshoe*, p. 310.
22. *Cape Parl. Papers*, G. 27–74, p. 22; Cape, G. H. 14/7: A. Davies to Bowker, 6 June 1869.
23. There was strong rivalry between the French Protestant and Catholic missionaries in attempts to convert Moshoeshoe, who for a long time delayed, not wishing to offend either. For the rival Catholic and Protestant versions of Moshoeshoe's conversion, see Sanders, *Moshoeshoe*, pp. 312–15; Thompson, *Survival in Two Worlds*, pp. 320–3.
24. C. W. Mackintosh, *Coillard of the Zambesi* (London, 1907) p. 193.
25. See p. 38.
26. Cape, U.B.R., vi. 81: Barkly to Kimberley, 18 May 1871.
27. Sometimes spelt Masupha or Masupa by contemporary writers.
28. Cape, U.B.R., vi. 123–4: returns of revenue received up to 31 May 1871.
29. P.R.O., C.O. 48/450: Wodehouse to Granville, no. 62, 14 May 1870, enclosing regulations.
30. Although by this date rape was almost never punished by the death penalty. See A. Sachs, *Justice in South Africa* (London, 1973) p. 57. Cape and Sotho law differed on which offences were punishable by death. In Sotho law murder and arson with intent to kill (capital offences in Cape law) were usually punishable by fines. Death was inflicted 'for acts of treason against the chief, and for being pronounced by a witchfinder guilty of having caused any great calamity. A man caught in the act of stealing cattle at night could be killed with impunity. A notorious thief whose conduct was likely to get the tribe into difficulty was usually put to death by order of his chief.' See G. M. Theal, *History of South Africa, 1854–1872* (London, 1900) pp. 312–13, n. 2. According to George Moshoeshoe, a thief who resisted when apprehended could be killed. See *Cape Parl. Papers*, 1873, Appendix III, Special Commission on the Laws and Customs of the Basutos, evidence, p. 47.
31. Later altered to three magistrates. See Proclamation 51, 23 Aug. 1871.

32. P.R.O., C.O. 48/450: minute of 1 July 1870 in enclosure 1 of Wodehouse to Granville, no. 62, 14 May 1870.
33. *Cape Parl. Papers*, C. 3–85, p. 7.
34. But see p. 70 below.
35. Cape, N.A. 272: Tsekelo to Griffith, 30 Aug. 1873, encl. in Griffith to Molteno, 11 Sept. 1873.
36. Ibid.
37. In addition, it directly affected the bride's senior maternal uncle (*malome*), who was in certain circumstances entitled to receive from the head of her family a portion of the *bohali* paid on her marriage, in return for which he had certain obligations to her and her children.
38. As a result of the earlier regulations, between March 1869 and June 1871, 64 marriages were registered in Basutoland. Cape, U.B.R., vi. 123–4: Revenue Return, 3 July 1871.
39. *Cape Parl. Papers*, A. 18–72, Report of the Select Committee on Basuto Regulations, evidence, pp. 7–8.
40. It is difficult to gauge what proportion of the Sotho paid this charge in practice after the regulations came into force, as income from registration fees did not form a separate item in the later annual revenue accounts. But in the 1873 commission report it was pointed out that 'the law with regard to the registration of marriage, as far as the heathen Basutos are concerned, has been quite inoperative', and at the 1874 annual *pitso* one headman remarked 'I see only the Christian people bringing their half crowns to register their marriages, but not the heathen people'. At the 1876 annual *pitso* Sotho rebuked their countrymen for not paying the registration fee. On the other hand, in December 1876 Austen was able to report that in his district the principal court work, of which there appears to have been no dearth, consisted of petty assaults, and civil cases arising from the marriage laws. It seems probable that as the magistrates tried an increasing number of cases, more marriages were registered. See *Cape Parl. Papers*, 1873, Appendix III, Report of the Commission on the Laws and Customs of the Basutos, evidence, p. 6; G. 21–75, p. 24; G. 12–77, pp. 13, 16, 19.
41. Lesotho, S9/1/3/1: Griffith to Surmon, 11 July 1872.
42. e.g. *Little Light of Basutoland*, no. 11, Nov. 1874, reporting on such protests at the 1874 annual *pitso*.
43. *Cape Parl. Papers*, A. 18–72, Report of the Select Committee on Basuto Regulations, evidence, p. 6.
44. Tylden, *The Rise of the Basuto*, p. 114; Brookes, *History of Native Policy*, p. 186. The regulations of 1871, to which Tylden and Brookes both refer, were identical on this point to the 1870 regulations.
45. This was not interpreted to include rainmakers, despite Rolland's recommendation in his memorandum. See J. Widdicombe, *Fourteen Years in Basutoland* (London, 1891) p. 63.
46. *Little Light of Basutoland*, no. 8, Aug. 1872, p. 31.
47. Theal, *History of South Africa, 1854–1872*, p. 313, n.1.
48. See p. 11.
49. Cape, G.H. 14/7: Austen to Bowker, 26 Jan. 1871.
50. Cape, U.B.R., v. 553–4: Sotho chiefs to Bowker, 22 Dec. 1870.
51. *Cape Parl. Papers*, A. 4–71, p. 2: Kimberley to Barkly, 17 Oct. 1870.

52. Cape, G.H. 14/7: Bowker to Southey, 10 Nov. 1870.
53. Cape, U.B.R., vi. 92–3: Barkly to Kimberley, 18 May 1871.
54. At his meeting with Letsie and his retinue on 16 March 1871, Letsie and the other chiefs, after hearing his plans for the future administration of Basutoland, professed themselves happy with whatever arrangements he chose to make. Cape, G.H. 14/7: minutes of meeting between Barkly and Letsie, 16 Mar. 1871; U.B.R., vi. 88: Barkly to Kimberley, 18 May 1871.
55. Ibid., vi. 99–100.
56. *Cape Parl. Papers*, C. 1–71: Report of the Select Committee on the Basutoland Annexation Bill.
57. Only Cape law had been officially recognised in the Ciskei, with the result that the Africans there had generally ignored the magistrates' courts and continued to take their cases to the chiefs' 'illegal' courts. See S. B. Burman, 'Cape Policies Towards African Law in Cape Tribal Territories, 1872–1883' (Oxford Univ. D.Phil. thesis, 1973).
58. P.R.O., C.O. 48/455: minutes encl. in Barkly to Kimberley, no. 53, 31 May 1871.
59. Lesotho, S9/1/1/1: Griffith to Barkly, 7 Aug. 1871.
60. Cape, U.B.R., vi. 224–5: Barkly to Griffith, 12 Aug. 1871; Lesotho, S9/1/3/1: Griffith to Letsie, 26 Aug. 1871.

CHAPTER 4   THE CAPE ADMINISTRATION

I am indebted to Dr C. Saunders for the loan of his B.A. Hons. thesis, which was especially useful for this chapter: C. C. Saunders, 'The Cape Native Affairs Department and African Administration on the Eastern Frontier under the Molteno Ministry, 1872–78' (Cape Town Univ. B.A. Hons. thesis, 1964).

1. Cape, G. H. 31/13: Barkly to Carnarvon, no. 33, 27 Mar. 1876, quoted in P. Lewsen, 'The First Crisis in Responsible Government in the Cape Colony', *Archives Year Book for South African History* (1942) ii. 234. The Governor/High Commissioner was paid from colonial revenues, which gave Cape parliamentarians a reason for querying his actions. See C.O. 48/510 (Treasury): Cole to Herbert, 29 Jan. 1884, and minute by Fairfield, 10 May 1889.
2. For an account of the way in which it led to the dismissal of the Molteno Ministry, see Benyon, 'Basutoland and the High Commission', pp. 326–42.
3. There is some confusion about the date of his birth, but he himself gives this date. See C. Brownlee, *Reminiscences of Kaffir Life and History* (Lovedale, 1896) p. 347. For the following details, see ibid., pp. 2–12. See also C. C. Saunders' biographical introduction to the Killie Campbell Reprint edition.
4. B. A. Tindall (ed.), *James Rose Innes—Autobiography* (Cape Town, 1949) p. 23.
5. Although he usually used an interpreter when colonists attended his meetings. See J. W. Macquarrie (ed.), *The Reminiscences of Sir Walter Stanford*, vol. i (Cape Town, 1958) p. 70.
6. e.g. In his report in the Cape Native Blue Book for 1875 Brownlee attributed to the Sotho as well as the Xhosa a prohibition on marriage between cousins. In fact the Sotho regarded marriages between cousins as highly desirable. See

Cape Parl. Papers, A. 6–79, Select Committee on Basutoland Hostilities, pp. xl–xlii: appendix D.

7. On all questions concerning Africans beyond the border the High Commissioner had retained overriding control.

8. In all, Brownlee spent more than a year of his five-year term of office on the frontier, and also spent over five months in England in 1875–6 for medical treatment.

9. e.g. *Cape Argus*, 11 Jan. 1881; *Graham's Town Journal*, 4 Apr. 1881.

10. Tindall, *James Rose Innes*, p. 22.

11. *Cape Parl. Papers*, G. 110–83, evidence, p. 414: questions 5717 & 5718.

12. *Cape Times*, vol. xii, no. 2657, 8 May 1884: General Charles Gordon's memo. of 1882.

13. Proclamation no. 51, 23 Aug. 1871.

14. *Government Gazette*, no. 4365, 25 Aug. 1871: government notice no. 311, 24 Aug. 1871, stated that the Governor had appointed *James* Surmon, Inspector of Armed and Mounted Police, to act as Resident Magistrate of the District of Berea, but judging from the correspondence files in the Cape and Lesotho Archives, this is a misprint for W. H. Surmon.

15. Cape, U.B.R., vi. 74: Surmon to Southey, 17 May 1871.

16. Cape, G. H. 14/7: minutes of meeting between Barkly and Letsie, 16 Mar. 1871; Cape, U.B.R., vi. 87: Barkly to Kimberley, 18 May 1871.

17. P. Hadley (ed.), *Doctor to Bosuto, Boer & Briton 1887–1906* (Cape Town, 1972) p. 91. He appears in Sotho praise-poems as 'Majorobello'.

18. Maseru, the 'Place of the Red Sandstone', became the headquarters of the Cape Administration in Basutoland after Bowker moved his camp there from Mokema in March 1869. See Sanders, *Moshoeshoe*, pp. 308–9.

19. Lesotho, S9/1/3/1: Griffith to Casalis, 17 Nov. 1871; E. W. Smith, *The Mabilles of Basutoland* (London, 1939) p. 205.

20. Samuel Rolland, b. Switzerland 13 May 1801; d. Hermon, Basutoland, 18 Jan. 1873. Arrived South Africa 1829, first established a mission station in Lesotho in 1835.

21. Cape, G. H. 14/7: Bowker to Southey, 10 Nov. 1870.

22. Tylden, *The Rise of the Basuto*, p. 116.

23. e.g. Cape, N. A. 272: Austen to Griffith, 31 Jan. 1873, encl. in Griffith to Molteno, no. 33, 14 Mar. 1873; N. A. 273: Austen to Griffith, 19 Apr. 1876.

24. Cape, N. A. 275: Rolland to Brownlee, no. 12, 25 Jan. 1878: Lesotho, S9/1/3/2: Griffith to Austen, 21 Oct. 1871; Griffith to Austen, 19 Jan. 1874.

25. Cape, G. H. 14/7: Surmon to Bowker, 13 Nov. 1868; Wodehouse to Bowker (Private), 4 Jan. 1870; *Cape Parl. Papers*, A. 43–71, A. 44–71 and A. 45–71: Petitions of Tozane, Tsueu Lepota, and George Parkies respectively.

26. Cape, G. H. 14/7: Bowker to Wodehouse, 23 Oct. 1868; Wodehouse to Burnet, 17 Nov. 1868; *Cape Parl. Papers*, A. 6–79, Select Committee on Basutoland Hostilities, evidence, pp. 15–16.

27. Lesotho, S9/1/1/1: Griffith to Southey, 8 Aug. 1871.

28. See Lesotho, S9/1/3/1: Griffith to Masopha, 12 Aug. 1871.

29. Cape, N.A.274: Griffith to Brownlee, no. 13, 21 Apr. 1876; N.A.273: no. 21, 31 May 1876.

30. Cape, N.A. 274: Letsie to Bartle Frere, 10 Sept. 1877, encl. in Rolland to Brownlee, no. 87, 22 Sept. 1877. Rolland reported that 'the petition is a

perfectly spontaneous one, without any prompting from any Government officer or European in the country. It was drawn up in English almost *verbatim* from the instructions of Letsie assisted by his brothers Tsekelo and Masupha and by some of his sons and Councillors.'

31. Ibid., Rolland to Brownlee, no. 87, 22 Sept. 1877.

32. But Basutoland does not appear to have been unique in this respect. The Chief Magistrate of the Transkei, for example, complained that he quite often was obliged to work from 9 a.m. to 12 midnight. See Cape, N.A. 2, p. 135: Blyth to Ayliff, no. 158, 21 Dec. 1878.

33. Lesotho, S9/1/3/2: Griffith to Civil Commissioner, Aliwal North, 24 June 1872.

34. Cape, N.A. 274: Griffith to Brownlee, no. 21, 27 Feb. 1877; N.A. 275: Bowker to Ayliff, no. 25, 18 March 1878; Griffith to Ayliff, no. 69, 4 Dec. 1878, minute by Ayliff, 17 Dec. 1878.

35. Cape, N.A. 273: Griffith to Brownlee, 2 Feb. 1875.

36. Lesotho, S9/1/3/2: Griffith to Rolland, 30 Apr. 1873; Griffith to Austen, 19 Jan. 1874; S9/2/2/3: Griffith to Rolland, 18 Feb. 1876.

37. Cape, N.A. 275: Bowker to Ayliff, no. 25, 18 Mar. 1878. The building about which Bowker was complaining was in fact an improvement on the one in which Griffith had worked until 1874, when some of the original sod and raw brick walls collapsed after heavy rains. See J. Walton, 'Old Maseru', *Basutoland Notes and Records*, 4 (1963–4) 7.

38. *Cape Parl. Papers*, G. 16–76, p. 18: Census Return, 28 Apr. 1875.

39. By the end of 1881 there were only twenty-seven traders left in Basutoland, as against twenty-two in the Thaba-Bosiu District alone the previous year. See Cape, N.A. 281: Return by Orpen, 21 Jan. 1882.

40. Orpen, *History of the Basutus*, p. 8. There were no professional traders in pre-*lifaqane* Sotho society, but itinerant white traders had made their appearance before this date.

41. Lesotho, S9/2/1/1: Griffith to Southey, 26 Aug. 1872; *Cape Parl. Papers*, G. 27–73, p. 1; G. 27–74, p. 23; Cape, N.A. 274: Rolland to Brownlee, 28 Dec. 1877.

42. As early as 1872 Griffith, after listing the main items purchased by the Sotho at trading stores, added: 'As nearly all these articles pay a considerable duty it will be seen that colonial revenue benefits largely by the Basuto trade'. See *Cape Parl. Papers*, A. 23–73, p. 2: Griffith to Southey, 26 Aug. 1872.

43. e.g. Undated article from unnamed newspaper, probably the *Northern Post*, encl. in Cape N.A. 275: Griffith to Brownlee, no. 72, 9 Dec. 1878.

44. Cape, N.A. 275: Griffith to Ayliff, no. 72, 9 Dec. 1878; N.A. 276; Griffith to Ayliff, no. 102, 3 Dec. 1879.

45. T. W. Irvine, *British Basutoland and the Basutos* (London, 1881) p. 22.

46. e.g. Cape, U.B.R., vi. 281–6: Mabille's statement encl. in Griffith to Barkly, 1 Sept. 1871; vi. 309–10: Southey to Griffith, 18 Sept. 1871; *Little Light of Basutoland*, no. 5, May 1872, pp. 17–20; no. 6, June 1872, pp. 21–4; no. 7, July 1872, pp. 25–8; no. 9, Sept. 1872, pp. 33–5; no. 11, Nov. 1873, pp. 41–4; no. 1, Jan. 1876, p. 2; no. 6, June 1876, pp. 23–5.

47. Lesotho, S9/1/3/2: Bright to Mabille, 28 Mar. 1872; Cape, N.A. 276: Mabille to Griffith, 6 Jan. 1879, encl. in Griffith to Ayliff, no. 4F, 17 Jan. 1879.

48. Cape, U.B.R., vi. 452: Barkly to Kimberley, 1 May 1872; *Cape Parl. Papers*, G. 27–73, pp. 4–5.

49. In 1871 *Leselinyana* had 480 subscribers. Between 1871 and 1877 the number of children attending school rose from 2,129 to approximately 3,000. Adults attended the mission schools as well. See *Cape Parl. Papers*, A. 23–73, p. 3: Griffith to Southey, 26 Aug. 1872; Cape, N.A. 274: Rolland to Brownlee, 28 Dec. 1877.
50. Lesotho, S9/1/3/1: Griffith to Casalis, 17 Nov. 1871; Smith, *The Mabilles*, p. 205.
51. e.g. *Little Light of Basutoland*, no. 1, Jan. 1875, p. 2; no. 11, Nov. 1877, p. 4; Cape, N.A. 276: Secretary, Paris Evangelical Missionary Society Conference to Griffith, 24 Apr. 1879, encl. in Griffith to Ayliff, 27 Apr. 1879.
52. Though both Catholic and Church of England missionaries viewed Sotho customs less severely, these missions were relatively newly established and small in this period. See Cape, N.A. 274: Rolland to Brownlee, 28 Dec. 1877.
53. Undated article from newspaper, probably the *Northern Post*, encl. in Cape, N.A. 275: Griffith to Brownlee, no. 72, 9 Dec. 1878. Sir Arthur Gordon was Governor of the Fiji Islands.
54. Lesotho, S9/1/3/2: circular by Griffith to Basutoland magistrates, 11 June 1872.
55. *Cape Parl. Papers*, G. 27–73, p. 2.
56. Cape, N.A. 272: Austen's and Rolland's annual reports for 1872, encl. in Griffith to Molteno, no. 33, 15 Mar. 1873.
57. *Cape Parl. Papers*, G. 12–77, p. 7.

CHAPTER 5   NEUTRALISING THE CHIEFS

1. Sanders, *Moshoeshoe*, pp. 116–17; Thompson, *Survival in Two Worlds*, pp. 180–1; both cite Arbousset to P.E.M.S. Committee, 21 Jan. 1848, *J.M.E.*, xxiii (1848) 29–302.
2. He was born in or about 1811.
3. Cape, N.A. 275: Rolland to Ayliff, no. 36, 19 July 1878.
4. Cape, U.B.R., vi. 397: Bell to Griffith, 17 Feb. 1872.
5. Sanders, *Moshoeshoe*, pp. 117–18.
6. Cape, N.A. 272: Bell to Griffith, 19 May 1873, encl. in Griffith to Molteno, no. 56, 26 May 1873. Molapo, by his submission to the Orange Free State, had escaped the devastating and humbling effects of the last two wars against the Boers, and displayed a more independent approach in his dealings with Cape officials than did the other chiefs. See Cape, U.B.R., vi. 411–12: Griffith to Southey, 27 Feb. 1872.
7. Cape, N.A. 273: Bell to Griffith, 3 May 1874, encl. in Griffith to Brownlee, no. 8, 11 May 1875.
8. Cape, N.A. 272: Bell to Griffith, 28 Aug. 1873, encl. in Griffith to Brownlee, no. 91, 9 Sept. 1873. These were in fact probably from the Swazi refugees who joined Molapo in the early 1860s. Until these police were recruited, Bell had no police at all. See Sanders, *Moshoeshoe*, p. 245; Cape, U.B.R., vi. 413: Griffith to Southey, 27 Feb. 1872. For an example of police being intimidated by Jonathan, Molapo's son, see Cape, N.A. 272: complaint by Jan Makhatlane, 17 Oct. 1873, encl. in Griffith to Molteno, no. 111, 28 Oct. 1873.

9. Ibid., Bell to Griffith, 8 Feb. 1874, encl. in Griffith to Brownlee, no. 3, 26 Feb. 1874.
10. Ibid., Bell to Griffith (Private), 19 Oct. 1873. Whether Molapo's motive was intimidation, as Bell claimed, is not entirely clear. The Rev. François Coillard, his missionary, wrote: 'my opinion is that he had some undefined fear at the thought of going to court, before a new and strange power whose attributions are not yet fully known to the people of the country. He would therefore feel some security in having with him some of his men. This is, I believe, the reason why he requested me also to be present.' See ibid., Coillard to Bell, 7 Nov. 1873, encl. in Griffith to Brownlee, no. 3, 26 Feb. 1874. In his covering letter, Griffith agreed with the Rev. Coillard. The correspondence on this incident is reproduced in full in S. B. Burman, *The Justice of the Queen's Government*, African Social Research Documents (Leiden/Cambridge, 1976) pp. 58–62.
11. e.g. Cape, N.A. 272, Bell to Griffith, 19 May 1873, encl. in Griffith to Molteno, no. 56, 26 May 1873; Bell to Griffith, 28 Aug. 1873, encl. in Griffith to Brownlee, no. 91, 9 Sept. 1873; Bell to Griffith, 8 Feb. 1874, encl. in Griffith to Brownlee, no. 3, 26 Feb. 1874; Cape, N.A. 273: Bell to Griffith, 3 May 1874, encl. in Griffith to Brownlee, no. 8, 11 May 1875.
12. e.g. Cape, N.A. 272: Griffith to Brownlee, no. 6, 13 May 1874.
13. Lesotho, S9/1/3/2: Griffith to Bell and Surmon, 15 July 1873.
14. *Cape Parl. Papers*, G. 46–75, p. 6.
15. Lesotho, S9/1/3/2: Griffith to Letsie, 22 Nov. 1873.
16. G. Lagden, *The Basutos*, vol. ii (London, 1909) p. 483. The Sotho were, however, eventually obliged to surrender about two-thirds of the stock they captured to the Natal forces. See J. M. Mohapeloa, *Government by Proxy* (London, 1971) p. 24.
17. Cape, N.A. 272: Bell to Griffith, 9 Dec. 1873.
18. *Cape Parl. Papers*, G. 27–74, p. 35.
19. 'Another version of the incident says that Molapo was intent on protecting Langalibalele and sent Jonathan to conduct him safely down, but that Jonathan, tempted by the cattle, arrested him and brought him to Lefi's Nek, and that he and not Molapo received the cattle as a reward.' R. Dove, 'The History of Basutoland "Camps": 2. Leribe (Hlotse)', *Basutoland Notes and Records* 1 (1959) 25.
20. Cape, N.A. 272: Bell to Griffith, 9 Dec. 1873, encl. in Griffith to Molteno, no. 124, 9 Dec. 1873.
21. Ibid.
22. Ibid., Molapo to Brownlee, 17 Feb. 1874.
23. Ibid., Griffith to Molteno, no. 93, 15 Sept. 1874, and enclosed statement.
24. Cape, N.A. 273: Bell to Griffith, 19 June 1875, encl. in Griffith to Brownlee, no. 78, 26 June 1875.
25. Lesotho, S9/1/1/1: Griffith to Barkly, no. 2, 18 Aug. 1871.
26. Cape, U.B.R., vi. 93: Barkly to Kimberley, 18 May 1871.
27. Lesotho, S9/1/1/1: Griffith to Barkly, no. 2, 18 Aug. 1871. See also Cape, U.B.R., vi. 376–8: Griffith to Southey, 3 Feb. 1872.
28. Cape, N.A. 272: Barkly to Griffith, 2 Sept. 1871, encl. in Griffith to Brownlee, no. 12, 21 Nov. 1873.
29. In 1871 Griffith was informed that Letsie had ordered Masopha to leave Thaba-Bosiu and that Masopha had replied that he would use force to resist

any attempt to move him: see Lesotho, S9/1/1/1: Griffith to Barkly, 7 Aug. 1871. Masopha and Letsie had always been rivals. See Smith, *The Mabilles*, p. 298.

30. Cape, N.A. 272: Bell to Griffith, 10 Nov. 1873, encl. in Griffith to Brownlee, no. 12, 21 Nov. 1873.
31. Ibid., Griffith to Brownlee, no. 1, 30 Jan. 1874.
32. *Cape Parl. Papers*, G. 27–74, p. 33.
33. Cape, N.A. 272: Griffith to Brownlee, no. 7, 14 May 1874.
34. Ibid., minutes of the annual *pitso*, 20 Aug. 1873, encl. in Griffith to Molteno, no. 85, 27 Aug. 1873, p. 44.
35. *Cape Parl. Papers*, G. 21–75, p. 9.
36. Ibid., G. 16–76, pp. 16–17.
37. Lesotho, S9/1/3/2: Griffith to Masopha, 8 Dec. 1875.
38. See Cape, N.A. 273: Griffith to Brownlee, no. 17, 20 Oct. 1876.
39. *Little Light of Basutoland*, no. 2, Feb. 1877, p. 1.
40. Cape, N.A. 277: C. G. H. Bell to Griffith, 3 Feb. 1880, encl. in Griffith to Ayliff, no. 26, 10 Feb. 1880.
41. The boy was born of a union with Molapo's eldest son, for which Molapo cattle had deliberately not been acepted. See *Cape Parl. Papers*, A. 6–79, Select Committee on Basutoland Hostilities, pp. xl–xliii: appendix D; Jones 'Chiefly Succession', op. cit., pp. 70–1; cf. J. Widdicombe, *In the Lesuto* (London, 1895) p. 332; Poulter, *Family Law*, pp. 149–53.
42. Surmon had moved there in mid-1877 to replace Rolland as Assistant Magistrate of Thaba-Bosiu.
43. Cape, N.A. 275: Rolland to Ayliff, no. 36, 19 July 1878. This description is closely corroborated by that of the Church of England missionary, the Rev. J. Widdicombe, in his book *In the Lesuto*, pp. 331–3.
44. These are the names given to them by the missionaries. Nehemiah (Sekhonyana) was the son of Moshoeshoe's third wife, George (Tlali) was the son of his fifth wife, and Sofonia (Pii) was the son of his sixth wife.
45. Cape, G. H. 14/7: Austen to Bowker, 26 Jan. 1871.
46. Proclamation no. 74, 6 Nov. 1871.
47. See p. 46.
48. *Cape Parl. Papers*, A. 18–72, Select Committee on the Basuto Regulations, pp. 20–2: Petition from the Basuto People praying for Representation in Parliament, 25 Feb. 1872.
49. Cape, U.B.R., vi. 449: Barkly to Kimberley, 1 May 1872, vi. 471–2: Griffith to Southey, 24 June 1872; vi. 516–18: Griffith to Southey, 7 Sept. 1872; *Cape Parl. Papers*, A. 18–72, Select Committee on the Basuto Regulations, appendix A, p. 17.
50. Rhodes House, MSS. Brit. Emp. s. 18 (Anti-Slavery Society Papers), C140/226a: Mabille to Chesson, 12 Jan. 1881.
51. *Cape Parl. Papers*. A. 18–72, Select Committee on the Basuto Regulations, pp. 22–3: Southey to Griffith, 25 Mar. 1872.
52. Ibid., pp. 17–18: appendix A.
53. It was revived in 1878, without result. See J. M. Orpen, *Some Principles of Native Government Illustrated* (Cape Town, 1880) pp. 52–5: Petition of the Chief of the People of Basutoland, 1878. However, as early as 1874 Tsekelo was advocating a council of chiefs and headmen to advise Griffith—again without result. See

Cape Parl. Papers, G. 21–75, p. 19; G. 17–78, p. 23.

54. See pp. 76–7.

55. i.e. Ntsane, son of Moshoeshoe's fourth wife, Tlali or George, Pii or Sofonia, and Tsekelo, a full brother of Sofonia. Nehemiah was not living in Basutoland at this time.

56. Cape, N.A. 275: Rolland to Ayliff, no. 37, 20 July 1878.

57. Cape, P.M. 259: Griffith to Scanlen, 12 Dec. 1881.

58. Cape, N.A. 279: George Moshoeshoe to Orpen, 27 Dec. 1881, encl. in Orpen to Sauer, no. 2/352, 30 Dec. 1881.

59. Cape, N.A. 272: Griffith to Brownlee, no. 11, 25 Nov. 1876; N.A. 274: Griffith to Brownlee, no. 40, 16 May 1877.

60. *Cape Parl. Papers*, G. 21–75, p. 2; see also pp. 17–18: Sofonia Moshoeshoe's speech at the 1874 annual *pitso* describing the visit.

61. e.g. Cape, U.B.R., vi. 360–1: Bell to Griffith, 22 Jan. 1872; vi. 380–1: Griffith to Southey, 7 Feb. 1872; N.A. 273: Griffith to Brownlee, no. 8, 18 Apr. 1876; N.A. 274: Griffith to Brownlee, no. 34, 9 May 1877.

62. Ibid., Griffith to Brownlee, no. 49, 19 June 1877.

63. *Cape Parl. Papers*, G. 27–74, p. 35; Lesotho, S9/1/3/2: Griffith to Letsie, 30 Jan. 1874.

64. e.g. *Cape Parl. Papers*, A. 49–79, p. 16: Rolland to Hope, 30 Nov. 1877.

65. e.g. Cape, N.A. 276: Griffith to Ayliff, no. 39, 26 Feb. 1879. Moshoeshoe had also used his junior sons as messengers and negotiators.

66. Lesotho, S9/1/3/2: circular from Griffith to Resident and Assistant Resident Magistrates, Basutoland, 22 Apr. 1873.

67. See p. 22. above.

68. J. T. Thomson, 'Capitation in Colonial and Post-Colonial Niger: Analysis of the Effects of an Imposed Head Tax System on Rural Political Organization' in S. B. Burman and B. E. Harrell-Bond (eds), *The Imposition of Law* (New York, 1979).

69. Lesotho, S9/1/3/2: circular from Griffith to Basutoland magistrates, 21 Aug. 1871.

70. See pp. 86–9.

71. e.g. Cape, N.A. 275: Rolland to Ayliff, no. 18, 25 Feb. 1878. In terms of s.5 of both the 1871 and 1877 regulations, the magistrate had an obligation to notify a chief of changes in land allocation.

72. e.g. Cape, U.B.R., vi. 355–6: Bell to Griffith, 17 Jan. 1872; Lesotho, S9/1/3/2: Griffith to Bell, 26 May 1875; Cape, N.A. 276: Surmon to Griffith, 17 Feb. 1879, encl. in Griffith to Ayliff, no. 31, 19 Feb. 1879; Austen to Griffith, no. 75, 29 Nov. 1879, encl. in Griffith to Ayliff, no. 108, 8 Dec. 1879; N.A. 277: Bell to Griffith, 3 Feb. 1880, encl. in Griffith to Ayliff, no. 26, 10 Feb. 1880.

73. After May 1875 messengers from chiefs outside Basutoland were required to report themselves at the nearest Basutoland magistracy to the border. See Cape, N.A. 273: Griffith to Molteno, no. 63, 26 May 1875, minute by Brownlee, 7 June 1875.

74. Apart from the fact that traders' stores were used as informal meeting places where a good deal of gossip took place, traders would report to magistrates if there was any sudden demand for saddles and blankets, items needed by the Sotho when campaigning, e.g. Cape, N.A. 276: A. Barkly to Griffith, 15 Feb. 1879, encl. in Griffith to Ayliff, no. 31, 19 Feb. 1879; Surmon to Griffith, 24

Feb. 1879, encl. in Griffith to Ayliff, no. 36, 26 Feb. 1879.

75. Ibid., Griffith to Ayliff, no. 34, 24 Feb. 1879.
76. Cape, G.H. 14/7: Tsekelo and George Moshoeshoe to Wodehouse, 19 Apr. 1868. For an account of their earlier education in the Cape, see M. Damane and P. B. Sanders (eds), 'The story of the Sotho–Part I', *Mohlomi, Journal of Southern African Historical Studies*, ii (1978)
77. Cape, G.H. 14/7: Austen to Bowker, 26 Jan. 1871.
78. Ibid., Barkly to Griffith, 8 July 1871. The Sotho, on the basis of an agreement with Faku, the Mpondo chief, claimed that the Matatiele district of Nomansland on the other side of the Drakensberg was part of Lesotho, and from the first objected to its exclusion from the area defined by the British as Basutoland. Nehemiah and his followers had moved there.
79. Lesotho, S9/1/1/1: Griffith to Barkly, no. 6, 16 Aug. 1871; Cape, U.B.R., vi. 238–40: Tsekelo's speech in the minutes of the meeting.
80. Ibid., vi. 354: Griffith to Southey, 15 Jan. 1872.
81. Cape, N.A. 272: Tsekelo to Griffith, 27 June 1873, encl. in Griffith to Molteno, no. 71, 10 July 1873; Tsekelo to Griffith, 30 Aug. 1873, encl. in Griffith to Molteno, 11 Sept. 1873.
82. Ibid., Griffith to Molteno, no. 71, 10 July 1873; Griffith to Brownlee, no. 11, 28 Oct. 1873.
83. Cape, N.A. 273: Barkly's memo. on Griffith's letter to Molteno, no. 16, 23 Feb. 1876.
84. [Original footnote to excerpt] Cape, G.H. 14/6: Orpen to Burnet, 29 Nov. 1862.
85. Majara was the fourth son of Moshoeshoe by his first wife, but died young.
86. [Original footnote to excerpt] op. cit., Orpen to Burnet, 14 Nov. 1862, and Burnet to Travers, 1 and 17 Dec. 1862; *Friend of the Free State*, 21 Nov. 1862.
87. Sanders, *Moshoeshoe*, p. 280. See also Wodehouse's testimony on his bad character and past behaviour, in P.R.O., C.O. 48/449: Wodehouse to Granville, no. 22, 21 Feb. 1870.
88. Cape, N.A. 274: Rolland to Brownlee, no. 109, 19 Nov. 1877.
89. Cape, N.A. 273: Griffith to Brownlee, no. 7, 13 Apr. 1876.
90. Cape, N.A. 274: Rolland to Brownlee, no. 109, 19 Nov. 1877.
91. Ibid., enclosing A. Barkly to Rolland, 16 Nov. 1877.
92. Ibid., see Brownlee's footnote.
93. Significantly Molapo was not informed of the petition. See *Cape Parl. Papers*, G. 33–79, pp. 33–5.
94. Cape, N.A. 275: Rolland to Ayliff, no. 37, 20 July 1878. Rolland's judgement was confirmed when the 1878 annual *pitso* indignantly repudiated the petition. See *Cape Parl. Papers*, G. 33–79, pp. 31–6.

CHAPTER 6   WINNING OVER THE PEOPLE

1. Lesotho, S9/1/3/2: circular by Griffith to Basutoland magistrates, 30 Jan. 1872.
2. Ibid.
3. Cape, U.B.R., vi. 408–9: Griffith to Southey, 27 Feb. 1872.
4. There is however no evidence that, until the Cape Administration took charge,

people had refused to render *letsema* service. MacGregor writing in 1910 of this earlier period, pointed out that beef and beer were always supplied and provided the occasion for an enjoyable social gathering. MacGregor, 'Some Notes on the Basuto Tribal System, Political and Social', op. cit., p. 278.

5. See J. M. Mohapeloa, *Africans and their Chiefs* (Cape Town, 1945) p. 4.
6. Thompson, *Survival in Two Worlds*, p. 15.
7. Cape, U.B.R., vi. 408–11: Griffith to Southey, 28 Feb. 1872.
8. Ibid., vi. 397–8: Bell to Griffith, 17 Feb. 1872.
9. Ibid., vi. 405–14: Griffith to Southey, 27 Feb. 1872.
10. Ibid., vi. 436: Southey to Griffith, 16 Mar. 1872.
11. Ibid., vi. 437.
12. Lesotho, S9/1/3/2: circular from Griffith to Basutoland magistrates, 11 June 1872. *Letsema* continued to be a respectable enough institution for Griffith in 1873, when trying to recruit labour for the railway works near Port Elizabeth, to use the concept of *letsema* to convey to Letsie that the Sotho had an obligation to provide labourers for the Government. See ibid., Griffith to Letsie, 20 May 1873.
13. Cape, N. A. 150: Griffith to Southey, no. 88, 18 Sept. 1872. See minute of 21 Oct. 1872. The Nguni population lived mostly in separate villages under their own headmen, and kept up their own language, dress and customs. Rolland characterised the Sotho attitude to them as 'a kind of good natured contempt for their inferior intelligence, industry and morality'. See Cape, N.A. 274: Rolland to Brownlee, 28 Dec. 1877.
14. Ibid., Griffith to Molteno, no. 109, 17 Dec. 1872.
15. Lesotho, S9/1/3/2: Griffith to Rolland, 23 June 1873.
16. *Cape Parl. papers*, G. 47–82, p. 158: Rolland to Orpen, 13 Mar. 1882.
17. A. Barkly to Sir Henry Barkly, 1 Oct. 1877, quoted in F. Barkly, *Among Boers and Basutos* (London, 1893) p. 18.
18. G. M. Theal, *History of South Africa since September 1795*, vol. vi (London, 1908) p. 335.
19. Rhodes House, MSS. Brit. Emp. s. 18 (Anti-Slavery Society Papers), C140/243a: Mabille to Chesson, 15 Apr. 1881.
20. Cape, N. A. 274: Rolland to Brownlee, no. 90, 18 Oct. 1877 and Brownlee's minute.
21. Cape, N. A. 272: Griffith to Molteno, no. 88, 27 Aug. 1873.
22. Thompson, *Survival in Two Worlds*, p. 209.
23. e.g. *Little Light of Basutoland*, nos. 10–12, Oct.–Dec. 1875, p. 47. There are, however, occasional indications that the Sotho may have become increasingly disillusioned with the extent to which they were able to influence policy through the *pitso*. For example, at the 1875 *pitso* one man demanded 'I want to know what answer the Queen has ever sent to our misgivings expressed at these annual meetings? And yet I have often heard misgivings expressed but never any answer.' See *Cape Parl. Papers*, G. 16–76, p. 15.
24. Casalis, *The Basutos*, p. 236.
25. Cape, N.A. 272: Griffith to Molteno, no. 100, 14 Oct. 1874.
26. e.g. Cape, N.A. 273: Austen to Griffith, no. 73, 11 Nov. 1876, encl. in Griffith to Brownlee, no. 54, 14 Nov. 1876.
27. e.g. Cape, N.A. 276: Griffith to Ayliff, no. 22, 5 Feb. 1879; Davies to Griffith, 15 Feb. 1879, encl. in Griffith to Ayliff, no. 31, 19 Feb. 1879.

28. Pierre-Joseph Maitin, b. Switzerland 17 June 1816, d. Ladybrand, South Africa, 1 April 1903. Arrived in Basutoland 1842.
29. Cape, N.A. 274: Rolland to Ayliff, 28 Dec. 1877.
30. *Cape Parl. Papers*, G. 17–78, p. 24.
31. Cape, N.A. 273: Griffith to Brownlee, 9 Sept. 1876.
32. Cape, N.A. 281: Letsie's speech in minutes of *pitso* held on 16 Jan. 1882, encl. in Orpen to Sauer, no. 2/377, 25 Jan. 1882.
33. For details, see U.B.R., vi. 519–20: Southey to Griffith, 11 Oct. 1872; Tylden, *The Rise of the Basuto*, p. 232.
34. Cape, U.B.R., vi. 413: Griffith to Southey, 27 Feb. 1872.
35. See p. 70.
36. Cape, N.A. 276: Letsie to Austen, 9 Feb. 1879, encl. in Griffith to Ayliff, no. 31, 19 Feb. 1879. See also *Little Light of Basutoland*, nos. 2–3, Feb. & Mar. 1875, p. 12; Cape, N.A. 283: minutes of *pitso*, 25 Apr. 1883, encl. in Blyth to Sauer, no. 41/83, 27 Apr. 1883.
37. *Cape Parl. Papers*, G. 27–73, p. 9.
38. e.g. Cape, U.B.R. vi. 270–1: Bell to Griffith, 25 Aug. 1871; vi. 311–12: Mills to Griffith, 20 Sept. 1871; Lesotho, S9/1/3/2: Griffith to President of Orange Free State, 30 June 1873.
39. *Cape Parl. Papers*, 1873, Appendix III, Special Commission on the Laws and Customs of the Basuto, p. 64: Supplementary paper by Austen.
40. Ibid., G. 27–73, p. 1. Most of the 1871 hut tax was also paid in cash, since the value of stock was purposely fixed low to discourage its use as a medium of payment. See U.B.R., vi. 455: Barkly to Kimberley, 1 May 1872.
41. Cape, N.A. 272: minutes of the annual *pitso*, encl. in Griffith to Molteno, no. 85, 27 Aug. 1873; Lesotho, S9/1/3/2: Rolland to Labour Agent, King William's Town, 4 Oct. 1875; *Cape Parl. Papers*, G. 12–77, pp.4, 8.
42. Cape, N.A. 274: Rolland to Brownlee, 28 Dec. 1877.
43. e.g. Cape, N.A. 272: statement by Jan Makhatlane, encl. in Griffith to Brownlee, no. 111, 28 Oct. 1873; N.A. 277: Surmon to Griffith, 28 June 1880.
44. Hadley, *Doctor to Basuto, Boer & Briton*, p. 44.
45. It is clear that protests were made *after* shops were established since it was customary to consult a chief before allowing a trader to open a shop on his land. The chiefs must therefore have initially consented to the shops. See Cape, N.A. 281: Orpen to Sauer, no. 2/438, 16 Mar. 1882; *Little Light of Basutoland*, no. 9, Sept. 1873, p. 27; no. 11, Nov. 1874, p. 43.
46. The census figure was an under-estimate. See Sanders, *Moshoeshoe*, p. 279 n. 43. R. C. Germond, *Chronicles of Basutoland* (Morija, 1967) p. 326.
47. Cape, N.A. 273: Rolland to Griffith, 30 May 1874, encl. in Griffith to Brownlee, no. 8, 7 July 1874.
48. Cape, N.A. 274: Rolland to Brownlee, 28 Dec. 1877.
49. Smith, *The Mabilles*, p. 187. Mabille succeeded Arbousset at Morija, the mission station near Letsie's village, in 1859.
50. See Sanders, *Moshoeshoe*, pp. 150, 161.
51. e.g. in 1874 Molapo was vociferously opposed to missionary schools on the grounds that they led to the abandonment of *bohali* and circumcision. See Cape, N.A. 295: Nixon's report, 12 Aug. 1874. On Masopha, see e.g. J. M. Mohapeloa, 'The Essential Masupha', *Lesotho Notes and Records*, 5 (1965–66) 11–12; *Cape Parl. Papers*, G. 16–76, pp. 6–7.

52. Smith, *The Mabilles*, pp. 186–193.

53. *Little Light of Basutoland*, no. 6, June 1876, pp. 23–5.

54. Ibid., p. 25.

55. Hadley, *Doctor to Basuto, Boer & Briton*, p. 43.

56. See Lesotho, S9/1/3/1: Griffith to Casalis, 14 Oct. 1871; *Cape Parl. Papers*, G. 27–74, p. 26: Griffith's report for 1871; Cape, U.B.R., vi. 524–6: Griffith to Barkly, 11 Nov. 1872; vi. 529–30: Report by Langham Dale, 3 Dec. 1872; vi. 533–4: Brownlee to Molteno, 20 Dec. 1872; N.A. 295: (Education) Langham Dale to Nixon, 26 Aug. 1874.

57. Ibid.; *Little Light of Basutoland*, nos. 2–3, Feb. & Mar. 1875, p. 9.

58. Cape, N.A. 274: Rolland to Brownlee, 28 Dec. 1877.

59. Cape, U.B.R., vi. 526–8: Griffith to Barkly, 11 Nov. 1872; N.A. 273: Griffith to Molteno, no. 108, 10 Dec. 1875.

60. Ibid., Griffith to Brownlee, no. 73, 11 Nov. 1876. See Brownlee's minute.

61. Barkly, *Among Boers and Basutos*, p. 32. Indigenous healers always charged a fee. See C. Griffith 'Some Observations on Witchcraft in Basutoland' (communicated by J. X. Merriman), *The Transactions of the South African Philosophical Society*, (1877–80) 89.

62. *Little Light of Basutoland*, no. 8, Aug. 1872, p. 32.

63. *Cape Parl. Papers*, G. 27–74, p. 22.

64. Ibid., p. 35. Barkly in 1877 described this system in his district: 'the chief constable is a good hand at settling such matters, and we generally make him try his hand outside the court before making a "case" of it, and he is very often successful'. A. Barkly to Sir Henry Barkly, 1 Oct. 1877, quoted in Barkly, *Among Boers and Basutos*, p. 20.

65. *Cape Parl. Papers*, G. 12–77, p. 8.

66. Ibid., G. 17–78, pp. 11–12.

67. Cape, N.A. 275: Bowker to Ayliff, no. 25, 18 Mar. 1878.

68. Ibid., Rolland to Ayliff, no. 37, 20 July 1878.

69. Partly it seems because the Phuthi, the clan occupying that part of Basutoland nearest Griqualand East, had no sympathy with Nehemiah's land grievances. Austen however took no chances, immediately visiting their chief, Moorosi, and various petty chiefs to explain the cause of Nehemiah's apprehension. See Cape, N.A. 273: Austen to Griffith, no. 73, 11 Nov. 1876.

70. Cape, N.A. 274: Rolland to Brownlee, no. 96, 24 Oct. 1877; *Cape Parl. Papers*, G. 17–78, p. 4.

71. Cape, N.A. 275: Rolland to Ayliff, no. 36, 19 July 1878.

72. Ibid.

73. *Cape Parl. Papers*, A. 49–79, pp. 30–1: Bowker to Ayliff, 18 Apr. 1878.

74. See pp. 86–7.

75. *Cape Parl. Papers*, G. 21–75, p. 8.

76. Ibid., G. 17–78, p. 7.

77. Cape, N.A. 275: Rolland to Ayliff, no. 47, 17 Sept. 1878.

78. Widdicombe, *Fourteen Years in Basutoland*, pp. 47–8. This may also be an indication of the chiefs' legal use of the considerable power they retained from the patronage provided by the *mafisa* system. Molapo, for example, withdrew all *mafisa* cattle from Christians who refused to do *letsema* service after the first P.E.M.S. Synod in 1872 ruled that Christians must 'refuse those tasks which identified them with heathen practices'. (Mackintosh, *Coillard of the Zambesi*, p.

199). His action was a severe blow to the Christians' economic position and status.

79. *Cape Parl. Papers*, G. 16–76, p. 17: minutes of the 1875 *pitso*, 4 Nov. 1875. This opinion was echoed by Duvoisin, the P.E.M.S. Berea missionary from 1861. See Germond, *Chronicles of Basutoland*, p. 404.

CHAPTER 7   CHANGING THE LAW

1. See pp. 82–3.
2. Lesotho, S9/1/3/2: Griffith to Letsie, 19 Dec. 1872.
3. e.g. Ibid., Griffith to Nehemiah, 9 Sept. 1871; Griffith to Masopha, 9 Sept. 1871 and 30 Apr. 1873.
4. Cape, U.B.R., vi. 462–4: Statement by Masopha, June 1872; vi. 468: Griffith to Southey, 11 June 1872; vi. 511–12: Griffith to Southey, 29 Aug. 1872; N.A. 272: Rolland to Griffith, 23 June 1873; Lesotho, S9/1/3/2: Rolland to Surmon, 13 Sept. 1875.
5. Cape, N.A. 275: Rolland to Ayliff, no. 47, 17 Sept. 1878.
6. Cape, N.A. 840: Brownlee to Griffith, no. 143, 3 July 1873.
7. Cape, N.A. 272: Griffith to Molteno, no. 100, 14 Oct. 1874.
8. *Little Light of Basutoland*, no. 6, June 1876, p. 25.
9. Lesotho, S9/1/3/2: Griffith to Austen, 19 Jan. 1874.
10. Ibid., Griffith to Bell, Dec. 1874. The father in this case was Molapo.
11. e.g. Lesotho S9/1/3/2: Griffith to resident magistrate, Aliwal North, 21 June 1875; *Cape Parl. Papers*, G. 16–76, p. 5. The 'Governor's Code', which had come into force on 1 Dec. 1871, was not exactly the same as the regulations originally drafted by Wodehouse and accepted by the Sotho, as various deficiencies had to be rectified and changes recommended by Griffith were incorporated. The most important (made at the suggestion of the magistrates) was that infanticide and concealment of birth were to be punishable by imprisonment, although not offences in Sotho law. When the magistrates enforced this, yet another foreign concept was imported into Basutoland's criminal law. See Lesotho, S9/1/1/1: Griffith to Barkly, no. 7, 16 Aug. 1871; no. 12, 22 Aug. 1871; Griffith to Southey, 30 Sept. 1871; *Cape Parl. Papers*, 1873, Appendix III, Special Commission on the Laws and Customs of the Basutos, evidence, pp. 44, 47.
12. P.R.O., C.O. 48/50: third minute on enclosure 1 of Wodehouse to Glanville, no. 62, 14 May 1870. Cape parliamentarians were later to express surprise when they realised (as a result of a rebellion in Basutoland) how wide were the powers of sentencing given to magistrates. See *Cape Parl. Papers*, A. 6–79, Select Committee on Basutoland Hostilities, pp. 75, 807–13: Rolland's evidence.
13. Hadley, *Doctor to Basuto, Boer & Briton*, pp. 21–2. 'Thlotsi' was an alternative spelling to 'Hlotse'.
14. *Cape Parl. Papers*, A. 18–72: Report and Evidence of the Select Committee of the House of Assembly on Regulations for the future Government of British Basutoland. Austen subsequently produced evidence to show that the chiefs had not wanted such an enquiry. See ibid., 1873, Appendix III, Special

Commission on the Laws and Customs of the Basutos, pp. 66–7; supplementary paper by Austen.

15. *Cape Parl. Papers*, 1873, Appendix III, Report and Evidence of the Special Commission on the Laws and Customs of the Basutos.
16. Also spelt 'Morosi' and 'Moirosi' by some nineteenth-century writers.
17. *Cape Parl. Papers*, 1873, Appendix III, Report and Evidence of the Special Commission on the Laws and Customs of the Basutos, p. 5.
18. Ibid.
19. Both missionaries were rather strait-laced and culture bound. See Thompson, *Survival in Two Worlds*, pp. 255, 317–18.
20. But see Bell's attack on these provisions: *Cape Parl. Papers*, G. 17–78, pp. 5–6.
21. Ibid., A. 18–72, Select Committee on the Basuto Regulations, appendix A, p. 17.
22. *Cape Parl. Papers*, 1873, Appendix III, Special Commission on the Laws and Customs of the Basutos, report, p. 6.
23. Ibid., p. 10: s. 11.
24. According to the evidence taken by the Commission, the only man known to have made an (oral) will was Moshoeshoe. However, the Chiefs Letsie and Jobo both favoured the idea.
25. This was the origin of a similar provision in the Transkeian Territories some years later. Stanford inaccurately believed it had originated from the 1883 Cape Native Laws and Customs Commission. See Macquarrie, *The Reminiscences of Sir Walter Stanford*, i. 100.
26. Cape, U.B.R., vi. 281–6: Mabille's statement encl. in Griffith to Barkly, 1 Sept. 1871.
27. *Cape Parl. Papers*, 1873, Appendix III, Special Commission on the Laws and Customs of the Basutos, report, p. 6.
28. *Cape Parl. Papers*, A. 18–72, Select Committee on the Basuto Regulations, evidence, p. 3.
29. Cape, U.B.R., vi. 315: Southey to Griffith, 28 Oct. 1871.
30. e.g. Lesotho, S9/1/3/2: Griffith to Letsie, 19 Dec. 1872; Cape, N.A. 275: petition from the chiefs enclosed in Rolland to Ayliff, no. 37, 20 July 1878; N.A. 276: Austen to Griffith, 7 May 1879, encl. in Griffith to Ayliff, 12 May 1879.
31. *Cape Parl. Papers*, 1873, Appendix III, Special Commission on the Laws and Customs of the Basutos, evidence, p. 56.
32. Cape, N.A. 275: Rolland to Ayliff, no. 37, 20 July 1878.
33. Lesotho, S9/1/3/2: Griffith to Basutoland magistrates and chiefs, 7 Sept. 1871.
34. Government Notice no. 2 of 1872, Basutoland, published in *Little Light of Basutoland*, no. 2, Feb. 1872.
35. Letsie claimed that he opposed the laws because men would impound each other's cattle out of spite, and that it was difficult to discern which were real strays on a large commonage, but Rolland replied that he had never heard of Sotho impounding neighbours' stock out of spite, and that in fact strays were reported to the magistrates by the headmen. See *Cape Parl. Papers*, G. 33–79, p. 32; Cape, N.A. 275: Rolland to Ayliff, no. 37, 20 July 1878 and encl. petition.
36. Theal, *History of South Africa since 1795*, iv. 339.
37. e.g. *Cape Parl. Papers*, G. 27–74, p. 37; G. 21–75, p. 11; Cape, N.A. 273: Griffith to Brownlee, no. 39, 27 Feb. 1875; *Cape Parl. Papers*, G. 16–76, p. 10.

38. Proclamation no. 44, 1 July 1877.
39. One alteration is of interest, more for the influence it had on subsequent Transkeian regulations than for its effect in Basutoland. It resulted from a suggestion by Griffith when returning a rough draft of the amended regulations to Brownlee:

> The only regulation which appears to me to require specific amendment is No. 7 under the head of Marriages—this clause provides for the registration of marriages according to Basuto Custom or 'Cattle Marriages'—I think this clause ought only to provide for the registration of the *first wife*—by this means we should be discountenancing polygamy—whereas by registering all the marriages of a polygamist we are encouraging this form of marriage—we should then be able to say, well, we recognize your first wife, but we cannot recognize any others as we don't approve of polygamy and therefore don't want to know anything about the other wives.

Cape, N.A. 274: Griffith to Brownlee, no. 11, 18 April 1876. As this suggestion was originally made by Rolland in his 1868 memorandum, it is possible that he gave Griffith the idea. The 1875 missionary conference at Bloemfontein, an account of which was published in the *Little Light of Basutoland*, had also advocated this measure. (See *Little Light of Basutoland*, nos. 10–12, Oct.–Dec. 1875, p. 42.) Brownlee agreed, (see Cape, N.A. 274: Brownlee's minute on Griffith to Brownlee, no. 11, 18 Apr. 1878) and the suggestion was embodied in the regulations but would apparently have been completely ineffective legally, since the regulations contained no provision that registration was necessary for magisterial recognition of a Sotho law marriage; the courts could still have heard cases dealing with all or any of the marriages of a polygamist. It is not clear, however, whether this was realised. Both Griffith's attitude in the passage quoted above and that of the missionaries' annual conference of 1879 seem to indicate that with Sotho law marriages the courts may in practice have entertained only cases arising from the first marriage. (See Cape, N.A. 176: Dieterlen to Griffith, 24 Apr. 1879 encl. in Griffith to Ayliff, 27 Apr. 1879.)
40. *Cape Parl. Papers*, A. 18–72, Select Committee on the Basuto Regulations, evidence, p. 9.
41. Section 24.

CHAPTER 8   PROPHESIES

1. *Cape Parl. Papers*, G. 17–78, pp. 23, 24: Tsekelo's and Ramatšeatsana's speeches at the 1877 annual *pitso*, 1 Nov. 1887.
2. *Cape Parl. Papers*, G. 27–74, p. 25.
3. Cape, N.A. 274: Rolland to Brownlee, 28 Dec. 1877.
4. Lesotho, S9/1/3/2: Griffith to Letsie, 19 Dec. 1872. The resolutions were so extreme that they caused a schism in the church in Basutoland; some of the Christians at the Hermon mission station refused to accept them and formed an independent church. See Cape, N.A. 272: Rolland's annual report for 1872 encl. in Griffith to Molteno, no. 33, 15 Mar. 1873. For a discussion of why this

happened, see P. E. Webber, 'The Church in Basutoland, 1833–1884' (Southampton Univ. M.A. thesis, 1967) pp. 199–203.

5. *Cape Parl. Papers*, G. 21–75, p. 26.
6. e.g. Cape, N.A. 272: minutes of annual *pitso*, 20 Aug. 1873, encl. in Griffith to Molteno, no. 85, 27 Aug. 1873; N.A. 274: Resident Magistrate, Herschel, to Austen, 3 Oct. 1877, encl. in Rolland to Brownlee, no. 97, 26 Oct. 1877. (In this case the complainant's claim was not good in African law, so no substantial injustice resulted; but in the many cases which must have arisen with Sotho living on both sides of the Border, the result cannot always have been so fortunate); N.A. 275: Rolland to Brownlee, no. 12, 25 Jan. 1878.
7. *Little Light of Basutoland*, no. 3, March 1876, p. 14.
8. Tylden, *The Rise of the Basuto*, p. 42; Smith, *The Mabilles*, pp. 120–1; Sanders, *Moshoeshoe*, pp. 168–9, 171, 174, 205, 275–6; Thompson, *Survival in Two Worlds*, pp. 10–11, 46, 102–3, 150–1, 207, 317.
9. It is difficult from the material available to glean how far the prophets were consciously politically inspired and how far they represented a more or less involuntary reaction to the impact of colonial rule, of the type analogous to cases of 'peripheral possession' in I. M. Lewis, 'A Structural Approach to Witchcraft and Spirit-Possession' in M. Douglas (ed.), *Witchcraft Confessions and Accusations* (London, 1970) pp. 293–309. But whatever the source was of the prophets' activities, the general enthusiasm with which they were received indicates the widespread disquiet of the Sotho at the effects of colonial rule and missionary influence.
10. Cape, N.A. 272: Tsekelo to Griffith, 30 Aug. 1873, encl. in Griffith to Molteno, 11 Sept. 1873.
11. *Little Light of Basutoland*, nos. 10–12, Oct.–Dec. 1875, p. 47.
12. Ibid., pp. 47–8.
13. Ibid., no. 3, Mar. 1876, pp. 13–14.
14. Ibid.
15. Ibid., nos. 4–5, Apr. & May 1876, p. 20.
16. Ibid., no. 10, Oct. 1876, p. 43.
17. Ibid., nos. 10–12, Oct.–Dec. 1875, p. 47.
18. Cape, N.A. 274: Barkly's farewell letter to the Basuto, Mar. 1877.
19. *Cape Parl. Papers*, G. 12–77, p. 4.
20. Ibid., G. 16–76, pp. 4, 8–9.
21. Ibid., G. 12–77, p. 4.
22. Cape, N.A. 274: Barkly's farewell letter to the Sotho, Mar. 1877.
23. Tylden, *The Rise of the Basuto*, p. 126.
24. Cape, N.A. 274: Griffith to Brownlee, no. 13, 21 Apr. 1876.
25. P.R.O., C.O. 48/478: Barkly to Carnarvon, no. 84, 12 July 1876.
26. Tylden, *The Rise of the Basuto*, p. 126.
27. Though he subsequently left the Church in 1848 when disillusioned with the missionaries' attitudes towards the war of that year. See Sanders, *Moshoeshoe*, p. 150.
28. See *Cape Parl. Papers*, G. 37–76; A. 6–79, Select Committee on Basutoland Hostilities, appendices B and D.
29. Rhodes House, MSS. Afr. s. 23 (J. C. Molteno Papers), ii. 146: Probart to Molteno, 25 Jan. 1876.
30. See p. 171.

31. *Little Light of Basutoland*, no. 2, Feb. 1877, p. 3.
32. See *Cape Parl. Papers*, A. 6–79, Select Committee on Basutoland Hostilities, Appendix B, pp. xxii–xxix.
33. *Little Light of Basutoland*, no. 12, Dec. 1876, p. 53.
34. *Cape Parl. Papers*, G. 17–78, pp. 20–1.
35. Germond, *Chronicles of Basutoland*, p. 391.

CHAPTER 9   MOOROSI REBELS

1. Sanders, *Moshoeshoe*, pp. 37–8, 119–21, 168; Thompson, *Survival in Two Worlds*, pp. 54–5, 88, 184–6, 259.
2. Cape, U.B.R., vi. 419–20: Austen to Griffith, 29 Feb. 1872.
3. Cape, N.A. 276: Austen to Griffith, 7 May 1879, encl. in Griffith to Ayliff, 12 May 1879.
4. Thompson, *Survival in Two Worlds*, p. 173.
5. Cape, N.A. 273: Griffith to Brownlee, 9 Sept. 1876; N.A. 274: Rolland to Brownlee, 28 Dec. 1877.
6. He had been born about 1795.
7. See Theal, *Basutoland Records*, ii. 263: Burnet to Secretary to High Commissioner, 14 Feb. 1857; Hadley, *Doctor to Basuto, Boer & Briton*, p. 48.
8. Cape, N.A. 274: Griffith to Brownlee, no. 34, 9 May 1877.
9. Cape, N.A. 276: Austen to Griffith, 7 May 1879, encl. in Griffith to Ayliff, 12 May 1879.
10. Cape, N.A. 274: Griffith to Hope, 4 July 1877, encl. in Griffith to Brownlee, no. 56, 11 July 1877.
11. Ibid., Griffith to Brownlee, no. 34, 9 May 1877. See Brownlee's minutes of 28 May 1877.
12. A. Atmore, 'The Moorosi Rebellion: Lesotho, 1879', in R. I. Rotberg and A. A. Mazrui (eds), *Protest and Power in Black Africa* (New York, 1970) p. 7: information supplied to Anthony Atmore by Mosebi Damane in a series of conversations in London, Feb. 1965.
13. Tyhali (or 'Tyali' or 'Chale', as his name was usually spelt by contemporary writers) was chief of the Vundle, a Nguni group which settled in Moorosi's district in 1846–7. In Sotho usage all southern Nguni are called Thembu, and the whites referred to Tyhali's people and the other recently arrived Nguni groups in the area as Thembu, Tembus, or Tambookies. Rolland estimated there were 'about a thousand Tembus' in Moorosi's territory. See Cape, N.A. 273: Rolland to Brownlee, 28 Dec. 1877; Thompson, *Survival in Two Worlds*, p. 174.
14. Also spelt Mafetoli. He was Moorosi's official messenger.
15. Cape, N.A. 274 and *Cape Parl. Papers*, A. 49–79, pp. 112–14. Many of the letters in the Cape Archives cited in this chapter are reproduced in *Cape Parl. Papers*, A. 17–79 and A. 49–79.
16. A potent alcoholic drink brewed locally (*Joala*). In the printed version this is misspelt as 'Tuata'. Atmore indicates (in 'The Moorosi Rebellion', op. cit., p.8) that Moorosi's objection to the sale of *joala* would have been that the white man's money economy should not be allowed to impinge upon one of the

traditional bonds of hospitality. Hope's concern would have been to prevent the consumption of alcohol.

17. The regulations did not actually debar chiefs from hearing criminal cases but provided that all such cases should be tried by magistrates, and made the enforcement of chiefs' decisions—whether fines or physical punishment— illegal. Magistrates therefore did their best to prevent the chiefs hearing criminal cases, for fear of the consequences.

18. Cape, N.A. 274 (and *Cape Parl. Papers.* A. 49–79, p. 115): Hope to Griffith, 25 June 1877.

19. Ibid., pp. 115–16.

20. Ibid., p. 116: Hope to Griffith, 26 June 1877.

21. Cape, N.A. 274: Griffith to Hope, 4 July 1877, encl. in Griffith to Brownlee, no. 56, 11 July 1877.

22. Ibid., Hope to Griffith, 5 July 1877, encl. in Griffith to Brownlee, no. 57, 11 July 1877.

23. Ibid., Griffith to Brownlee, no. 57, 11 July 1877 and enclosed letter of Griffith to Hope, 7 July 1877.

24. Ibid., Griffith to Brownlee, no. 74, 18 Aug. 1877, and encl. statement by Moorosi, 16 Aug. 1877.

25. *Cape Parl. Papers*, G. 49–79, pp. 9–10: Hope to Rolland, 24 Nov. 1877.

26. Ibid., pp. 10–11; Hope to Moorosi, 23 Nov. 1877.

27. Ibid., p. 11: Moorosi's reply to Hope.

28. Ibid., pp. 12–13: Rolland to Moorosi, 28 Nov. 1877.

29. Ibid., p. 13: Rolland to Hope, 28 Nov. 1877.

30. *Cape Parl. Papers*, A. 49–79, pp. 8–9: Rolland to Brownlee, 5 Dec. 1877.

31. Ibid., p. 18: Rolland to Brownlee, no. 11, 25 Jan. 1878.

32. Ibid., p. 22: Hope to Rolland, 16 Feb. 1878.

33. Ibid.

34. Cape, N.A. 273: Griffith to Brownlee, 9 Sept. 1876.

35. *Cape Parl. Papers*, A. 49–79, p. 29: Bowker to Ayliff, 18 Apr. 1878.

36. See Cape, N.A. 275: Rolland to Ayliff, no. 17, 15 Feb. 1878, and Bright's minutes on this letter.

37. *Cape Parl. Papers*, A. 49–79, p. 22: Hope to Rolland, 16 Feb. 1878.

38. Ibid., p. 24: Hope to Rolland, 28 Feb. 1878.

39. Atmore, 'The Moorosi Rebellion', op. cit., p. 15.

40. *Cape Parl. Papers*, A. 49–79, p. 25, Ayliff to Rolland, no. 121, 16 Mar. 1878; S.A.P.L., Noble Papers: Hope to Bailie, 24 Apr. 1878.

41. *Cape Parl. Papers*, A. 49–79, p. 27: Hope to Ayliff, 14 Mar. 1878.

42. Atmore, 'The Moorosi Rebellion', op. cit., p. 16, n. 48. See also Hadley, *Doctor to Basuto, Boer & Briton*, p. 48.

43. *Cape Parl. Papers*, A. 6–79, Select Committee on Basutoland Hostilities, pp. 58–9, 654–7: Bowker's evidence.

44. Hope had not built his house in the place that Griffith had selected in 1877. Instead he had moved nearer to Moorosi's mountain to a site which was commanded on all sides by hills close to it and was impossible to defend if attacked. See Cape, N.A. 276: Austen to Griffith, no. 24, 21 Jan. 1879, encl. in Griffith to Ayliff, no. 20, 5 Feb. 1879; Griffith to Ayliff, no. 28, 10 Feb. 1879; Griffith to Ayliff, no. 11F, 18 Feb. 1879.

45. Hadley, *Doctor to Basuto, Boer & Briton*, pp. 50–1. Hope subsequently became

magistrate with Mhlontlo, the Mpondomisi chief in the Transkei. During the 1880 rebellion he attempted, with characteristic bravery and lack of judgment, to persuade Mhlontlo and his men to fight for the Government and was killed on Mhlontlo's orders. See the eye-witness account by A. E. Davies in the (U.C.T.) Standford Papers, F(e)3, 29 Oct. 1880.

46. Hadley *Doctor to Basuto Boer & Briton*, p. 51.

47. *Cape Parl. Papers*, A. 6–79, Select Committee on Basutoland Hostilities, pp. 59, 658–9: Bowker's evidence.

48. Bowker reported that the fine was twenty-four head of cattle: *Cape Parl. Papers*, A. 6–79, Select Committee on Basutoland Hostilities, pp. 49, 567.

49. Hadley, *Doctor to Basuto, Boer & Briton*, pp. 52–3.

50. Cape, N.A. 275: Bowker to Ayliff, no. 31, 8 May 1878, and enclosure; *Cape Parl. Papers*, A. 6–79 Select Committee on Basutoland Hostilities, pp. 50, 572: Bowker's evidence.

51. Ibid., pp. 74, 796: Rolland's evidence.

52. Cape, N.A. 275: Austen to Griffith, 28 Sept. 1878, encl. in Griffith to Ayliff, 22 Oct. 1878.

53. *Cape Parl. Papers*, A. 6–79 Select Committee on Basutoland Hostilities, pp. 74–5, 801–4: Rolland's evidence.

54. Thlali, a grandson of Moorosi, was charged at the same time with receiving stolen property.

55. Cape, N.A. 275: Austen to Griffith, 23 Nov. 1878, encl. in Griffith to Ayliff, no. 71, 9 Dec. 1878.

56. Letuka was now back in the Quthing District, though the files contain no further mention of him replacing Moorosi before the latter's death. As a result of assisting the Government to bring three of his brothers to trial, Letuka incurred his father's displeasure. He had until recently been living in Griqualand East, and Moorosi refused to give him land in the Quthing District, as he feared that Letuka, by working with the magistrate in suppressing crime, would strengthen Government influence. Austen, in keeping with the Administration's tradition of securing the loyalty of heirs, promptly suggested that the district be divided into wards and that Letuka be made a ward master. This was approved by Ayliff. See ibid., Austen to Griffith, no. 8, 20 Nov. 1878, encl. in Griffith to Ayliff, no. 77, 26 Dec. 1878.

57. Ibid., Austen to Griffith, 23 Nov. 1878, encl. in Griffith to Ayliff, no. 71, 9 Dec. 1878.

58. Cape, N.A. 276: Griffith to Ayliff, no. 15, 28 Jan. 1879, and enclosures; Griffith to Ayliff, no. 20, 5 Feb. 1879, and enclosure.

59. Ibid., Austen to Griffith, 4 Jan. 1879, encl. in Griffith to Ayliff, no. 7, 14 Jan. 1879.

60. Ibid., Griffith to Ayliff, no. 15, 28 Jan. 1879; Letsie to Austen, 9 Feb. 1879, encl. in Griffith to Ayliff, no. 31, 19 Feb. 1879; Germond, *Chronicles of Basutoland*, p. 333, quoting Casalis.

61. Cape, N.A. 276: Griffith to Ayliff, no. 23, 5 Feb. 1879.

62. *Cape Parl. Papers*, A. 49–79, pp. 67–9; Griffith to Ayliff, no. 35, 24 Feb. 1879, and enclosures.

63. e.g. ibid., pp. 103–7.

64. Cape, N.A. 276: Austen to Griffith, no. 41, 22 Feb. 1879, encl. in Griffith to Ayliff, no. 37, 26 Feb. 1879.

65. Cape, N.A. 276: Griffith to Ayliff, no. 38, 26 Feb. 1879.
66. Ibid.
67. *Cape Parl. Papers*, A. 49–79, p. 55: Ayliff to Brownlee, Elliot and Blyth, 26 Feb. 1879; pp. 131–2: Austen to Ayliff, 8 July 1879.
68. Ibid., p. 86: Griffith to Ayliff, received 9 Mar. 1879.
69. *Cape Parl. Papers*, G. 33–79, p. 30. How far this was a cause of Moorosi's rebellion was much disputed, opinions ranging from Austen's and Mabille's that it played no part in the decision to rebel, to Rolland's belief that it was the basic cause of the disquiet among the Phuthi that made the rebellion possible. However, it seems clear that even Rolland believed that had Austen remained at his post, no rebellion would have occurred. See Cape, N.A. 276: Austen to Ayliff, 31 July 1879; 7 Aug. 1879; Rhodes House, MSS. Brit. Emp. s.18 (Anti-Slavery Society Papers) C140/254a: Mabille's notes on the Basuto, n.d., probably encl. in C140/251, Mabille to Chesson, 30 Dec. 1881; *Cape Parl. Papers*, A. 6–79, Select Committee on Basutoland Hostilities, evidence, pp. 76–8.
70. Smith, *The Mabilles*, p. 245.
71. Cape, N.A. 276: Austen to Griffith, no. 41, 22 Feb. 1879, encl. in Griffith to Ayliff, no. 37, 26 Feb. 1879; Austen to Ayliff, 31 July 1879.
72. Austen believed Letsie had encouraged Moorosi to defy the Government but had not intended him to carry matters so far. See Cape, N.A. 276: Austen to Ayliff, 19 June 1879.
73. *Cape Parl. Papers*, A. 49–79, p. 56: Griffith to Ayliff, 26 Feb. 1879.
74. Cape, N.A. 274: Rolland to Brownlee, 28 Dec. 1877.
75. *Cape Parl. Papers*, A. 49–79, pp. 26–7: Hope to Ayliff, 14 Mar. 1879.
76. Cape, N.A. 276: Letsie to Austen, 9 Feb. 1879, encl. in Griffith to Ayliff, no. 31, 19 Feb. 1879.
77. *Cape Parl. Papers*, A. 49–79, pp. 26–7: Hope to Ayliff, 14 Mar. 1879.
78. Cape, N.A. 277: Griffith to Ayliff, no. 46, 12 Mar. 1880 and enclosed letter from Letsie to Griffith.
79. [Original footnote to excerpt] The Hounds were Letsie's regiment.
80. See M. Damane and P. B. Sanders (eds), *Lithoko, Sotho Praise-Poems* (Oxford, 1974) pp. 152–4, 165.
81. Atmore, 'The Moorosi Rebellion', op. cit., p. 29 citing an article by Ellenberger in *Leselinyana*, August 1915.
82. Ibid., p. 30.
83. Tylden, *The Rise of the Basuto*, p. 132; Rhodes House, MSS. Afr. 5969 (Kennan Papers): Robert Kennan to his mother, 28 Nov. 1879.
84. A. Wilmot, *The History of Our Own Times in South Africa*, vol. i (London, 1897) p. 324.
85. Germond, *Chronicles of Basutoland*, p. 338, quoting F. Ellenberger, 31 July 1879.
86. Ibid., p. 340, quoting Emma Ellenberger.
87. Cape, N.A. 276: statement of Nkuetsana, a surrendered rebel, 10 Dec. 1879. Arthur Barkly wrote that Moorosi 'had apparently been deserted by most of his people, or starvation had compelled them to leave the mountain'. A. Barkly to Sir Henry Barkly, 25 Nov. 1879, quoted in Barkly, *Among Boers and Basutos*, p. 105.
88. Rhodes House, MSS. Afr. 5969 (Kennan Papers): Robert Kennan to his mother, 28 Nov. 1879.

89. Ibid., Cape N.A. 276: statement by Nkuetsana, 10 Dec. 1879; Austen to Griffith, 22 Nov. 1879, encl. in Griffith to Ayliff, no. 105, 3 Dec. 1879. Moorosi's head was subsequently cut off (and sent to the Cape Colony for dissection) and his body dismembered by the troops.
90. Cape, N.A. 280: Clarke to Orpen, no. 116, 24 Dec. 1881, encl. in Maitin (for Orpen) to Sauer, no. 2/349, 29 Dec. 1881. H. V. Woon claimed that Lehana had been found dying of his wounds in a cave during the week after the mountain was captured (see A Colonial Officer, *Twenty-Five Years' Soldiering in South Africa* [London, 1909] p. 75) but Atmore, citing Damane, reports that Lehana fled up the Orange River Valley, was pardoned much later, and died in 1906 (Atmore, *The Moorosi Rebellion*, p. 31).
91. Cape, N.A. 267: statement by Nkuetsana, a surrendered rebel, 10 Dec. 1879.

CHAPTER 10   THE COLLAPSE OF MAGISTERIAL RULE

1. U.C.T., Stanford Papers, F(i)4: Walker to Stanford, 20 May 1884.
2. Benyon, 'Basutoland and the High Commission', p. 374.
3. Ibid., p. 375. For the socio-economic factors underlying the scheme, see Atmore and Marks, 'The Imperial Factor in South Africa', op. cit. For opinions expressed by some of the interested parties in southern Africa on the desirability and practicality of the scheme, see Mohapeloa, *Rule by Proxy*, pp. 38–43.
4. Cape, N.A. 272: Tsekelo to Griffith, 27 June 1873, encl. in Griffith to Molteno, no. 71, 10 July 1873.
5. Lagden, *The Basutos*, ii, 486; Lesotho, S9/2/1/1: Griffith to Southey, 26 Aug. 1872.
6. *Cape Parl. Papers*, A. 49–79, p. 11: Moorosi's reply to Hope.
7. Significantly, that barometer of Sotho opposition to white civilisation, circumcision, was much in evidence in the magistrates' reports for 1879. A. Barkly and Surmon both remarked on the strength of the custom in their districts, and Davies wrote of the great increase in his district of the number of circumcision lodges established for both males and females in 1879. See *Cape Parl. Papers*, G. 13–80, pp. 23, 25, 26.
8. Ibid. G. 13–80, pp. 38–65.
9. [Original footnote to excerpt] Light material wound round the hat and hanging down behind as a shade.
10. Hadley, *Doctor to Basuto, Boer & Briton*, p. 56; for the official report of the *pitso*, see *Cape Parl. Papers*, G. 13–80, pp. 38–65. Sprigg also devised a system of ticketing surrendered guns so that compensation could subsequently be paid for them, and this gave rise to a contemptuous nickname (used by those who refused to surrender their guns) for those who cooperated with the Government: *Mateketa* or *Mateketoa* (lit. 'The Ticketed Ones'). See Cape, Griffith Papers (Acc. 1554): Sprigg to Griffith, 8 Dec. 1879; Hadley, p. 57; Damane and Sanders, *Lithoko*, p. 150 n.8.
11. e.g. Cape, N.A. 276: Griffith to Ayliff, no. 104, 27 Nov. 1879; Griffith to Ayliff, no. 111, 13 Dec. 1879 and enclosed letter from Letsie to Griffith; N.A. 277: Griffith to Ayliff, no. 22, 31 Jan. 1880; Letsie to Griffith, 6 Feb. 1880, encl. in

Griffith to Ayliff, no. 37, 1 Mar. 1880; Letsie to Griffith, 9 Mar. 1880, encl. in Griffith to Ayliff, no. 46, 12 Mar. 1880.

12. *Cape Parl. Papers*, A. 6–79, Select Committee on Basutoland Hostilities, evidence, pp. 81, 83–5.

13. Cape, N.A. 278: Griffith to Ayliff, no. 116, 24 Dec. 1879.

14. Announced at the 1879 annual *pitso* by Sprigg. See *Cape Parl. Papers*, G. 13–80, pp. 40–1.

15. Cape, N.A. 277: Griffith to Ayliff, no. 17, 6 Jan. 1880.

16. *Little Light of Basutoland*, no. 8, Aug. 1877, pp. 1–2; no. 10, Oct. 1877, p. 2.

17. Ibid.

18. *Cape Parl. Papers*, A. 6–79, Select Committee on Basutoland Hostilities, evidence, pp. 81–2.

19. Cape, N.A. 277: Griffith to Ayliff, no. 17, 6 Jan. 1880.

20. Cape, N.A. 279: Sprigg to Griffith, 26 Feb. 1880.

21. *Cape Parl. Papers*, A. 12–80, pp. 10–11: Bright to Griffith, 4 Mar. 1880.

22. Proclamation no. 49, 12 Apr. 1880.

23. Cape, N.A. 275: Griffith to Ayliff, no. 72, 9 Dec. 1878.

24. Cape, N.A. 277: Griffith to Ayliff, no. 17, 6 Jan. 1880.

25. P.R.O., C.O. 879/17, *African Confidential Print*, no. 255, p. 61: memo by Frere, 19 July 1880, encl. in Frere to Kimberley, no. 174, 20 July 1880; Cape, N.A. 279: Ayliff to Griffith (semi-official), 6 Apr. 1880.

26. Benyon, 'Basutoland and the High Commission', p. 387.

27. Cape, N.A. 277: Letsie to Griffith, 27 Feb. 1880, encl. in Griffith to Ayliff, no. 38, 1 Mar. 1880.

28. Cape, N.A. 277: Griffith to Ayliff, no. 16, 26 Jan. 1880, and enclosures. See also Mabille's private letters to Griffith in Cape, Griffith Papers (Acc. 1554).

29. P.R.O., C.O. 48/494: see Hicks Beach's minute, 9 Apr. 1880, on (missing) Frere to Hicks Beach (confidential), 2 Mar. 1880; Hicks Beach's minute, 21 Apr. 1880, on (missing) Frere to Hicks Beach (confidential), 15 Mar. 1880. For the missing despatches, see *Brit. Parl. Papers* 1880, li [C. 2569], pp. 6–9, 17–22.

30. Cape, N. A. 277: Ellenberger to Griffith, 19 Feb. 1880, encl. in Griffith to Ayliff, no. 42, 3 Mar. 1880; Griffith to Ayliff, 26 May 1880, with enclosures.

31. P.R.O., C.O. 879/17, *African Confidential Print*, no. 255, p. 9: Frere to Kimberley, no. 98, 10 May 1880, and enclosures.

32. Rhodes House, MSS. Brit. Emp. s.18 (Anti-Slavery Society Papers), C128 and C140: letters from Mabille and Casalis. For an account of the Society's campaign, see Benyon, 'Basutoland and the High Commission', pp. 397–400; Mohapeloa, *Rule by Proxy*, pp. 48–51.

33. Benyon, 'Basutoland and the High Commission', pp. 399–400.

34. *Brit. Parl. Papers* 1880, 1 [C.2482], p. 1: Morisse to Hicks Beach, 13 June 1879.

35. *Hansard*, 3rd series, 1880, cclii. 455–8.

36. *Brit. Parl. Papers* 1880, li [C.2569], p. 6: Hicks Beach to Frere (tel.), 10 Mar. 1880; pp. 49–51: Kimberley to Frere, 20 May 1880.

37. P.R.O., C.O. 48/494: Frere to Hicks Beach (confidential), 22 June 1880.

38. Cape, N. A. 277: Griffith to Ayliff, no. 55, 5 Apr. 1880, and enclosures.

39. P.R.O., C.O. 879/17, *African Confidential Prints*, no. 225, p. 25: Frere to Kimberley (confidential), 30 May 1880; Smith, *The Mabilles*, pp. 258, 260–1.

40. See p. 49.
41. Cape, N. A. 277: Letsie to Griffith, 16 Mar. 1880, encl. in Griffith to Ayliff, no. 48, 19 Mar. 1880; Letsie to Griffith, 11 Apr. 1880, encl. in Griffith to Ayliff, no. 63, 16 Apr. 1880; Letsie to Griffith, 11 May 1880, encl. in Griffith to Ayliff, no. 87, 18 May 1880.
42. Cape, N. A. 277: Letsie to Griffith, 11 May 1880 and 17 May 1880, encl. in Griffith to Ayliff, no. 87, 18 May 1880.
43. Ibid., A. Barkly to Griffith, 8 May 1880.
44. *Brit. Parl. Papers* 1881, lxvi [C.2755].
45. P.R.O., C.O. 48/494: Frere to Hicks Beach (confidential), 22 June 1880.
46. Cape, N. A. 277: Griffith to Ayliff, no. 2/104, 29 June 1880.
47. Widdicombe, *Fourteen Years in Basutoland*, pp. 136–7; Smith, *The Mabilles*, p. 261.
48. Cape, N. A. 282: Bailie to Orpen, 29 Oct. 1882, encl. in Orpen to Sauer, no. 2/587, 18 Nov. 1882.
49. Widdicombe, *Fourteen Years in Basutoland*, p. 99. Joel was relying on an alternative school of thought which believed that the eldest son of the second house should succeed if that of the first house was dead or incapable. I am indebted to Dr. P. B. Sanders for this information.
50. Hadley, *Doctor to Basuto, Boer & Briton*, p. 46.
51. Widdicombe, *Fourteen Years in Basutoland*, p. 216.
52. Cape, N. A. 278: minutes of meeting held on 3 July 1880, encl in Griffith to Ayliff, no. 2/109, 14 July 1880. (The minutes are reproduced in full in Burman, *The Justice of the Queen's Government*, pp. 93–104.) The remaining members of the delegation had remained in Cape Town to try to prevent the confiscation of the Quthing District.
53. See Damane and Sanders, *Lithoko*, p. 149.
54. Cape, N. A. 278: Griffith to Ayliff, no. 2/108, 13 July 1880.
55. For numerous examples, see Cape, N.A. 278; *Cape Parl. Papers*, A. 22–81 and A. 29–81.
56. Ibid., A. 29–81, p. 41: Davies to Griffith, 18 July 1880.
57. Cape, N. A. 278: Griffith to Ayliff, no. 2/129, 2 Aug. 1880, and enclosures.
58. *Cape Parl. Papers*, G. 20–81, p. 7.
59. V. Ellenberger, *A Century of Mission Work in Basutoland, 1833–1933*, (Morija, 1938) p. 218; Rhodes House, MSS. Brit. Emp. s.18 (Anti-Slavery Society Papers) C140/253c: Mabille's notes on the Basuto, n.d., probably encl. in C140/251: Mabille to Chesson, 30 Dec. 1881; Cape, N.A. 281: Leribe Catholic Mission report, 5 Jan. 1882, encl. in Orpen to Sauer, no. 2/410, 19 Feb. 1882.
60. Cape, N. A. 278: Griffith to Ayliff, no. 2/148, 18 Aug. 1880.
61. Widdicombe, *Fourteen Years in Basutoland*, p. 146.
62. *Cape Parl. Papers*, A. 22–81, p. 9: Griffith to Sprigg (tel.) no. 385, 26 July 1880.
63. Cape, N. A. 277: Griffith to Ayliff, no. 2/114, 21 July 1880.
64. Cape, N. A. 278: Griffith to Ayliff, no. 2/107, 7 July 1880.
65. *Cape Parl. Papers*, G. 20–81, p. 19.
66. Hadley, *Doctor to Basuto, Boer & Briton*, pp. 57–8.
67. *Cape Parl. Papers*, A. 22–81, p. 8: Griffith to Sprigg (tel.) no. 354, 21 July 1880.
68. Ibid., A. 29–81, pp. 90–1: Surmon to Griffith, 8 Aug. 1880. The reserve was the area round the magistracy reserved for the Government.

69. Ibid., p. 80: Griffith to Letsie, 27 July 1880; A. 22–81, p. 13: Griffith to Sprigg (tel.) no. 411, 1 Aug. 1880.

70. Ibid., Griffith to Sprigg (tel.) no. 420, 2 Aug. 1880.

71. Cape, N. A. 278: Griffith to Ayliff, no. 2/148, 18 Aug. 1880.

72. *Cape Parl. Papers*, A. 22–81, pp. 14–15: Griffith to Sprigg (tel.) no. 431, 4 Aug. 1880.

73. Ibid., p. 117: Sprigg to Griffith (tel.) no. 455, 13 Aug. 1880.

74. Ibid., p. 18: Griffith to Sprigg (tel.) no. 457e, 13 Aug. 1880.

75. Ibid., pp. 17–20: telegrams between Griffith and Sprigg, nos. 456–71: A. 29–81, pp. 87–9: Griffith to Ayliff, no. 2/140, 16 Aug. 1880, and enclosures; pp. 95–6: Griffith to Ayliff, no. 2/146, 18 Aug. 1880, and enclosures; Cape, N. A. 278: message of Letsie encl. in Griffith to Ayliff, no. 2/145, 18 Aug. 1880.

76. Ibid., Griffith to Ayliff, no. 2/148, 18 Aug. 1880.

77. *Cape Parl. Papers*, G. 20–81, pp. 5, 12–14; Cape, N. A. 280: C. H. Bell to Griffith, 10 Jan. 1881, and C. G. H. Bell to Griffith, 4 Oct. 1881, encl. in Griffith to Sauer, no. 2/327, 3 Dec. 1881; *Cape Parl. Papers*, G. 47–82, pp. 172–3: Dyke to Sprigg, 27 Aug. 1880.

78. Cape, N. A. 278: Griffith to Ayliff, no. 2/145, 18 Aug. 1880.

79. *Cape Parl. Papers*, A. 22–81, p. 14: Sprigg to Griffith (tel.), no. 432, 4 Aug. 1880.

80. Minutes of interviews by Sprigg and other information on his visit are in ibid., pp. 21–43.

81. Ibid., pp. 34–5: Griffith to Letsie, 5 Sept. 1880; pp. 42–3: Orpen to Sprigg, 6 Sept. 1880.

82. Benyon, 'Basutoland and the High Commission', p. 423.

83. Tylden, *The Rise of the Basuto*, p. 146.

84. A. Barkly to Sir Henry Barkly, 15 Sept. 1880, quoted in Barkly, *Among Boers and Basutos*, pp. 182–6.

CHAPTER 11   DEFEATING DISARMAMENT

1. C.C.Saunders, 'The Annexation of the Transkeian Territories (1872–1895) with special reference to British and Cape Policy', (Oxford Univ. D.Phil. thesis 1972) pp. 244–5.

2. Brownlee, *Reminiscences*, pp. 208–9; D.B.Hook, *With Sword and Statute* (London, 1906) p. 278.

3. Barkly, *Among Boers and Basutos*, pp. 168–9, 198.

4. [Footnote to original excerpt] Rainfall $4\frac{1}{2}$ inches in December and $7\frac{1}{2}$ inches in both January and February, and 28 inches January to June; average annual rainfall being 30 inches.

5. Tylden, *The Rise of the Basuto*, p. 149.

6. Hadley, *Doctor to Basuto, Boer & Briton*, p. 84.

7. Tylden, *The Rise of the Basuto*, p. 164.

8. Sir George Pomeroy-Colley—High Commissioner for South-Eastern Africa—suffered two initial reverses on 29 Jan. and 9 Feb. 1881. On 27 February, shortly after this letter was written, he was killed at Majuba.

9. Rhodes House, MSS. Afr. 5969 (Kennan Papers) p. 48: Robert Kennan to his mother, no. 63, 17 Feb. 1881. See also Mohapeloa, *Rule by Proxy*, p. 64.

10. Benyon, 'Basutoland and the High Commission', pp. 471–6.
11. Robinson took up his post on 22 Jan. 1881.
12. Germond, *Chronicles of Basutoland*, p. 376, quoting Dieterlen.
13. *Cape Parl. Papers*, A. 44–81, p. 27: Griffith to Robinson, no. 49 (tel.), 17 Apr. 1881; Germond, *Chronicles of Basutoland*, pp. 377–8.
14. *Cape Parl. Papers*, A. 44–81, pp. 29–30: Griffith to Robinson, no. 54 (tel.) 20 Apr. 1881.
15. Ibid., p. 30: Robinson to Griffith, no. 55 (tel.) 20 Apr. 1881.
16. Ibid., pp. 35–6: Minute from Ministers to Robinson, 29 Apr. 1881.
17. Ibid., G. 26–82, p. 5: Award of 29 Apr. 1881.
18. Cape, N.A. 278: Barkly to Griffith, 22 Sept. 1880, encl. in Griffith to Ayliff, no. 2/160, 28 Sept. 1880.
19. e.g. Ibid., Letsie to Griffith, 5 Dec. 1880, encl. in Griffith to Ayliff, no. 2/186, 13 Dec. 1880; various letters in N.A. 279 in February and March.
20. e.g. Cape, N.A. 278: Letsie to Griffith, 13 Dec. 1880, encl. in Griffith to Ayliff, no. 2/190, 18 Dec. 1880; various letters in N.A. 279 in February and March.
21. *Cape Parl. Papers*, G. 20–81, p. 14.
22. Widdicombe, *Fourteen Years in Basutoland*, p. 220.
23. Rhodes House, MSS. Brit. Emp. s. 18 (Anti-Slavery Society Papers), C140/242: Mabille to Chesson, 7 Apr. 1881.
24. Cape, N.A. 279: Griffith to Sauer, no. 2/257, 27 June 1881.
25. Cape, N.A. 280: Griffith to the Resident Magistrates and other gentlemen in the civil service, Basutoland, 26 Aug. 1881.
26. Cape Archives, acc. 1624 (3) (Wiid Collection) item I: memorandum by Sauer on Basutoland, 14 May 1881.
27. Lesotho, S9/1/3/2: Griffith to Gladwin, 9 July 1875.
28. E. Bradlow, 'The Cape Government's Rule of Basutoland, 1871–1883', *Archives Year Book for South African History* (1968) ii. 114.
29. Orpen, *Reminiscences*, pp. 208–17, 248; *Cape Parl. Papers*, A. 18–72, Select Committee on the Basutoland Regulations, pp. 11–12: Appendix A. In\1863\he had offered his 'permanent services to government as agent among the Basutos should such an office be constituted'. Cape, G.H. 10/7: Orpen to Wodehouse, 8 July 1863.
30. e.g. Cape, N.A. 280: Davies to Orpen, 20 Sept. 1881, encl. in Orpen to Sauer, no. 2/289, 27 Sept. 1881; Masopha to Orpen, 15 Oct. 1881, encl. in Orpen to Sauer, no. 2/306; 26 Oct. 1881; Orpen to Sauer, no. 2/325, 29 Nov. 1881; Surmon to Orpen, 30 Nov. 1881, encl. in Orpen to Sauer, no. 2/326, 3 Dec. 1881.
31. Printed in full in the *Eastern Star* and reproduced verbatim in Tylden, *The Rise of the Basuto*, pp. 173–8.
32. Cape, N.A. 280: C.G.H. Bell to Orpen, 29 Sept. 1881; Orpen to Sauer, no. 2/328, 4 Dec. 1881.
33. Ibid., Davies to Orpen, 17 Nov. 1881, encl. in Orpen to Sauer, no. 2/318, 18 Nov. 1881.
34. Ibid., Cape, N.A. 281: article from the *Kaffrarian Watchman*, of 4 Jan. 1882, encl. in Orpen to Sauer, 20 Jan. 1882.
35. Ibid., Maitin to Orpen, 15 Jan. 1882, encl. in Orpen to Sauer, no. 2/367, 19 Jan. 1882.
36. Cape, N.A. 282: Rolland to Sauer, no. 2/495, 15 May 1882, and enclosures;

Cape, N.A. 281: F. Bell to Orpen, 9 Mar. 1882, encl. in Orpen to Sauer, no. 2/430, 11 Mar. 1882.

37. Cape, N.A. 280: Davies to Orpen, 21 Dec. 1881, encl. in Orpen to Sauer, no. 2/346, 26 Dec. 1881; N.A. 281: Davies to Rose Innes, 20 Mar. 1882.

38. Lesotho, S9/2/2/3: Orpen to C.G.H. Bell, 30 Sept. 1882.

39. Cape, N.A. 279: Griffith to Sauer, no. 2/251, 8 June 1881; N.A. 280: A.Barkly to Sauer, 1 Dec. 1881.

40. Cape, N.A. 279: Griffith to Sauer, no. 2/261, 4 July 1881; Hadley, *Doctor to Basuto, Boer & Briton*, p. 90. Dove records that even the rebel leaders mourned his death and followed his body to the grave. See Dove, 'The History of Basutoland "Camps"', op. cit., p. 31.

41. Cape, N.A. 274: Griffith to Brownlee, no. 26, 11 Apr. 1877; *Cape Parl. Papers*, G. 47–82, p. 157: enclosure A in Orpen to Sauer, no. 28, 16 Mar. 1882.

42. Cape, N.A. 282: Carlisle to Clarke, 22 Aug. 1882, encl. in Orpen to Sauer, no. 2/549, 26 Aug. 1882; N.A. 283: Blyth to Sauer, no. 65/A, 8 Apr. 1883, minute, 30 Apr. 1883.

43. Ibid., Blyth to Sauer, no. 33/83, 7 Apr. 1883.

44. Cape, N.A. 282: Orpen to Sauer, no. 2/495, 15 May 1882 and enclosure; Hadley, *Doctor to Basuto, Boer & Briton*, p. 93.

45. e.g. Cape, N.A. 281: Orpen to Sauer, no. 2/413, 2 Feb. 1882; 6 Mar. 1882 and enclosures; 11 Mar. 1882 and enclosure; no. 2/439, 16 Mar. 1882; N.A. 282: Orpen to Sauer, 25 Mar. 1882; 4 Apr. 1882 and enclosures; 9 May 1882; no. 2/590, 25 Nov. 1882 and enclosure. See also J.W. Matthews, *Incwadi Yami or Twenty Years' Personal Experience in South Africa* (London, 1887) pp. 373–90.

46. *Cape Parl. Papers*, G. 26–82, pp. 50–1; Mohapeloa, *Rule by Proxy*, pp. 68–9.

47. Probably by Dr. Eugène Casalis. See Germond, *Chronicles of Basutoland*, p. 397. The expedition to capture Masopha had run into difficulties from the beginning. After various delays, it had marched to Thaba-Bosiu, but Orpen then had great difficulty persuading certain of its members to make the final move against Masopha. When Letsie was finally induced to order his force up the mountain, they found it undefended, Masopha having had most of his cattle driven into the mountains, while he himself retired to his village below Thaba-Bosiu. When summoned to attend Letsie on the mountain, he refused, but the Sotho could not be persuaded to attack him personally and by 19 January the expedition dispersed. See *Brit. Parl. Papers* 1882, xlvii [C.3112] pp. 128–32: telegrams of Orpen to Sauer.

48. Smith, *The Mabilles*, p. 309.

49. Cape, N. A. 281: Bailie's report for 1881, 7 Jan. 1882, encl. in Orpen to Sauer, no. 2/410, 19 Feb. 1882.

50. Cape, N. A. 280: Surmon's report, 30 Nov. 1881, encl. in Orpen to Sauer, no. 2/326, 3 Dec. 1881.

51. Ibid., Bailie's report, 29 Nov. 1881, encl. in Orpen to Sauer, no. 2/326, 3 Dec. 1881.

52. Cape, N. A. 281: Hatchard to Orpen, 9 Jan. 1882, for Cape Native Blue Book.

53. e.g. Ibid., Surmon's annual report, 6 Jan. 1882, encl. in Orpen to Sauer, no.2/410, 19 Feb. 1882; Nettleton to Orpen, 26 Jan. 1882, encl. in Orpen to Sauer, no. 2/396, 11 Feb. 1882; *Cape Parl. Papers*, G. 47–82, p. 192; Cape, N. A. 280: Bailie's report, 29 Nov. 1881, encl. in Orpen to Sauer, no. 2/326, 3 Dec. 1881.

54. Cape, N. A. 281: Reports by Surmon, Clarke and Fr. Gerard, encl. in Orpen to Sauer, no. 2/410, 19 Feb. 1882; Widdicombe, *Fourteen Years in Basutoland*, pp. 238–9.
55. e.g. Smith, *The Mabilles*, pp. 302, 304–5, 309.
56. Cape, N. A. 280: C. G. H. Bell's report, 30 Nov. 1881, encl. in Orpen to Sauer, no. 2/326, 3 Dec. 1881.
57. Even the old Christian chief, Moletsane, joined the rebels rather than surrender his arms. See Germond, *Chronicles of Basutoland*, p. 364.
58. Ibid., p. 376. The Catholics also remained in contact with them. See Webber, 'The Church in Basutoland', p. 257.
59. Cape, N. A. 281: Widdicombe's report, 4 Jan. 1882, encl. in Orpen to Sauer, no. 2/410, 19 Feb. 1882.
60. Benyon, 'Basutoland and the High Commission', pp. 509–13.
61. *Brit. Parl. Papers* 1883, xlix [C. 3717], pp. 28–9: Orpen to Sauer 15 Feb. 1882.

CHAPTER 12   THE TRIUMPH OF THE CHIEFS

1. *Votes and Proceedings of the Cape Legislative Council*, 1882, Minute I, p. 1: Governor's speech, 17 Mar. 1882.
2. *Cape Parl. Papers*, G. 8–83, p. 294: Orpen to Sauer, 31 Aug. 1882; G. 54–83, p. 58: Letsiè's speech on Quthing at the meeting with Scanlen and Sauer on 26 Mar. 1883.
3. Ibid., A. 24–83, p. 96.
4. Ibid.
5. Ibid., p. 97; Smith, *The Mabilles*, p. 304.
6. *Cape Parl. Papers*, A. 24–83, p. 97.
7. Ibid., pp. 97–8.
8. Benyon, 'Basutoland and the High Commission', pp. 516–7.
9. *Cape Parl. Papers*, G. 8–83, pp. 294–7: Orpen to Sauer, 13 Sept. 1882.
10. Charles George Gordon, a Major-General in the Royal Engineers, had suppressed the Taiping Rebellion in China in 1863–4, been Governor of the Equatorial Provinces of Central Africa in 1873, and Governor-General of the Soudan in 1877–9.
11. E. Bradlow, 'General Gordon in Basutoland', *Historia*, xv (1970) no. 4, p. 227, citing Gordon Correspondence.
12. P. Lewsen, *Selections from the Correspondence of J. X. Merriman 1870–1890* (Cape Town, 1960) pp. 107–9: Merriman to Scanlen, 30 July 1882.
13. *Cape Parl. Papers*, Special Session, G. 5–83, p. 16: Proposed Convention between the Cape and the Basuto, encl. in Gordon to Scanlen, 19 July 1882. On his earlier memorandum on Basutoland, dated 21 May 1882, see A. E. Hake, *The Story of Chinese Gordon*, vol. i (London, 1884) p. 191.
14. Lewsen, *Selections*, pp. 107–9: Merriman to Scanlen, 30 July 1882.
15. *Cape Parl. Papers*, Special Session, G. 6–83, p. 35: report of meeting, 18 Oct. 1882.
16. Ibid., Special Session, G. 9–83 (cont.) p. 6: Orpen's annual report for 1882.
17. Ibid., G. 8–83, p. 293: Orpen to Sauer, 31 Aug. 1882; pp. 294–7: Orpen to Sauer, 13 Sept. 1882.

18. Ibid., Special Session, G. 6–83, p. 5: report of meeting, 16 Sept. 1882.

19. Ibid., p. 6.

20. Cape, N. A. 282: Rolland's report of Letsie's message of 17 Sept. 1882, encl. in Orpen to Sauer, 30 Sept. 1882. See also Orpen Papers (Acc. 302), 1: Nehemiah to Orpen, 16 Aug. 1897.

21. *Cape Parl. Papers*, Special Session, G. 6–83, p. 4.

22. Ibid., pp. 9–10: The Basuto Embroglio, 19 Sept. 1882. He was referring to the earlier 1882 attempt to subdue Masopha: see p. 158.

23. Benyon, 'Basutoland and the High Commission', p. 539.

24. For a discussion of Sauer's role in Gordon's visit to Masopha, see ibid., pp. 541–5, 548–52; Bradlow, 'General Gordon in Basutoland', pp. 233–5.

25. *Cape Parl. Papers*, Special Session, G. 6–83, p. 7: Gordon to Sauer, 24 Sept. 1882.

26. Ibid., p. 21: Gordon to Scanlen (tel.) 11 Oct. 1882.

27. Ibid., Sauer to Gordon, 26 Sept. 1882, and enclosure.

28. Ibid., pp. 11–13: annexure A, no. 7.

29. Ibid., p. 11: Garcia to Sauer, 25 Sept. 1882.

30. Ibid., p. 7: Sauer to Gordon, 26 Sept. 1882; p. 16: Garcia to Sauer, 26 Sept. 1882.

31. Ibid., p. 7: Sauer to Gordon, 26 Sept. 1882.

32. Ibid., p. 16: Garcia to Sauer, 26 Sept. 1882; p. 15: Sauer to Garcia, 26 Sept. 1882.

33. Ibid., p. 17: Garcia to Sauer, 27 Sept. 1882.

34. Benyon 'Basutoland and the High Commission', p. 555, citing J. M. Orpen's 'General Gordon's Visit and my Administration', p. 78, in the Cory Library.

35. *Cape Parl. Papers*, Special Session, G. 6–83, p. 8: Sauer to Gordon, 26 Sept. 1882.

36. Ibid., p. 28: Letsie to Sauer, 17 Oct. 1882.

37. Ibid., p. 35: Report of meeting on 18 Oct. 1882.

38. For a vivid description of the attack, see Hadley, *Doctor to Basuto, Boer & Briton*, pp. 85–7.

39. *Cape Parl. Papers*, Special Session, G. 9–83: pp. 7–30; G. 6–83: reports of magistrates and missionaries in Basutoland for 1882.

40. Ibid., G. 9–83 (cont.), p. 5.

41. Lagden, *The Basutos*, ii, 539–40.

42. See Benyon, 'Basutoland and the High Commission', pp. 568–74, for a detailed account of various parliamentarians' attitudes towards the policy.

43. See *Cape Parl. Papers*, G. 54–83, A. 24–83, A. 24A–83, and A. 24B–83 for reports on the meetings.

44. To judge from the accounts of the meetings of 19 and 20 March 1883, the commoners generally would have preferred some sort of Government presence to protect them from the arbitrary powers of their chiefs, but would probably have loyally accepted their chiefs' decision.

45. Cape, N. A. 282: Orpen to Sauer, no. 2/600, 25 Dec. 1882, and enclosures; *Cape Parl. Papers*, G. 8–83, pp. 271–2.

46. Ibid., G. 96–83; Hadley, *Doctor to Basuto, Boer & Briton*, p. 95.

47. Ibid., A. 24–83, p. 10: Sauer to Orpen (tel.) 9 Feb. 1883.

48. F. N. Streatfield, *Reminiscences of an Old 'Un* (London, 1911) p. 235.

49. *Cape Parl. Papers*, G. 54–83, p. 39.

50. Lesotho, S9/2/2/3: Scanlen to Letsie, 31 Mar. 1883, enclosing proposed terms for the future government of Basutoland.
51. Smith, *The Mabilles*, pp. 315–16.
52. Hamilton Moore Dyke, 1817–98. He joined the French Protestant Mission in Lesotho in 1839, and from 1869 until 1874 was the Director of the Normal School run by the mission. He returned to Europe from 1875 to 1877 and retired in 1878, after which he remained at Morija until his death.
53. Smith, *The Mabilles*, pp. 315–16, citing the J.M.E., vol. lviii, p. 250 *et seq.*
54. *Cape Parl. Papers*, G. 8–83 (cont.), pp. 19–20.
55. Cape, N. A. 283: Blyth to Sauer, no. 41/83, 27 Apr. 1883. 'Mama' is a spelling of 'Maama' sometimes used by contemporary writers.
56. *Cape Parl. Papers*, A. 24–83, p. 73: Blyth to Sauer (tel.) no. 192, 1 May 1883. Blyth believed Masopha was 'the prime mover' behind Joel's attack. See ibid., G. 3–84, pp. 82–3: Blyth's report, 12 Jan. 1884.
57. Widdicombe, *Fourteen Years in Basutoland*, p. 227. There are dramatic descriptions of the attack in Hadley, *Doctor to Basuto, Boer & Briton*, pp. 98–103; Widdicombe, *Fourteen Years in Basutoland*, pp. 227–34.
58. Rhodes House, MSS. Afr. 5969 (Kennan Papers): Thomas Kennan to his father, no. 76, 30 July 1883; *Cape Parl. Papers*, A. 24–83, p. 78: Blyth to Sauer (tel.) no. 231, 27 May 1883. For minutes of the meeting, see Cape, N. A. 283: Blyth to Sauer, no. 53/83, 30 May 1883, and enclosure. Joel proved reluctant to accept Letsie's ruling and sporadic fighting continued between the brothers even after the *pitso*.
59. *Brit. Parl. Papers* 1883, xlviii [C.3708], pp. 1–3 Smyth to Derby, 1 May 1883, enclosing Scanlen's minute of 30 Apr. 1883; Cape, N. A. 283: Blyth to Sauer, no. 68/83, 1 July 1883, and enclosed letter to Letsie, no. 310E.
60. Hadley, *Doctor to Basuto, Boer & Briton*, p. 108; Cape, N. A. 283, Blyth to Sauer, no. 115/83, 1 Dec, 1883, and enclosures.
61. Under the new regulations apparently, Letsie legally retained all fines he imposed. In the three months from 1 July–30 Sept. 1883, Blyth received only £14–16s.–3d. in fines. See Cape, N. A. 283: Blyth to Sauer, no. 129/AF, 13 Sept. 1883; statement of actual revenue received, encl. in Blyth to Sauer, no. 135/AF, 13 Oct. 1883.
62. Ibid., Blyth to Sauer, no, 63/83, 22 June 1883.
63. Ibid., Blyth to Sauer, no. 73/83, 15 July 1883.
64. Ibid., Blyth to Sauer, no. 80/83, 6 Aug. 1883; no. 102/83, 20 Oct. 1883.
65. Ibid., Blyth to Sauer, no. 93/83, 15 Sept. 1883.
66. Ibid., Blyth to Sauer, no. 73/83, 15 July 1883.
67. E.g., ibid., Blyth to Sauer, no. 87/83, 26 Aug. 1883; no. 129/AF, 13 Sept. 1883; no. 106/83, 27 Oct. 1883.
68. Ibid., See also his report on a witchcraft case in August in ibid., no. 87/83, 26 Aug. 1883.
69. Ibid., Letsie to Blyth, 20 Oct. 1883, encl. in Blyth to Orpen, no. 106/83, 27 Oct. 1883.
70. Ibid., Blyth to Sauer, no. 109/83, 17 Nov. 1883.
71. Ibid., Blyth to Letsie, no. 507 E, 22 Oct. 1883, encl. in Blyth to Sauer, no. 106/83, 27 Oct. 1883.
72. Smith, *The Mabilles*, pp. 317–18.
73. P.R.O., C.O. 48/507: Smyth to Derby, no. 369, 12 Dec. 1883, enclosing report

of the *pitso* from the *Friend of the Free State*, 6 Dec. 1883. Blyth's report of the *pitso* is enclosed in Lesotho, S7/7/1: Blyth to Robinson, no. 116/83, 1 Dec. 1883.

74. RaManella was a nephew of Moshoeshoe who had proved difficult to control even in Moshoeshoe's day, when his cattle-raiding activities had caused Moshoeshoe considerable problems with the Free State and Natal.

75. *Brit. Parl. Papers* 1884, lvi [C. 3855] p. 47: Smyth to Derby (tel.), received 12 Dec. 1883. In contrast, after the national *pitso* Joel and RaManella sent word that 'they followed Letsea', although RaManella apparently soon changed his mind. See *Cape Parl. Papers*, G. 3–84: Blyth's report, 12 Jan. 1884; Cape, N. A. 284: Blyth to Sauer, no. 12/83 [sic], 16 Feb. 1884.

76. *Friend of the Free State*, 6 Dec. 1883: report of the *pitso*.

77. Benyon, 'Basutoland and the High Commission', pp. 617–19.

78. Cape, N. A. 284: Blyth to Sauer, no. 12/83 [sic], 16 Feb. 1884.

79. Ibid., enclosure Letsie to Blyth, 11 Feb. 1884.

80. Ibid., Letsie to the Cape Government via Blyth, 14 Feb. 1884, encl. in no. 13/84, 16 Feb. 1884.

81. Order in Council, 2 Feb. 1884, proclaimed as Proclamation No. 75a, 1884.

82. Cape, N. A. 284: Blyth to Sauer, no. 16/84, 18 Mar. 1884. Clarke had served as a magistrate in Basutoland from September 1881 to April 1882.

83. *Brit. Parl. Papers* 1884–5, lvi [C. 4263] pp. 75–80: proclamation by Robinson.

84. Lagden, *The Basutos*, ii. 598.

85. For an account of these years, see ibid., pp. 576–94.

86. Cape, Orpen Papers (Acc. 302), 1: Goring to Orpen, 8 Feb. 1898.

87. For a description of this action, see ibid.; Tylden, *The Rise of the Basuto*, pp. 198–9.

EPILOGUE

1. Cape, N.A. 284: annotated copy of Basutoland regulations; Burman, 'Cape Policies towards African Law', p. 362.

2. See R. L. Kidder's discussion of the mechanisms of imposing law in 'Towards an Integrated Theory of Imposed Law' in Burman and Harrell-Bond, op. cit.

3. See pp. 76–7.

4. See p. 82.

5. See p. 78.

6. See p. 118.

7. See pp. 91–3.

8. Tylden, *The Rise of the Basuto*, p. 175, quoting the report in the *Eastern Star*. Both George and Sofonia Moshoeshoe subsequently decided that there was no future for them in Basutoland. They each accepted land in Griqualand East, granted to them by the Cape Government, and left Basutoland.

Bibliography

A   Manuscript Sources
    1. Official
    2. Unofficial
B   Printed Sources
    1. Primary Sources
       a. Official Records
       b. Newspapers and Periodicals
       c. Contemporary Books and Pamphlets
       d. Documents subsequently published
    2. Secondary Sources
       a. Books, Pamphlets and Articles
       b. Unpublished Theses

A MANUSCRIPT SOURCES

1 OFFICIAL

a ***In the Public Record Office, London.***

i Cape of Good Hope, Original Correspondence from Cape Town to London: Despatches and enclosures (including Offices and Individuals). vol. C.O. 48/162 (1835)–vol. C.O. 48/510 (1884).

ii Cape of Good Hope, Entry Books of Correspondence from London to Cape Town. vol. C.O. 49/41 (1847)–vol. C.O. 49/61 (1872) (end of C.O. 49 series).

iii Cape of Good Hope, Minutes of the Cape Executive Council. vols. C.O. 51/126 (1866–8) and 51/163 (1869–72).

b ***In the Cape Archives, Cape Town.*** (Papers are listed as in the Archives. At the time research for this book was done, files originally numbered up to 119 had been split up and renumbered. Numbers below from NA 150 are the original numbers.)

i Native Affairs Department Papers

N.A. 1–10: Letters from Chief Magistrate, Transkei (1878–81).

N.A. 272–84: Letters from Governor's Agent, Basutoland (1873–84).
N.A. 294–309: Letters from Government Departments (1873–84).
N.A. 840–1: Letter Books (1873–6).
N.A. 932: Letters despatched (1879–80).
N.A. 1050: Circulars, Native Affairs Department.
ii Government House Papers
G.H. 10/7: Letters Received, Private and Semi-Official (1863–9).
G.H. 14/7: Letters from Native Chiefs and British Officials in Basutoland (1864–83).
G.H. 17/2: Letters from Supreme Court, Attorney General, and other departments (1850–84).
iii Prime Minister's Office Papers
P.M. 259: Prime Minister's correspondence, minutes, memoranda, etc. (1875–81).
iv Colonial Office Papers
C.O. 5488: Basutoland Letter Book.
C.O. 5489: Index.
v Unpublished Basutoland Records (Collected by G. M. Theal) vols. iv–vi (1868–72) – contains unofficial material too.

c *In the Lesotho Archives, Maseru*

i Governor's Agent to High Commissioner and Colonial Secretary. S9/1/1/1–S9/1/1/2 (1871–81).

ii Governor's Agent to Secretary for Native Affairs. S9/1/2/1–S9/1/2/3 (1873–84).

iii Governor's Agent: miscellaneous correspondence despatched. S9/1/3/1–S9/1/3/2 (1871–84).

iv Chief Magistrate and Resident Magistrates to Colonial Secretary. S9/2/1/1 (1872–4).

v Chief Magistrate to Magistrates. S9/2/2/1 and S9/2/2/3 (1872–4 and 1876–84).

vi Resident Magistrate, Maseru (out). S9/2/3/1 (1876–83).

vii Miscellaneous. S7/7/1 (1883–4).

viii Pitso Book. S11/1 (1875–6).

ix Leribe: Letters despatched. L2/1/1–L2/1/4 (1872–84).

2 UNOFFICIAL

a *Rhodes House Library, Oxford*

British and Foreign Anti-Slavery and Aborigines Protection

Society (MSS. Br. Emp. s. 18: letters received), (MSS, Br. Emp. s.22).
Hall Papers (MSS. Afr. s.54).
Kennan Papers (MSS. Afr. 5969).
J.C. Molteno Papers (MSS. Afr. s.23).
C.J. Rhodes Papers (MSS. Afr. t.5: Misc. material re Rhodes).
H. Waller Papers (MSS. Afr. s.16)–vol. 2: correspondence with General Gordon.

b **Foreign and Commonwealth Office Library, London**
Wodehouse Papers (13015: Correspondence relative to his term at the Cape).

c **Cape Archives**
Unpublished Basutoland Records (unofficial material).
Brabant Collection (Acc. 459).
Garcia Papers (Acc. 250).
Gordon Papers (Acc. 6).
Griffith Papers (Acc. 1554).
Pattison Papers (Acc. 88).
Orpen Papers (Acc. 302).
Southey Papers (Acc. 611).
Wiid Collection (Acc. 1624 (3)).

d **South African Public Library, Cape Town**
J.X. Merriman Papers.
J.C. Molteno Papers.
J. Noble Papers.

e **Jagger Library, University of Cape Town**
W.E. Stanford Papers.

B. PRINTED SOURCES
1. PRIMARY SOURCES
a **Official Records**
British
i *Colonial Office Confidential Print*—Africa vols. C.O. 879/1–C.O. 879/21.
ii *British Parl. Papers*
1851 xxxvii [1360] Correspondence re Assumption of Sovereignty

over the Territory between the Vaal and Orange Rivers.

1851 xxxviii (424) [1334, 1352, 1380] Correspondence re Kafir tribes.

1852 xxxiii [1428] War of 1850–3 and dubious conduct of Moshesh.

1852–3 lxvi [1635] Correspondence re Kafir tribes.

1852–3 lxvi [1646] Papers re Orange River Territory.

1854 xliii [1758] Correspondence re Orange River Territory.

1854–5 xxxviii [1969] Papers re Kafir tribes.

1856 xlii [2096] Papers re Kafir tribes.

1857 x [2202] Correspondence re Kafir tribes.

1857–8 xl [2352] Papers re Kafir tribes.

1868–9 xliii [4140] Despatches on recognition of Moshesh.

1870 xlix [C.18, C.99] Despatches on recognition of Moshesh.

1870 xlix (181) Correspondence re Responsible Government at Cape.

1871 xlvii [C.459] Correspondence re Cape of Good Hope.

1873 xlix [C.732] Correspondence re Cape of Good Hope.

1877 lx [C.1748, C.1776] Correspondence re Native Affairs in South Africa.

1878 lv [C.1961, C.2000] Correspondence re South Africa.

1878 lvi [C.2079, C.2100, C.2144] Correspondence re South Africa.

1878–9 liii [C.2252, C.2260, 2318] Correspondence re South Africa.

1878–9 liv [C.2374, C.2454] Correspondence re South Africa.

1880 l [C.2482, C.2505] Correspondence re South Africa.

1880 li [C.2569] Correspondence re Basutoland.

1880 li [C.2676, C.2695] Correspondence re South Africa.

1881 lxvi [C.2740] Correspondence re South Africa.

1881 lxvi [C.2754] Instructions to Sir H. Robinson on assuming office.

1881 lxvi [C.2755, C.2821] Correspondence re Basutoland.

1881 lxvii [C.2964] Correspondence re Basutoland.

1882 xlvii [C.3112, C.3175] Correspondence re Basutoland and Territories to Eastward of Cape Colony.

1882 xlvii [C.3113] Correspondence re Basutoland etc.

1883 xlviii [C.3493] Correspondence re Basutoland and the Native Territories.

1883 xlviii [C.3708] Correspondence re Basutoland.

1883 xlix [C.3717] Correspondence re Cape and Adjacent Territories.
1884 lvi [C.3855] Correspondence re Cape and Adjacent Territories.
1884–5 lvi [C.4263, C.4589] Correspondence re Cape and Adjacent Territories.
Hansard's Parliamentary Debates 3rd series.
iii. *The Colonial Office List*
1873–1884

Cape
  i *Votes and Proceedings of the Legislative Council* 1872–1884
  ii *Votes and Proceedings of the House of Assembly* 1872–1884
iii *Annexures and Appendices to the Votes and Proceedings of the Cape Parliament* (cited in the footnotes as *Cape Parl. Papers*).
The series number 'C' papers were printed by order of the Legislative Council, 'A' papers by order of the Assembly, and 'G' papers by order of the Government.
A. 37–68 Despatch re Moshesh's offer to Natal.
G. 30–68 Correspondence re annexation of Basutoland.
G. 32–68 Further correspondence re annexation of Basutoland.
G. 40–68 Further correspondence re annexation of Basutoland.
A. 4–71 Despatches from Secretary of State re South African Federation.
A. 43, 44, 45–71 Petitions of Tozane, Tsueu Lepota, and George Parkies respectively.
C. 1–71 Report of the Select Committee on the Basutoland Annexation Bill.
C. 1–72 Minutes of Executive on Responsible Government.
C. 6–72 Petition of the Basuto praying for Representation in Parliament.
A. 18–72 Report of the Select Committee on the Basuto Regulations.
A. 12–73 Report of the Select Committee on Native Affairs.
A. 23–73 Report of Governor's Agent on working of Basuto regulations.
G. 25–73 Basutoland Estimates, 1873.
G. 27–73 Report of Governor's Agent.
(Appendix III) Report of Special Commission on the Laws and Customs of the Basuto (1873).
G. 27–74 Blue Book on Native Affairs.

G. 41–74 Basutoland Estimates, 1974.

C. 17–75 Census Returns for Basutoland (population).

C. 18–75 Census Returns for Basutoland (stock).

G. 21–75 Blue Book on Native Affairs.

G. 33–75 Statement of Revenue and Expenditure in Basutoland during 1874.

G. 46–75 Correspondence relating to the rebel chief Langalibalele.

G. 48–75 Basutoland Estimates, 1875.

A. 19–76 Petition of the P.E.M.S. against cession of Basutoland to the Orange Free State.

G. 16–76 Blue Book on Native Affairs.

G. 19–76 Revenue and Expenditure, Basutoland, 1875.

G. 37–76 Report of a Commission on the Affairs of Griqualand East.

G. 52–76 Appendix to Blue Book on Native Affairs.

G. 55, 56–76 Basutoland Estimates for half year ended 30 June 1876 and for 1876/77.

A. 7–77 Petition of Letsie and others.

A. 9–77 Papers re Nehemiah Moshesh.

G. 1–77 Report and Proceedings of the Colonial Defence Commission.

G. 12–77 Blue Book on Native Affairs.

G. 52–77 Basutoland Estimates, 1877/78.

A. 12–78 Petition of Chief of People of Basutoland.

G. 17–78 Blue Book on Native Affairs.

G. 56–78 Basutoland Estimates, 1877.

A. 6–79 Report of the Select Committee on Hostilities in Basutoland.

A. 17, 49, 50–79 Papers on the Basutoland Rebellion.

A. 27–79 Statement showing the Total Expenditure on Account of . . . the Campaign against Moorosi.

G. 33, 33A, 43–79 Blue Book on Native Affairs and Appendix.

G. 57–79 Basutoland Estimates, 1879/80.

A. 10–80 Petition of Letsie and other chiefs to retain arms.

A. 11–80 Petition of Letsie, other chiefs and headmen against the confiscation of Moorosi's land.

A. 12–80 Correspondence re disarmament.

A. 17–80 Balance to the credit of Basutoland (Revenue) Deposit Account in the Treasury.

A. 31–80 Proclamations of Laws of Native Territories annexed.

A. 38–80 Disposal of Quthing to the Cape.
A. 52–80 Basutoland Affairs.
G. 13–80 Blue Book on Native Affairs.
G. 57–80 Basutoland Estimates, 1880/81.
A. 6–81 Correspondence on Command of Troops.
A. 7–81 Correspondence on Bright and Rose Innes.
A. 22–81 Telegraphic Correspondence between Cape Colonial Secretary and Col. C. D. Griffith.
A. 24–81 Correspondence re Basuto.
A. 25–81 Reports from Chief Magistrates and Resident Magistrates on Basutoland and Transkeian Affairs.
A. 29–81 Correspondence and Telegrams on Disarmament.
A. 44–81 Minutes etc. on Basuto Peace Negotiations.
A. 64, 77, 81–81 Petitions against war and for transfer of Basutoland.
G. 20–81 Blue Book on Native Affairs.
G. 38–81 Native Laws Commission Report.
G. 43–81 Basutoland Estimates, 1881/82.
A. 2–82 Petition of Jonathan Molapo for relief.
A. 8–82 Telegraphic Correspondence re Masupha's acceptance of High Commissioner's Award.
A. 19–82 Message from the President of the Orange Free State re Basutoland Policy.
A. 30–82 Correspondence between Griffith and Sprigg.
C. 5–82 Select Committee on Basutoland Affairs.
G. 12–82 Correspondence on Basutoland Affairs.
G. 26–82 Report of Secretary for Native Affairs on visit of June 1881.
G. 33–82 Blue Book on Native Affairs, Part I.
G. 47–82 Blue Book on Native Affairs, Part II.
G. 74–82 Report of *Pitso* held at Maseru by Hatchard with the loyal Basuto.
G. 83–82 Basutoland Estimates, 1882/83.
G. 89–82 Correspondence called for by Dr. Matthews, M.L.A. on Basutoland.
G. 97–82 Supplementary Estimates for Basutoland, 1882/83.
Special Session 1883
A. 1–83 Petition of Jonathan Molappo.
A. 3–83 Minutes of Governor and Official Correspondence on Basutoland.
A. 6–83 Statement of Revenue and Expenditure in Basutoland.

A. 7–83 Correspondence with Secretary of State on Native Affairs.
C. 4–83 Return of Basutoland Revenue, from 1 Jan.–30 Nov. 1882.
G. 4–83 Report of the Commission on Native Laws and Customs.
G. 5–83 Correspondence between Gordon and the Government on Basutoland Affairs, and the Colonial Forces.
G. 6–83 Minutes of meetings and correspondence on Affairs in Basutoland by Sauer.
G. 9, 9 (cont.)–83 Basutoland Reports.
G. 10–83 Parts I & II Basutoland: Telegrams on progress of events, 17–24 Jan. and 25 Jan.–1 Feb. 1883.
Ordinary Session 1883
A. 27, 36–83 Despatches re annexation of Basutoland.
A. 29, 34, 40–83 Correspondence with President and Administrator of Orange Free State and Volksraad resolutions.
C. 3–83 Correspondence between Jonathan Molapo and Gordon; Cost of Lerothodi's movement against Masupha; Payments to members of Parliamentary Commissions.
G. 8, 8(cont.)–83 Blue Book on Native Affairs.
G. 54, A. 24, A. 24A, A. 24B–83 Interviews of Basuto Chiefs and Headmen with Sprigg and Sauer.
G. 96–83 Report of Commission or War Losses.
G. 106–83 Correspondence re stolen cattle traced to Basutoland.
G. 109–83 Report re Threatened Combination in Extra-Colonial Territories.
G. 110–83 Report of the Civil Service Commission.
G. 3–84 Blue Book on Native Affairs.
C. 3–85 Basutoland Report of the Resident Commissioner.
iv *The Cape of Good Hope Government Gazette* 1872–1884
 v *Statutes of the Cape of Good Hope 1652–1895*
H. Tennant and E. Jackson (eds), 3 vols. (Cape Town, 1895).

b Newspapers and Periodicals
The only newspaper in Basutoland during the period covered by this book was the missionary newspaper *Leselinyana la Lesotho*, and its slightly modified English version The *Little Light of Basutoland*, published at Morija between 1872–7. Newspapers in the Orange Free State and Cape carried original articles on Basutoland, such as the *Friend of the Free State* (Bloemfontein), *De Express en Oranjevrijstaatsch Advertentieblad* (Bloemfontein), the *Cape Times* (Cape Town), the *Cape Argus* (Cape Town), the *Eastern Star* (Grahamstown), the *Graham's Town Journal* (Grahamstown), the

Kaffrarian Watchman (King William's Town) and the *Christian Express* (Lovedale). Towards the end of the period covered, articles appeared in the Transvaal and Natal newspapers too. In Britain, *The Times* was the best source, but a few articles on Basutoland also appeared in periodicals, e.g. the *Nineteenth Century* and the *Gentleman's Magazine*, and illustrations in such publications as the Graphic and the *Illustrated London News*. The Paris Evangelical Mission Society's *Journal des Missions Evangéliques* (Paris) published many articles on Basutoland.

c Contemporary Books, Pamphlets and Articles

A Colonial Officer (Woon, H. V.). *Twenty-Five Years Soldiering in South Africa* (London, 1909).

Arbousset, T. *Relation d'un voyage d'exploration au nord-est de la colony du Cap de bonne–esperance* (Paris, 1842). An English translation by J. C. Brown, *Narrative of an Exploratory Tour to the North-East of the Colony of the Cape of Good Hope*, was published in Cape Town in 1846 and in London in 1852.

Backhouse, J. *Extracts from the letters of James Backhouse* (London, 1841).

Barkly, F. *Among Boers and Basutos* (London, 1893).

Brownlee, C. *Reminiscences of Kaffir Life and History* (Lovedale, 1896; 2nd ed. Lovedale, n.d.; Killie Campbell Africana Library Reprint Series, Pietermaritzburg, 1977).

Bryce, J. *Impressions of South Africa* (London, 1897).

Caldecott, A. *The Government and Civilization of the Native Races of South Africa* (Cape Town, 1884).

Casalis, E. *Les Bassoutos* (Paris, 1859: reprinted 1930). An English translation, *The Basutos*, was published in London in 1861.

——, *Mes Souvenirs* (Paris, 1882). An English translation by J. Brierley, *My Life in Basutoland*, was published in London in 1889.

Chalmers, J. *The Native Question* (Grahamstown, 1878)

Chesson, F. W. *The Basuto War* (London, 1881).

Cunynghame, A. T. *My Command in South Africa, 1874–1878* (London, 1879).

Ellenberger, D. F. *History of the Basuto, Ancient and Modern* (rewritten in English by J. C. Macgregor, London, 1912).

Frere, B. *On the Laws affecting the Relations between Civilized and Savage Life* (pamphlet, London, 1882).

Griffith, C., 'Some Observations on Witchcraft in Basutoland' (communicated by J. X. Merriman), *The Transactions of the South African Philosophical Society*, i (1877–80).

Hook, D. B. *With Sword and Statute* (London, n.d. (?1907)).

Irvine, T. W. *British Basutoland and the Basutos* (London, 1881).

Mabille, H. E. 'The Basuto of Basutoland', *Journal of the Africa Society*, v, 19 and 20 (1906).

Macgregor, J. C. *Basuto Traditions* (Cape Town, 1905; Hiddingh Reprint Series, Cape Town, 1957).

——, 'Some Notes on the Basuto Tribal System, Political and Social', *The South African Journal of Science*, v, 7 (1910).

Mackenzie, J. *Austral Africa, Losing it or Ruling it*, 2 vols. (London, 1887).

Maclean, C. B. (ed.), *A Compendium of Kafir Laws and Customs* (Mount Coke, 1858; Cape Town, 1866; Grahamstown, 1906).

Malan, C. H. *South African Missions* (London, 1876).

Martin, M. *Basutoland: Its Legends and Customs* (London, 1903).

Matthews, J. W. *Incwadi Yami or Twenty Years' Personal Experience in South Africa* (London, 1887).

Moletsane, A. A. *An Account of the Autobiographical Memoir* (privately printed for Capt. R. S. Webb, Paarl, 1967).

Mosh[o]esh[oe], Nehemiah. *Statement made by Nehemiah when in prison for the guidance of counsel* (pamphlet, Kind William's Town, 1877).

——, 'A Little Light from Basutoland', *Cape Monthly Magazine*, (1880) pp. 221–33; 280–92.

Noble, J. *South Africa, Past and Present* (London, 1877).

Orpen, J. M. *History of the Basutus in South Africa, by the Special Commissioner of the Cape Argus* (Cape Town, 1857).

——, *Our Relations with the Imperial Government* (Cape Town, 1879).

——, *Some Principles of Native Government Illustrated* (Cape Town, 1880).

——, *Reminiscences of Life in South Africa from 1845 to the Present Day* (Durban, 1908; enlarged edition by Struik, Cape Town, 1964).

Streatfield, F. N. *Reminiscences of an Old 'Un* (London, 1911).

Trollope, A. *South Africa*, 2 vols (London, 1878).

Widdicombe, J. *Fourteen Years in Basutoland* (London, 1891).

——, *In the Lesuto* (London, 1895).

d   Documents subsequently published

Berthoud, P. *Lettres missionaires de M. & Mme. Paul Berthoud, de la Mission romande, 1873–1879* (Lausanne, 1900).

Buckle, G. E. (ed.), *Correspondence between Major General Gordon and Mr. Scanlen* (Cape Town, 1905).

Damane, M. and Sanders, P. B. (eds), 'The Story of the Sotho – Part I', *Mohlomi, Journal of Southern African Historical Studies*, ii (1978).

Gérard, J. *Le Père Gérard nous parle . . .*, vol. 2: *Son Premiere Sejour a Roma 1862–1875* (Roma, 1969); vol. 3: *Son Sejour a Ste-Monique 1876–1897* (Roma, 1970). (Father Gérard's diaries, edited by the Roman Catholic Mission in Lesotho.)

Germond, R. C. *Chronicles of Basutoland* (Morija, 1967).

Hadley, P. (ed.), *Doctor to Basuto, Boer & Briton 1877–1906* (Cape Town, 1972).

Herstlet, E. (ed.), *The Map of Africa by Treaty*, 2 vols, 2nd rev. edn (London, 1896).

Lewsen, P. (ed.), *Selections from the Correspondence of J. X. Merriman 1870–1890*, vol. i (Cape Town, 1960).

Macquarrie, J. W. (ed.), *The Reminiscences of Sir Walter Stanford*, 2 vols (Cape Town, 1958).

Martineau, J. *The Life and Correspondence of the Right Hon. Sir Bartle Frere*, 2 vols (London, 1895).

Theal, G. M. (ed.), *Basutoland Records*, 3 vols (Cape Town, 1883).

Tindall, B. A. (ed.), *James Rose Innes—Autobiography* (Cape Town, 1949).

2 SECONDARY SOURCES

*a **Books, Pamphlets and Articles***

Allott, A. *Essays in African Law* (London, 1960).

Ashton, E. H. 'Medicine, Magic, and Sorcery among the Southern Sotho', *Communications of the School of African Studies*, University of Cape Town, new series, 10 (Dec. 1943).

——, *The Basuto* (London, 1952).

Atmore, A. 'The Passing of Sotho Independence' in L. M. Thompson (ed.), *African Societies in southern Africa* (London, 1969).

——, 'The Moorosi Rebellion: Lesotho 1879' in R. I. Rotberg and A. A. Mazrui (eds), *Protest and Power in Black Africa* (New York, 1970).

Atmore, A. and Marks, S. 'The Imperial Factor in South Africa in the Nineteenth Century: Towards a Reassessment', *Journal of Imperial and Commonwealth History*, iii, 1 (Oct. 1974).

Atmore, A. and Sanders, P. B. 'Sotho Arms and Ammunition in the Nineteenth Century', *Journal of African History*, xii, 4 (1971).

Benians, E., Butler, J. and Carrington, C. (eds), *The Cambridge History of the British Empire*, iii: *The Empire–Commonwealth, 1870–1919* (Cambridge, 1959).

Bradlow, E. 'The Cape Government's rule of Basutoland 1871–1883', *Archives Year Book for South African History*, 1968, part II.

——, 'General Gordon in Basutoland', *Historia*, xv, 4 (1970).

Breytenbach, W. J. *Crocodiles and Commoners in Lesotho*, Communications of the Africa Institute (Pretoria, 1975).

Brookes, E. *The History of Native Policy in South Africa from 1830 to the Present Day* (n.p., 1924; 2nd edn, Pretoria, 1927).

Brookes, E. and Webb, C. *A History of Natal* (Pietermaritzburg, 1965).

Burman, S. B. (ed.), *The Justice of the Queen's Government*, African Social Research Documents Series, vol. 9 (Leiden/Cambridge, 1976).

——, 'Symbolic Dimensions of the Enforcement of Law', *British Journal of Law and Society*, iii, 2 (1976).

——, 'Masopha' in C. C. Saunders (ed.), *African Leaders in Southern African History* (London, 1979).

Burman, S. B. and Harrell-Bond, B. E. (eds), *The Imposition of Law* (New York, 1979).

Campbell, W. B. 'The South African Frontier 1865–1885: A Study in Expansion', *Archives Year Book for South African History*, 1959, part I.

Crisp, W. *Some Account of the Diocese of Bloemfontein in the Province of South Africa from 1863 to 1894* (pamphlet, Oxford, 1895).

Damane, M. and Sanders, P. B. (eds), *Lithoko: Sotho Praise-Poems* (Oxford, 1974).

Davenport, T. R. H. *The Afrikaner Bond* (Cape Town, 1966).

De Kiewiet, C. W. *British Colonial Policy and the South African Republics 1848–1872* (London, 1929).

——, *The Imperial Factor in South Africa* (London, 1937).

——, 'Social and Economic Development in Native Tribal Life' in E. Walker (ed.), *The Cambridge History of the British Empire*, 2nd edn, vol. viii (Cambridge, 1963).

De Kock, W. 'Ekstra Territoriale Vraagstukke van die Kaapse Regering 1872–85', *Archives Year Book for South African History*, 1948, part I.

De Kock, W., Krüger, D. W. and Beyers, C. J. (eds), *Dictionary of South African Biography*, vols i–iii (Cape Town, 1968–77).

Dieterlen, H. *Eugène Casalis (1812–1891)* (Paris, 1930).

——, *Adolphe Mabille (1836–1894)* (Paris, nouvelle édition, 1933).

Dove, R. 'The History of Basutoland "Camps": 2. Leribe (Hlotse)', *Basutoland Notes and Records*, 1 (1959).

——, *Anglican Pioneers in Lesotho* (Maseru, 1975).

Duncan, P. *Sotho Laws and Customs* (Cape Town, 1960).

Dutton, E. A. T. *The Basuto of Basutoland* (London, 1923).

Elias, T. O. *The Nature of African Customary Law* (Manchester, 1956).

Ellenberger, V. *A Century of Mission Work in Basutoland, 1833–1933* (translated from the French by E. M. Ellenberger, Morija, 1938).

Fairclough, T. L. 'Notes on the Basuto, their history, country, etc.', *Journal of the Africa Society*, iv, 14 (1905).

Favre, E. *Les vingt-cinq ans de Coillard au Lessouto* (Paris, 1931).

Galbraith, J. S. *Reluctant Empire* (Berkeley, 1963).

Gallienne, G. *Thomas Arbousset (1810–1877)* (Paris, 1933).

Gluckman, M. *Politics, Law and Ritual in Tribal Society* (Oxford, 1965).

——, *Ideas and Procedures in African Customary Law* (London, 1969).

Goodfellow, C. *Great Britain and South African Confederation (1870–1881)* (Cape Town, 1966).

Guest, W. R. *Langalibalele: The Crisis in Natal 1873–1875* (Durban, 1976).

Hake, A. E. *The Story of Chinese Gordon*, vol. i (London, 1884).

Haliburton, G. *Historical Dictionary of Lesotho* (New Jersey, 1977).

Hamnett, I. *Chieftainship and Legitimacy: An Anthropological Study of Executive Law in Lesotho* (London, 1975).

Hicks Beach, V. *Life of Sir Michael Hicks Beach*, i (London, 1932).

Jones, G. I. *Basutoland Medicine Murder* (London, 1951).

——, 'Chiefly Succession in Basutoland' in J. Goody (ed.), *Succession to High Office* (Cambridge, 1966).

Kerr, A. J. 'The Reception and Codification of Systems of Law in Southern Africa', *Journal of African Law*, 2 (1958).

Kidder, R. L. 'Towards an Integrated Theory of Imposed Law' in S. B. Burman and B. E. Harrell-Bond (eds), *The Imposition of Law* (New York, 1979).

Kuper, H. and Kuper, L. (eds), *African Law: Adaptation and Development* (Berkeley, 1965).

Lagden, G. *The Basutos*, 2 vols (London, 1909).

Laurence, P. *The Life of John Xavier Merriman* (London, 1930).

Lee, R. W. *Introduction to Roman-Dutch Law* (Oxford, 1915).

Lewin, J. *Studies in African Native Law* (Cape Town, 1947).
——, *An Outline of Native Law*, 4th edn (Cape Town, 1966).
Lewis, I. M. 'A Structural Approach to Witchcraft and Spirit-Possession' in M. Douglas (ed.), *Witchcraft Confessions and Accusations* (London, 1970)
Lewsen, P. 'The First Crisis in Responsible Government in the Cape Colony', *Archives Year Book for South African History*, 1942, part II.
——, *The Cape Liberal Tradition—Myth or Reality?* (pamphlet, Johannesburg, 1969).
Livre d'Or de la Mission du Lessuto, soixante-qunize ans de l'histoire d'un tribu Sud-Africaine, 1833–1908 (Paris, 1912).
Lockhart, J. and Wodehouse, C. *Rhodes* (London, 1963).
Mackintosh, C. W. *Coillard of the Zambesi* (London, 1907).
Macmillan, M. *Sir Henry Barkly: Mediator and Moderator* (Cape Town, 1970).
Macmillan, W. M. *Complex South Africa* (London, 1930).
——, *Bantu, Boer and Briton*, 2nd edn (London, 1963).
Mohapeloa, J. M. *Africans and their Chiefs* (pamphlet, Cape Town, 1945).
——, 'The Essential Masupha', *Lesotho Notes and Records*, 5 (1965–66).
——, *Government by Proxy* (Morija, 1971).
Molteno, P. A. *The Life and Times of Sir John Charles Molteno*, 2 vols (London, 1900).
Newton, A. and Benians, E. (eds), *The Cambridge History of the British Empire*, viii: *South Africa* (Cambridge, 1936: 2nd edn, E. Walker [ed.], 1963).
Omer-Cooper, J. D. *The Zulu Aftermath* (London, 1966).
Poulter, S. *Family Law and Litigation in Basotho Society* (Oxford, 1976).
Ramolefe, A. 'Customary Law Inheritance and Succession', *Basutoland Notes and Records*, 5 (1966).
Roberts, S. A. (ed.)., *Law and the Family in Africa* (The Hague, 1977).
Robertson, H. M. '150 Years of Economic Contact between Black and White', *South African Journal of Economics*, ii, 4 (1934) and iii, 1 (1935).
Robinson, R. and Gallagher, J. 'The Imperialism of Free Trade', *Economic History Review*, 2nd ser. iv, 1 (1953).
Rutherford, J. *Sir George Grey* (London, 1961).
Sachs, A. *Justice in South Africa* (London, 1973).

Sanders, P. B. *Moshoeshoe: Chief of the Sotho* (London, 1975).

——, 'Sekonyela and Moshweshwe: Failure and Success in the Aftermath of the Difaqane', *Journal of African History*, x, 3 (1969).

Schapera, I. (ed.), *The Bantu-Speaking Tribes of South Africa* (London, 1937).

——, *Government and Politics in Tribal Society* (London, 1956).

Seymour, S. M. *Native Law in South Africa* (Cape Town, 1953).

Sheddick, V. G. J. *The Southern Sotho* (London, 1953).

Simons, H. J. *African Women: Their Legal Status in South Africa* (London, 1968).

Smith, E. W. *The Mabilles of Basutoland* (London, 1939).

Solomon, W. E. G. *Saul Solomon 'The Member for Cape Town'* (Cape Town, 1948).

Stow, G. *The Native Races of South Africa* (London, 1905).

Theal, G. M. *A Fragment of Basuto History, 1854–1871* (Cape Town, 1886).

——, *History of South Africa, 1854–1872*, 2nd edn (London, 1900).

——, *History of South Africa since September, 1795*, 5 vols (London, 1908).

——, *History of South Africa from 1873–1884*, 2 vols (London, 1919).

Thompson, L. M. (ed.), *African Societies in southern Africa* (London, 1969).

——, *Survival in Two Worlds: Moshoeshoe of ·Lesotho 1786–1870* (Oxford, 1975).

Thomson, J. T. 'Capitation in Colonial and Post-Colonial Niger: Analysis of the Effects of an Imposed Head Tax System on Rural Political Organization' in S. B. Burman and B. E. Harrell-Bond (eds), *The Imposition of Law* (New York, 1979).

Tylden, G. 'The Basutoland Rebellion of 1880–1881', *Journal of the Society for Army Historical Research*, 15 (1936).

——, 'The Capture of Morosi's Mountain, 1879', *Journal of the Society for Army Historical Research*, 21 (1942).

——, *A History of Thaba Bosiu: 'A Mountain at Night'* (pamphlet, Maseru, 1945).

——, *The Rise of the Basuto* (Cape Town, 1950).

Van der Poel, J. 'Basutoland as a Factor in South African Politics (1858–1870)', *Archives Year Book for South African History* (1941) part I.

Walker, E. A. *Historical Atlas of South Africa* (Cape Town, 1922).

Walton, J. 'Villages of the Paramount Chiefs of Basutoland: II.

Thaba Bosiu, the Mountain Fortress of Chief Moshesh', *Lesotho*, ii (1960).

——, 'Old Maseru', *Basutoland Notes and Records*, 4 (1963–4).

Whitfield, G. M. B. *South African Native Law*, 2nd edn (Cape Town, 1948).

Wille, G. *Principles of South African Law* (Cape Town, 1937).

Williams, B. *Record of the Cape Mounted Riflemen* (London, 1909).

Wilmot, A. *History of Our Own Times in South Africa* (Cape Town, vol. i, 1897, vol. ii, 1898).

——, *The Life and Times of Sir Richard Southey* (London, 1904).

Wilson, M. and Thompson, L. (eds), *The Oxford History of South Africa*, 2 vols (Oxford, 1969 and 1971).

Worsfold, B. *Sir Bartle Frere* (London, 1923).

b *Unpublished theses*

Benyon, J. A. 'Basutoland and the High Commission with particular reference to the years 1868–1884: The Changing Nature of the Imperial Government's "Special Responsibility" for the Territory' (Oxford Univ. D.Phil., 1968).

Burman, S. B. 'Cape Policies Towards African Law in Cape Tribal Territories, 1872–1883' (Oxford Univ. D.Phil., 1973).

Matthews, Z. K. 'Bantu Law and Western Civilization in South Africa; A Study in the Clash of Cultures' (Yale Univ. M.A., 1934)—on microfilm in Rhodes House, Oxford.

Sanders, P. B. 'The Life and Times of Moshoeshoe from his Birth c. 1786 to the Proclamation of the Orange River Sovereignty in February 1848' (Oxford Univ. D.Phil., 1969).

Saunders, C. C. 'The Cape Native Affairs Department and African Administration on the Eastern Frontier under the Molteno Ministry, 1872–1878' (Cape Town Univ. B.A. Hons., 1964).

——, 'The Annexation of the Transkeian Territories (1872–1895) with special reference to British and Cape Policy' (Oxford Univ. D.Phil., 1972).

Webber, P. E. 'The Church in Basutoland, 1833–1884' (Southampton University M.A., 1967).

Index

Adultery, *see* Marriage
Alcohol, 194n.36, 207–8n.4, 215–16n.16; *see also* Joala
Aliwal North Convention, (1869), 39–41, 72, 109
Arbousset, Rev. T. (PEMS), 7, 8, 12, 84
Austen, John, 42, 54, 58, 82, 106, 108, 114, 119, 121, 124–6, 135, 144, 149–50, 210n.69, 217n.56, 218nn.69, 72
Ayliff, William, Cape Secretary for Native Affairs, (1878–81), 121, 132

Baphuti, *see* Phuthi
Barkly, Arthur, 81, 89, 142–5, 156
Barkly, Sir Henry, Governor of Cape Colony (1870–7), 46–7, 64, 72, 77, 104
Basutoland Mounted Police Force (1872), 43, 82, 186, 203n.8, 210n.64
Bell, Charles George Harland, 142, 144, 156, 159
Bell, Major Charles Harland (d.1881), 53, 58, 61–4, 69, 78, 89, 140, 144, 156–7, 201n.17, 203n.8, 224n.40
Bell, Fitzwilliam, 81, 156
Berea District, 53, 64–5, 73, 78, 94, 142–3
Bereng, son of Letsie, 141, 143, 176
Blyth, Captain Matthew, Acting Governor's Agent, (1883–4), 120, 171–81
Boers, 13–15, 38, 40, 150; *see also* Orange Free State, Transorangia
Bohali, 10, 20, 24, 37, 43, 45, 58, 83, 85, 96, 193n.17, 195n.8, 199n.37,

209n.51; *see also* Cattle, Marriage, Regulations
Botha-Bothe, 7
Bowker, James Henry, 38–48, 54, 56, 64, 88–90, 100, 108, 120–7, 133, 175, 197n.10, 201n.18
Brand, J. H., President of Orange Free State, (1864–88), 15
Bright, H. E. R., 52–3
British annexation (1868), 15–16, 36, 41
annexation (1884), 177, 179–83
British High Commissioner (Governor of Cape Colony), 15, 34, 49, 200n.1, 201n.7; *see also* Barkly, Frere, Robinson, Wodehouse
Brownlee, Charles Pacalt, Cape Secretary for Native Affairs (1872–8), 50, 98, 121, 132, 200–1n.6, 201n.8, 213n.39
Buchanan, David Dale, 39

Caledon River, 13, 39, 62
Cannibals, 10
Cape Colony administration (1871–84), 1, 3, 15–16, 41–3, 47–60, 94, 127, 133–7, 162–4, 177–8, 181, 185–91
    Department of Native Affairs, 49, 52–3, 58, 132
    Legislative Council, 47–8
    Responsible Government, 48–9
    Secretary for Native Affairs, 49, 52
    see also specific subjects
Cape Frontier Armed and Mounted Police, 36, 38, 82
Cape Frontier War (1877), 118

Cape law, 68, 96, 99, 196n.15, 200n.57, 212n.25, 213n.39
Cape Mounted Rifles, 145–8, 150, 165
Carrington, Colonel F., 145–7
Casalis, Rev. Eugene (PEMS), 7, 9, 12–13, 20, 84
Cattle, 10, 14, 31–3, 58, 98, 212n.35; *see also* Bohali, Mafisa, Marriage
Census (1875), 57, 209n.46
Cetshwayo, Zulu chief, 64
Chiefs and headmen, 6, 11, 26–30, 37, 42–3, 46, 75–7, 82–100, 193n.22, n.27, 196n.27, 209n.45, 210–11n.78, 212n.35, 226n.44
　neutralisation, 61–74
　triumph, 162–84
　see also names of chiefs

Clarke, Colonel Marshall James, Resident Commissioner (1884), 181–2, 228n.82
Cochet, Rev. I. (PEMS), 139, 143
Coillard, Rev. F. (PEMS), 204n.10
Confederation policy, 3, 105, 133
Courts, 27–31, 32, 42, 56–7, 61, 62, 86–90, 193n.21, 196n.25, n.27, 199n.40, 210n.64; *see also* Justice, administration of, Regulations
Cornet Spruit District, 54, 81–2, 94, 158, *see also* Mohale's Hoek
Currie, Sir Walter, 35, 38, 48, 53
Custody and guardianship, 22, 25, 44–5, 92, 95, 97

Daniel, Rev. John, 35, 197n.7
Daumas, Rev. F., 39
Davies, Henry Lee, 56, 141, 155
Diamond fields, 3, 83, 105
Disannexation (1884), 163, 177–8, 181–2
Disarmament, 2–3, 133–6, 140, 142, 218n.69, 219n.10
　defeating disarmament, 148–61
　see also Gun War
Divorce, *see* Marriage
Doda, *see* Lehana
Dyke, Hamilton Moore (PEMS), 173, 227n.52

Economy, 1–3, 17, 32–3, 38, 48, 83, 104–5, 163, 170, 187, 197n.30, 202n.42; *see also* Cattle, Hut tax, Taxation, Traders
Education, 3, 59, 85–6, 157, 203n.49, 209n.51
Ellenberger, Rev. Frederic (PEMS), 10, 22, 121, 137
English, W. H., 52

Family Law, 17–20, 28, 33, 43; *see also* Custody and guardianship, Marriage, Widows, Women, position of,
Fines, 30, 42, 46, 77–8, 198n.30, 216n.17, 227n.61
Franchise, 68
Frere, Sir Bartle, Governor of Cape Colony (1877–80), 133, 137
Friend of the Free State, 104, 179–80, 182

Garcia, Arthur, 167–9
George (Tlali), son of Moshoeshoe, 68–9, 72, 118, 144, 155, 205n.44, 228n.8
Gordon, General Charles, 164–8, 225n.10
Governor's Agent, 81, 154; *see also* Blyth, Bowker, Griffith, Orpen, Rolland,
Governor's Code, *see* Regulations
Governors of Cape Colony, *see* Barkly, Frere, Robinson, Wodehouse,
Griffith, Charles Duncan, Governor's Agent (1871–81), 44, 46, 48, 54–66, 69, 72–82, 86, 89, 91, 93, 95, 98, 100, 104, 110, 117–18, 126–31, 135–44, 151, 154–6, 171, 180, 213n.39.
Griqualand East, 63, 72–3, 88, 105–6, 120, 135, 148, 207n.78, 210n.69, 217n.56, 228n.8
Guardianship, *see* Custody and guardianship
Gun War (1880–1), 3, 57, 147–9, 185
　guns, 32, 83, 93, 133–4, 140, 142, 193n.31, 218n.69

Health, 86, 149

High Commissioner, *see* British High Commission

Hlotse (Leribe District), 62, 92–3, 159, 172, 211n.13; *see also* Leribe

Hlubi, 62–3; *see also* Langalibalele

Hope, Hamilton, 110–28, 148, 216nn.16, 44, 216–17n.45

Hut tax, 38, 41, 47, 65, 70–1, 82, 83, 89, 97, 110, 135, 163, 167, 180, 197n.9, 209n.40

Imprisonment, 31, 211n.11, 227n.61

Inheritance, 25–6, 67, 96, 205n.41, 212n.24, 221n.49; *see also* Widows

Initiation (*Lebollo*), 13, 19, 32, 37, 58, 85, 94, 102–3, 158, 194n.36, 209n.51, 219n.7

Innes, James Rose, 50, 52

Interpreters, 56, 79

Joala, 80, 115, 194n.36, 215–16n.16; *see also* Alcohol

Joel, son of Molapo, 63, 139, 148, 151, 166, 169, 176–7, 180, 221n.49, 227nn.56, 58, 228n.75

Jonathan, son of Molapo, 63, 139, 142, 144, 148, 153, 166, 169, 176–7, 203n.8, 204n.19, 221n.49

Joseph, son of Molapo, 139

Justice, administration of, 11, 13, 27–32, 42, 47–70, 86–90, 196nn.25, 27, 199n.40, 210n.64, 211nn.11, 12, 213n.39, 214n.6, 216n.17, 217n.56
changing the law, 91–9, 211, 213n.39
see also Magisterial system, Regulations

Khoikhoi, 5, 31, 193n.31

Kora, 12, 193n.31

Land law, 14, 26–7, 37, 77, 196n.12, 206n.71

Langalibalele, Hlubi chief, 62–3, 88, 123, 204n.19

Lebollo, see Initiation

Lehana (Doda), son of Moorosi, 111, 117, 119–21, 124–6, 130, 219n.90

Leribe District, 53, 78, 86, 94, 142, 158–9, 176

Lerotholi (Lerothodi), son of Letsie, (1837–1905), 67, 69, 123, 129, 140–1, 143, 145–6, 148–9, 151, 157–9, 165–6, 168–9, 175, 182–3

Lesaona, *see* RaManella

Leselinyana la Lesotho, 58, 203n.49; *see also Little Light of Basutoland*

Letsema, 68, 76–7, 90, 207–8n.4, 208n.12, 210–11n.78

Letsie (Letsea), son of Moshoeshoe, (1810–91), 39–41, 46–8, 55, 61, 63–5, 67, 69, 74, 77, 82, 84–5, 88, 91, 101, 117–18, 122, 126, 128–9, 134–9, 142–4, 148, 150, 153, 157–8, 160, 162–4, 165–6, 171–82, 200n.54, 210–12n.30, 204–5n.29, 212n.35, 218n.72, 224n.47, 227n.61

Letuka, son of Moorosi, 120, 125, 127, 217n.56

Levirate, *see* Marriage

Lifaqane, 7, 31, 101

Lingoetsi, 22–3

Little Light of Basutoland, 58, 92, 101–4, 106; *see also Leselinyana la Lesotho*

Maama (Mama), son of Letsie, 143, 175, 176, 178

Mabille, Rev. Adolph (PEMS), 68, 84–5, 93, 137, 158, 173–4, 218n.69

Maboella, 76

Mafeteng (Thaba-Bosiu District), 53, 67, 81, 146–8; *see also* Thaba-Bosiu

Mafetoli (Mafetodi), 114, 215n.14

Mafisa, 10–11, 26, 193nn.13, 17, 210–11n.78

Magisterial system, 1–3, 16, 29, 37, 42, 56–9, 61, 71–82, 87–9, 156–8, 162–3, 168, 172, 182–3, 185–6, 211n.12, 216n.17, 221n.68
changing the law, 91–9
collapse of the system, 131–48
see also Justice, administration of, names of magistrates

Maikela, headman, 119–20

Maitin, Charles, 81, 110, 112–17, 156

Majara, son of Moshoeshoe, 207n.85

Malome, 199n.37

'MaMohato, principal wife of Moshoeshoe, 20, 22–23

Manthunya, prophetess, 104
Marriage, 18–24, 31–2, 43–4, 92, 94–7, 100, 199nn.38, 40, 200–1n.6, 213n. 39
  adultery, 23, 31, 66
  divorce, 23, 25, 85, 96, 194n.40
  levirate, 31, 45, 85, 111
  sororate, 31, 85
  see also Bohali, Polygamy, Widows
Masopha (Masupha, Masupa), son of Moshoeshoe, (1820–99), 41, 46–7, 54, 63–7, 69, 72, 74, 79, 84, 90, 105, 107, 128, 134, 139–45, 148, 151, 157–8, 162–3, 166–9, 173, 176, 180–4, 204–5n.29, 224n.47, 227n.56
Maseru, capital (from 1869), 53, 86, 131, 133–4, 142–3, 148, 151, 155, 158, 201n.18
Matsieng, 64
Merriman, John Xavier, 164–5
Missionaries, 12–13, 31–2, 36–7, 40–1, 44, 58–9, 84–5, 95–6, 101, 103, 105, 133, 137, 142, 159–60, 187, 193n.33, 197n.33, 198n.23, 203n.49, 210–11n.78, 213n.39, 213–4n. 4, 214n.9
  Church of England (1875), 159, 203n.52
  Paris Evangelical Mission Society (PEMS) (1833), 12, 39, 58–9, 84, 100, 151, 157–9, 163, 193n.33, 193–4n.34, 194n.40, 198n.23, 203n.49, 210–11n.78, 213–14n.4
  Roman Catholics (1862), 12, 159, 193n.33, 198n.23, 203n.52, 225n.58
  see also Morija, names of individual missionaries
Mohale's Hoek (Cornet Spruit District), 86, 110, 148; *see also* Cornet Spruit District
Molapo (Molappo), son of Moshoeshoe, (1814–80), 15, 39, 41, 46–7, 53, 61–4, 69, 78, 84, 89, 104, 128, 134, 139–40, 177, 194n. 44, 203n. 6, 204nn. 10, m 19, 207n. 93, 209n.51, 210–11n.78, 211n.10

Moletsane, Taung chief, 39, 94, 225n.57
Molteno, John Charles, Cape Prime Minister, (1872–78), 50, 79, 132
Moorosi (Morosi), Phuthi chief, (1795–1879), 2, 94, 133–5, 215–16n.16, 217n.56, 218n.72
  rebellion, 108–31, 218n.87, 219n.89
Morija (PEMS headquarters), 12, 137, 148, 159, 167
Moshoeshoe (1786–1870), 1, 7–16, 20, 22–3, 26–7, 33, 39–41, 45–6, 67, 101–2, 105, 192nn.4, 6, 8, 12, 193n.17, 194nn.35, 36, 39, 41, 42, 197nn.9, 10, 198n.23, 206n.65, 212n.24, 228n.74
Motsapi, son of Moorosi, 125

Natal, 15–16, 35, 37, 63
Nehemiah (Sekhonyana), son of Moshoeshoe, 10, 68, 73, 88, 105–6, 162, 171, 175, 205n.44, 206n.55, 207n.78, 210n.69, 214n.27,
Nguni, 5, 6, 10, 78, 94, 108–10, 203n.8, 208n.13, 215n.13; *see also* Phuthi, Zulu
Nkoebi, son of Letsie, 143, 171
Nomansland, *see* Griqualand East
Ntalimi, son of Moshoeshoe, 20
Ntsane, son of Moshoeshoe, 144, 206n.55

Orange Free State, 38–9, 48, 83, 87–8, 104, 139, 150, 170, 184, 194n.44; *see also* Boers, Transorangia
Orpen, Joseph Millard, Acting Governor's Agent (1881–83), 8, 11, 54, 68, 93, 95, 138, 144, 154–8, 160, 164–5, 168–9, 171–2, 179, 223n.29

Paris Evangelical Mission Society (PEMS), *see* Missionaries
Peace Preservation Act (Cape), 136–41, 156, 160–1
Pedi (N. Sotho), 5, 128
Phuthi, 6, 94, 108–10, 120, 122, 124, 127–31, 210n.69, 218n.69; *see also* Moorosi, Quthing

Pii, *see* Sofonia

Pitsos (Lipitso), 27, 36, 38–40, 65–6, 79–81, 90, 91, 100, 106–7, 111, 127, 133, 136, 144, 162–3, 165, 172–6, 179–80, 196n.21, 208n.23

Polygamy, 13, 18, 31, 32, 37, 43, 58, 67, 85, 94, 193n.29, 194nn.40, 41, 195n.1, 196n.11, 213n.39; *see also* Bohali, Marriage, Widows

Prophesy movement, 101–7, 214n.9

Punishments, 11, 30–1, 42, 45–6, 66, 78, 92–3, 189, 193n.21, 196n.23, 197nn.32, 10, 198n.30, 211n.12, 216n.17; *see* *also* Fines, Imprisonment

Quthing (Cornet Spruit District), 83, 89–90, 112, 124, 129, 131, 137–8, 160, 162, 171, 217n.56, 221n.52; *see also* Cornet Spruit District, Hope, Hamilton, Moorosi, Nkoebi, Phuthi,

Raisa, headman, 110–11, 117–18

RaManella (Lesaoana), 176, 180, 182, 228nn.74, m75

RaMatšeatsana, 11, 197n.35, 213n.1

Regulations
1868, 36–48, 175, 227n.61
1871 – Governor's Code, 53, 55, 68, 78, 92, 101, 199nn.40, 44, 206n.71, 211n.11, 216n.17
1877, 98–9, 206n.71, 216n.17
commission (1872), 93–9
see also Justice, administration of, Magisterial system

Rhodes, Cecil John, 171

Robinson, Sir Hercules, Governor of Cape Colony (1881–89), 151, 153, 223n.11

Rolland, Rev. Emile (PEMS), 37–8, 42–3, 45, 53, 58–9, 67, 83–4, 88, 90, 100, 105, 118–22, 125, 131, 135, 157, 162–3, 205n.42, 212n.35, 218n.69

Roman Catholics; *see* Missionaries

San (Bushmen), 5, 6, 108–10

Sauer, J. W., Cape Secretary for Native Affairs (1881–94), 150, 154, 157–8, 165–72

Scanlen, Thomas Charles, Cape Prime Minister (1881–4), 164–5, 170, 172

Sekake, nephew of Letsie, 10, 69

Sekhonyana, *see* Nehemiah

Shaka, Zulu chief, 6, 7

Sofonia (Pii), son of Moshoeshoe, 20, 68, 98, 118, 144, 205n.44, 228n.8

Sororate, *see* Marriage

Sotho law, 26–30, 67–8, 75–6, 85, 91–9, 101–7, 198n.30; *see also* specific subjects

Sprigg, Gordon, Cape Prime Minister (1878–81), 130, 132–5, 143–4, 146, 150, 219n.10

Surmon, James, 81

Surmon, William Henry, 40–4, 53, 66–7, 105, 141–2, 157–8, 201n.14, 205n.42

Taung, 39, 94

Taxation, 68, 70–1, 135–6, 142, 181; *see* *also* Hut tax

Thabi-Bosui, 7, 9, 12, 16, 35, 38–9, 41–2, 64–5, 73, 100, 140, 142–3, 167, 183, 192n.5, 204–5n.29, 224n.47
District, 53, 55, 81, 87, 141, 202n.39, 205n.42
Treaty (1866), 15

Thembu, 120, 148, 215n.13

Tlali (Thlali, Thladi), *see* George

Trade, 32, 56–8, 83, 135, 193n.31, 202nn.39, 40, 42, 206–7n.74, 209n.45; *see also* Cattle, Economy

Transorangia, 5, 7, 13–15; *see also* Boers, Orange Free State

Tsekelo, son of Moshoeshoe, 39, 43, 72–4, 101–2, 144, 205–6n.53, 206n.55, 213n.1

Tyhali (Tyali, Chale) 112, 215n.13

Vote, *see* Franchise

Widdicombe, Rev. John, 90, 159–60, 176–7

Widows, 24, 25, 43–5, 92, 97, 111, 119;
    see also Bohali, Marriage,
    Polygamy
Witchcraft, 30–1, 37, 45–6, 158,
    193n.22, 194n.36, 195n.4,
    197nn.28, 31, 6, 198n.30, 199n.45
Wittebergen (Herschel) Reserve, 42,
    54, 109

Wodehouse, Sir Philip, Governor of
    Cape Colony (1862–70), 15, 16,
    35, 37–42, 87, 108
Women, position of, 17–18, 21–2, 25,
    44–5, 85; *see also* Custody and
    guardianship, Marriage, Poly-
    gamy, Widows
Zulu, 6–7, 62, 63–4, 128, 203n.8